Marketing Technologies

'Simakova has produced an absolutely excellent, theoretically sophisticated, empirically rich account of the production of emerging technologies. It is a fascinating read for those interested in organizational ethnography, marketing practice and critical marketing studies. I cannot recommend it highly enough.'

Professor Mark Tadajewski, *Durham University, UK.*

Global corporations initiate, join and maintain socio-technological change and hence, alter the ways in which we organize our lives. Demanding significant investment of resources and time, the development and implementation of new technologies on different levels must take into consideration these subtle processes. As such, it is particularly important that we have a greater insight into the practices of hi-tech corporations, in view of the often inflated promises of and concerns about the destiny of technological breakthroughs, especially those promising sizeable economic outcomes and societal transformation.

Elena Simakova undertook a lengthy ethnographic study, working alongside marketing managers in a global IT corporation in their Europe, Middle East and Africa (EMEA) headquarters in the UK. Using the experience gained through a close participation in their everyday corporate rituals and routines, her account challenges common perceptions of how corporations make the world think and act with regard to technologies in particular ways. The book contains an interesting case study on the launch of a radio frequency identification (RFID) based solution.

Unravelling the construction of expectations, inclusions and exclusions around emerging technologies, this reflexive account also tackles uneasy practical and methodological questions pertinent to corporate ethnography. This book is an essential read for scholars in science and technology studies, economic sociology, anthropology, as well as management and organizational studies and research policy.

Elena Simakova is Lecturer in Innovation at the University of Exeter Business School, UK. Her research focuses on policy and politics of emerging technologies and the creation of market values. Her publications have appeared in *Social Studies of Science*; *Science, Technology & Human Values*; and *Science as Culture*.

Routledge Studies in Innovation, Organization and Technology

RIOT!

Marketing Technologies

Corporate cultures and
technological change

Elena Simakova

Routledge
Taylor & Francis Group

LONDON AND NEW YORK

First published 2013
by Routledge
2 Park Square, Milton Park, Abingdon, Oxon OX14 4RN

Simultaneously published in the USA and Canada
by Routledge
711 Third Avenue, New York, NY

Routledge is an imprint of the Taylor & Francis Group, an informa business

British Library Cataloguing in Publication Data
A catalogue record for this book is available from the British Library

Library of Congress Cataloging in Publication Data
Simakova, Elena, 1973-
Marketing technologies: corporate cultures and technological change / Elena Simakova.
  p. cm. – (Routledge studies in innovation, organization, and technology)
Includes bibliographical references and index.
  1. Organizational change. 2. Electronic commerce. 3. Technological innovations—
Economic aspects. 4. Management–Technological innovations. I. Title.
HD58.8.S576 2012
381–dc23   2012006972

ISBN: 978-0-415-62477-0 (hbk)
ISBN: 978-0-203-10203-9 (ebk)

Typeset in Times New Roman
by Cenveo Publisher Services

MIX
Paper from
responsible sources
FSC® C004839

Printed and bound by CPI Group (UK) Ltd, Croydon, CR0 4YY

Contents

5 Marketing texts as discursive objects, or do texts speak for themselves? 85

Technology as text or text as technology? 85
Marcom materials as discursive objects 90
Discussion 103

6 'Softly, softly' tagging the world 106

Introduction/transition 106
RFID as a tellable story 112
Product launch as organisational practice 115
Preparing a product launch 118
Tentative launch 122
Discussion 128

7 RFID 'theatre of the proof' 130

The organisational politics of technology demonstration 130
Holding marketing and engineering together 133
Locations, audiences and selling cycles 137
Cometh the moment, cometh the artefact? 139
RFID Expo: tentative opening 141
Discussion 144

8 Concluding remarks 146

Revision of the post-essentialist approach to the market 146
Markets, technology and accountability 147
Marketing knowledge: an ethnographic perspective 149
Marketing technologies and intervention 151
Living with unrest: research strategies and tellability 154

Acknowledgements

Marketing Technologies is, in the first instance, an outcome of research conducted for my doctoral thesis at the Saïd Business School, University of Oxford, in 2002–2007, under the supervision of Professor Steve Woolgar, who offered a tremendous amount of inspiration and support. The assistance and support received from faculty and staff at the SBS, St Cross College, and the legal office of the University of Oxford were crucial to taking the doctoral thesis to its completion. I also thank anonymous marketing managers and engineers at *Virtual World* (a pseudonym) for providing opportunities for access to the corporate activities during my initial field research in 2003–2005. Kristen Ebert-Wagner's help was indispensable during the preparation of the manuscript for submission.

Developing the research into the book was possible because of interest from and collaboration with numerous institutions and individuals, whose contribution is gratefully acknowledged. My joint postdoctoral fellowship at the Centre for Sociology of Innovation (CSI) at Ecole des Mines and at the Department of Economics and Social Sciences (SES) at Telecom-ParisTech in Paris, France – in 2006 and 2007 – helped me to refine some of the ideas expressed in the thesis, and eventually in this book. The seminars and discussions devoted to the anthropology of the market held at the CSI with Michel Callon's group were essential for the elaboration of many of the arguments. The presentations of fragments of this study at the Centre for Sociology of Innovation (CSI) Colloquium *'Expérimenter, éprouver, assembler'* at Ecole des Mines, Paris (September 2007); the *'Boundary Object, Boundary Work'* workshop at the University of Grenoble (May 2007); the 4th International Critical Management Studies Conference, Cambridge (July 2006); and the Philosophy of Management Conference at St Anne's College, Oxford (July 2005) were particularly valuable occasions for thinking about the directions this book would take. My thanks go to the organisers and audiences of these events.

Since the beginning of the project, I have benefited from discussions with many individuals who acted as examiners, editors, reviewers, discussants, colleagues and co-authors. I am particularly grateful to Catelijne Coopmans, Catherine Grandclément-Chaffy, Keith Grint, Claes-Fredrik Helgesson, Stephen Hilgartner, Douglas Holt, Hans Kjellberg, Christian Licoppe, Fabian Muniesa, Mike Lynch, Dan Neyland, Trevor Pinch, Paolo Quattrone, Brian Rappert, Steve

Rayner, Wally Smith, Lucy Suchman, and Marc Ventresca as well as to anonymous reviewers, whose valuable comments at various stages of the draft helped me to shape the arguments I present in the book.

This work was supported by a Science and Technology Studies studentship, Saïd Business School, University of Oxford (2002–2005), and partially by the Center for Nanoscale Systems in Information Technologies, Cornell University, a NanoScience and Engineering Center of the National Science Foundation under Award # EEC-0117770, 0646547. I would also like to acknowledge the research grants from the Administration of the Ile-de-France region and GET-ParisTech that supported my research fellowships in France (2006–2007). The key final work on the manuscript was accomplished during my time as a postdoctoral associate with the Department of Science & Technology Studies and the Center for Nanoscale Systems in Information Technologies at Cornell University (2007–2010).

Preface

In the spirit of current public and scholarly attempts at rethinking the foundations, successes, and failures of economic systems, the careful examination of corporate practices acquires special significance. It is particularly important – for academics, students, business practitioners, citizens, and policymakers – to have greater insight into the practices of hi-tech corporations in view of the often inflated promises of and concerns about the destiny of technological breakthroughs, especially those promising sizeable economic outcomes and societal transformation. Improving this understanding becomes a particularly meaningful effort in the context of demands for and attempts to achieve responsible innovation. Global corporations initiate, join, and maintain cultural technological discourses that provide for socio-technical change and hence alter the ways in which we organise our lives. Demanding significant investment of resources and time, the informed development and implementation of new technologies on different levels must take into consideration the subtle processes providing for the emergence of technological change.

Marketing Technologies offers an ethnographic account of encounters with technology marketing in the course of a lengthy participant observation with a global supplier of IT solutions. As such, the book examines a variety of ethnographic episodes and issues associated with the construction of technology discourses in the context of market relations. In order to do so, it raises and discusses a number of analytic questions that contribute to the current debate on the nature of the market, marketing knowledge, materiality, accountability, and technological change. In particular, the book offers a discussion of such practices as product launch and technological demonstration in the corporate attempts to intervene in societal discourses and practices. While corporations appear to act as a single entity to outsiders, much deliberation is involved in the creation of winning technological claims behind the corporate walls. Technological change, as it is seen from a corporate-insider perspective, is a matter of contesting opinions and versions of the outside world that underpin corporate decision-making. Technology marketing is one such corporate site where these deliberations take place. What this book is trying to do in the first instance is to offer an ethnographic account of what it means and what it takes to become a competent member of the technology marketing community through engaging with the participants' ways of making sense of socio-technical orders. The book is thus an attempt to understand the local construction of globally promoted and adopted technological assemblages (Ong and Collier, 2005), or, in Riles's terms, 'the internal possibilities for generating scale' (2000: 183).

The book also advances and interrogates a post-essentialist understanding of technology by way of examining a number of analytic premises in science and technology studies (STS). The rationale and motivation for the book were developed in the course of my work on my doctoral thesis at the University of Oxford between 2002 and 2007. In addition to the stimulating task of addressing the current concerns in science and technology studies, the inspiration for the study of technology marketing in practice was sustained as a result of my excitement about the social science research on markets, marketing, and financial institutions shared with STS colleagues especially in the UK, France, Sweden, and in the United States.[1] The approach to marketing by analogy with the sociology of scientific knowledge also provided a basis for a useful conversation with such emerging streams of research as critical marketing (e.g. Brownlie *et al.*, 1999b; Neyland and Simakova, 2009) and the practice-based approach (Araujo *et al.*, 2010). The book can be seen as a contribution to an increasingly visible post-positivist critique of the traditional normative approaches in marketing and management disciplines.

In this regard, the general purpose of the book is to examine how STS can enrich current understandings of technology marketing, and how a study of technology marketing can inform science and technology studies research. I contend that a study of technology marketing practice can contribute to a further exploration of the anti-essentialist premises in STS concerning the nature of technical artefacts and scientific facts. In the context of market studies informed by post-essentialist STS, the argument can be generally recast as follows: the supposedly intrinsic properties of a product are contingent and thus not a reliable basis for explaining market success. In other words, the market success of technologies is not due to the intrinsic properties of these artefacts or to the laws of the market, but derives from the performance of relationships across organisational boundaries. Technology marketing is one such site where the co-construction of properties both of technical artefacts and of the markets takes place through boundary work. The nature of such boundary work is explored through the book. My choice of technology marketing as research site was also informed by a recognition of the lack of in-depth ethnographic studies of these settings that would be informed by STS. Despite the existence of a range of theories of technology in STS and the increasing anthropological attention to markets and marketing, technology marketing has surprisingly received little attention so far. Furthermore, although numerous literatures in innovation management and hi-tech marketing exist, they are rarely based on thorough empirical studies, nor do they attempt to converse with ethnographic STS. Therefore, I contend that if we look at technology marketing as a cultural phenomenon, both marketing theory and STS can inform each other.

Thus, marketing offers a convenient opportunity to explore the merits of post-essentialist arguments in STS concerned with the constitution of technological boundaries and the ways in which winning technological claims are produced and sustained. I will discuss in what sense, in attempts to intervene in existing societal discourses, corporations accomplish boundary work through offering and maintaining membership in marketed products by way of creating and offering for interpretation technology narratives. The questions about the construction of corporate statements about new technologies became the main focus of the book. This line of inquiry opens up a series of further questions about social ordering and interpretation, which I will specifically address. Technology marketing is thus approached as an interpretive work of constructing and maintaining boundaries vis-à-vis technological artefacts. While the properties of novel technologies and applications are still in flux, participants must evaluate statements made by others, as well as come up with their own appraisals, commercial and societal evaluations, and critique of the new developments. It is these practices of creating what I call the *tellable stories* of emerging technologies that compose the main argument of the book.

The ethnographic approach that I develop examines corporate assumptions, beliefs, and practical issues concerning technology dissemination. Along with the earlier STS critique of the linear model of innovation coming from a number of perspectives, it would certainly be simplistic to suggest that marketing departments simply *disseminate* technologies. First, marketing managers often interact with engineers and other R&D specialists, thus influencing technology design. And second, the work of marketing managers is importantly about *interpreting* a technology and the corporate expertise, including the meanings and images of the corporation itself in these discourses, which are made available for others to interpret. The nature of and possible responses from the interpretive communities who will become exposed to the corporate discourse, such as sellers, adopters, and users of these technologies, as well as analysts and media, become a matter of consideration inside marketing departments that results in the work of categorisation and ordering bearing on the eventual presentation of technologies. In other words, marketing practices can be said to be *constitutive* of the technologies in question. This perspective will inform the ways in which the book addresses technology marketing in practice.

One particular technology that emerged as a focus for marketing practice is radio frequency identification (RFID). As an example of emerging technologies, RFID is associated with a transformative promise of profoundly changing societal and economic mobility patterns. In the early 2000s RFID technologies were perceived as 'enabler' technologies for all kinds of tracing and tracking activities, with the likely consequence of changing patterns of mobility of objects and people as well as providing ways to manage data about these movements. At the same time, the public discourses of RFID exhibit uncertainties, and concerns, about its potential impact and implications. As such, RFID has attracted the attention of privacy activists and governments. Taken up by corporations as potentially profitable applications, these technologies may or may not eventually affect the lives of broader publics drawn into the discourse of the benefits, consumption, implementation, and everyday use of RFID, such as in managing supermarket inventories, or in locating individuals. Thus, the central goal of the book to understand the corporate assumptions behind technological change undoubtedly speaks to broader concerns about the nature of technological adoption by society. In this book, corporations are mostly discussed as engaging in business-to-business exchanges, which may or may not later provide for framings of technologies proliferating into the public domain.

The book's title, *Marketing Technologies,* thus reflects two mutually implicated empirical concerns around 'marketing technologies': everyday life in a hi-tech marketing department, as well as marketing knowledge in its practical and theoretical aspects. The latter of course assumes that marketing 'technologies' or 'tools of the trade' can be approached and described ethnographically. The book, however, is intended neither as a contribution to the normative marketing theory nor as a 'realistic' portrayal of how marketing works in practice. On the contrary, in an anthropological spirit, the book offers an individual, if not idiosyncratic, ethnographic experience of participating in marketing rituals and of learning the signs of competent membership in corporate life. As an exercise in corporate anthropology, I will try to show in what sense the 'tricks of the trade' in marketing are matters of local evaluation and assessment and can be challenged; that the rhetoric of marketing knowledge is constitutive of boundary relations in and of marketing.

Below I offer a brief outline of the book chapters.

Chapter 1 begins with a discussion of the 'market turn' in STS as a contribution to the more general intellectual effort that has recently become known as market studies (Araujo *et al.,* 2010) to reassess the reliance of the academic discourse on the economic notions of the market. Examining the French and the British anthropological approaches to the market, the chapter develops a post-essentialist understanding of the market as text. In doing so, the questions of agency and accountability in the analytic treatments of the market are considered as central to the reappraisal of market relations from STS perspectives. Addressing the need for the empirical examination of the boundaries of markets and marketing, technology marketing is proposed as a strategic site to undertake research that will inform current academic debate.

Chapter 2 prepares the reader for a further anthropological discussion by offering an analysis of literatures on marketing as a societal and corporate phenomenon. As a culture and as a cultural artefact, marketing is a part of deliberations – by both marketing insiders and outsiders – about the nature of change in societal discourses and practices. As such, the debates on marketing power and marketing knowledge, as well as on the boundaries of marketing, receive special attention in the chapter. From an analytic point of view, the issues concerning the role of marketing in social ordering are reconsidered in terms of the creation of the interpretive constraints and of the performative properties of narratives. The chapter argues that technological discourses need to be seen in terms of the ongoing work of the production of texts, their audiences, purposes, and the assessment of these textual practices, which I approach in terms of the creation of *tellable stories.*

The suggestion of technology marketing as a strategic research site entails a number of practical and analytic questions about the nature of ethnographic inquiry. What features of the ethnographic project undertaken in a corporation made it distinct from laboratory studies? How were the ethnographic and marketing knowledges mutually configured in negotiating access to the corporation? Such rarely discussed but crucial for corporate anthropology questions as the rhetoric of access, the inscription of ethnography into non-disclosure agreements, and the creation of a place for ethnography in the corporation are discussed in Chapter 3. Three specific methodological issues – virtual ethnography, multi-sited ethnography, and data gathering and organising – receive special attention in the discussion of the constitution of the field in the ethnographic encounters.

Between February 2003 and July 2005, I conducted participant observation with *Virtual World*, one of the world's largest IT corporations, at the company's EMEA (Europe, the Middle East, and Africa) headquarters near London. In this book, as well as in other publications, I had to anonymise the name of the corporation since I conducted the study under a non-disclosure agreement (NDA) with the company. Reflections on the writing strategies under the NDA became a productive part of the ethnography. Chapter 4 begins an empirical analysis of technology marketing in practice by examining a neophyte marketer experience with the 'vertical' marketing team at Virtual World. One of the marketing approaches adopted by the corporation in order to sell IT solutions to various businesses involved building relations with a large number of distribution channels, potential customers, as well as its own sales force, categorised into distinctive 'vertical' markets. The chapter offers a discussion of marketing practice through an account of participating in a so-called organising activity purported to create encounters between corporation and customers through events and the distribution of promotional materials. In order to produce an anthropological perspective on 'organising', and to situate it as a specific marketing practice as opposed to a more general cultural practice adopted in a variety of settings, the chapter looks at organising through the lens of documentary analysis. As such, the discussion of marketing knowledge takes place in the context of organisational accounting as participants, including myself, provide input in a weekly report. Enriching the discussion of marketing and accountability provided in Chapter 1, technology marketing is discussed in Chapter 4 as a practice made amenable to, and constructed through, a variety of accountability systems and procedures in attempts at organisational change.

One attribute of the practice of organising, and of marketing in general, is the production of so-called marketing communication ('marcom') materials. These promotional materials, such as invitations, are prepared for and sent to those identified as relevant audiences who are to be compelled to take certain desired actions in relation to a corporate product (e.g. visit a trade show). The role of marcom materials is examined in Chapter 5 in view of more general analytic concerns about the functioning of textual artefacts in social ordering. Two analytic responses to these concerns are contrasted: the approach to textual artefacts in the material culture studies, and the approach in the post-essentialist tradition in science and technology studies. Asking whether texts speak for themselves, the chapter looks in detail at the deliberations concerning textual agency taking place inside the marketing department. The chapter also discusses in what sense the practical debates in marketing contribute to the analytic discussion about the role of materiality in social ordering.

Chapters 6 and 7 offer an analysis of a particular ethnographic episode that follows the ethnographic transition to a project devoted to the marketing of RFID-related technological 'solutions'. The main goal of the chapters is to examine the construction of the corporate discourse around the emerging technology. One particular practice that is examined in detail is product 'launch'. The deliberations around the launch of RFID by Virtual World are conceptualised in the chapters as the creation of *tellable stories* about RFID to be told on behalf of the corporation. Chapter 6 situates product launch in the organisation and analyses the construction of the first corporate statement about RFID. Chapter 7 more specifically looks at the organisational politics of technology demonstration. Managerial practices and beliefs analysed in these chapters prompt analytic questions about the role of material technical artefacts, such as the demonstration kit, in the construction of business technological discourses. Illustrating the debate, an analysis of the interactions between marketers and engineers around the construction of the RFID demonstration kit where the ethnographer served as project manager is presented. Consequently, product launch is discussed in detail in terms of accounting for tentative encounters between the corporation and its audiences.

In addition to a summary of themes and questions discussed in the book, the concluding Chapter 8 offers a revision of the post-essentialist approach to the market. In particular, through recounting the post-essentialist premises of the analysis offered earlier in the book, the chapter offers a discussion of the market and of technology in terms of the practical management of accountability relations. The chapter also brings together earlier observations about the nature of technology marketing knowledge as attempts to intervene in societal technological discourses. The discussion of the boundaries of marketing highlights the main implications of the book for our understanding of organisational beliefs and rituals. Finally, the chapter raises and discusses questions about the nature of social science research with corporations via a discussion of research strategies and tellability that takes into account audiences for ethnographic writing.

1 The 'market turn' in science and technology studies

A post-essentialist approach to the market

Science and technology studies have played an important role in informing recent scholarship in market studies.[1] At the same time, the phenomenon of the market has become a meeting point for STS concepts, theories, and empirical stances. Although a common feature of the concerted criticism was to confront the economic understandings of the market epitomised in Adam Smith's metaphor of the market's invisible hand, a variety of approaches to the market have been offered and explored. The interest in the market in STS has already been labelled (sceptically) the 'market turn' (e.g. Fine, 2003; Mirowski and Nik-Khah, 2007). The 'turn', like the earlier 'turn to technology' in STS (Woolgar, 1991b), attempts to translate earlier works in science and technology studies for empirical studies of the market. Callon speaks of 'simply the continuation' of the anthropology of sciences with regard to the anthropology of social sciences, of which market-making activities is a particular case: 'The way we are now studying social sciences is only an extension of the work done on the natural sciences. It's simply the continuation of the anthropology of science, but an anthropology of science which is concerned with economics in the broadest sense of the term, including, for example, marketing and accountancy' (Callon in Barry and Slater, 2002: 285).

What does it mean to translate STS continuously for the studies of the market? To what extent can this statement be taken up for a study of technology marketing, the main empirical focus of this manuscript? The metaphor of the 'turn' certainly cannot pass unnoticed for STS students. Science and technology studies have already known at least two critical debates called 'turns' – the 'semiotic turn' (Lenoir, 1999; Latour, 1999b) and the 'turn to technology' (Woolgar, 1991b; Pinch, 1993; Winner, 1993; Woolgar, 1993b). Neither of the two previous 'turns' was unproblematic; each highlighted analytic points that provoked productive critical exchange. The main lesson from the previous debates is that science and technology studies are not uniform with regard to their theoretical and empirical approaches to science and technology. Similarly, the 'market turn' in STS has provoked equally important questions about the relations between science, technology, and society. The market as object of STS research has not only put STS sensibilities and approaches, such as actor-network theory, on trial

(Callon, 1998b). Establishing market relations as an object of research for STS has also provoked questions and reflections about the nature of the engagement of STS with the new academic (such as business schools) and empirical (corporate, financial) settings (Woolgar *et al.*, 2009b).

Technology marketing can arguably be seen as a constitutive element in the market relations around a technological product. What are the roles of technology marketing in the emergence and commodification of technological innovation? How exactly does technology marketing participate in the creation of relations between corporation, technology, and markets? What can STS offer to a study of technology marketing?

Questions about the nature of innovation and socio-technical change have received extensive attention in science and technology studies. As I will discuss below, these questions can be productively recast in terms of the problem of content (of technology) and context (the market), thus lending themselves to the analyses informed by science and technology studies. One may wonder which approach in STS to select in order to inform one's line of inquiry. The aim of this, and the next, chapter is not to offer an exhaustive list of STS approaches possibly relevant to the analysis of markets and marketing, but rather to provide an overview of my sources of inspiration and to highlight some critical points that may help to turn such analysis into a productive analytic inquiry. Before beginning an analysis of technology marketing in practice, these two chapters seek to outline an approach to the market, to marketing, and to technology, and to the relationships between these notions. As contributors to Araujo *et al.* (2010) observe, the relations between markets and marketing are neither straightforward – in the sense that marketing does not simply 'produce' markets – nor analytically plain in terms of the complex interplay of the two in the domains of both marketing and economic theory, and in marketing practice. Hence, a better understanding of markets, marketing, and technology is needed before approaching technology marketing. The sections below first examine how some existing approaches to the market can be useful for the STS-informed analysis of technology marketing; and next offer a brief discussion of what makes technology marketing a strategic research site for STS.

The market as actor network

Actor-network theory (ANT) has been particularly influential in informing recent market studies (Callon, 1998b; 1999; Callon and Muniesa, 2005; MacKenzie *et al.*, 2007; Kjellberg, 2001; Lien, 1997; Araujo, 2007). The actor-network semiotic approach is associated with Latour's introduction of the notion of the 'actant' in *Science in Action* (Latour, 1987) and with Callon's study of the domestication of scallops in St Brieuc Bay (Callon, 1986). This approach generally relates to the debates on the nature of technology content and context, where artefacts are understood as sets of contingent negotiations between human and non-human network *actants*. Callon (1986) introduced the so-called principle of generalised symmetry, related to the symmetry between human and non-human actants, to extend the Strong Programme's symmetry requirement about falsity or truthfulness of beliefs (Bloor, 1976). According to Callon (1986), the principle of generalised symmetry derives from the French semiotic tradition (Greimas and Courtes, 1979).

Actor-network theory can be seen as an attempt to clarify one of the major premises of the social approaches to technology – namely, to acknowledge the contingency of the constituencies of technological context, whose identities and interests are constantly negotiated during the process of translation (Callon, 1986). Indeed, approaches such as SCOT (the social construction of technology) and the social shaping of technology (Pinch and Bijker, 1984; MacKenzie and Wajcman, 1985, respectively) prefer to see technological context as existing 'out there' in the form of social groups that influence the shaping or construction of technology and its functions. As Jordan and Lynch observed, this approach assumes seeing 'a technical thing in a social context' (Jordan and Lynch, 1998: 778). As they put it, 'the relevant way to reveal the culture of an artefact is to specify how the context determines, shapes, affects, circumscribes, sets conditions for the use of, provides resistance to or sustains the technical object in question' (ibid.).

Common to the SCOT-informed approaches is the recognition that the technical properties of an artefact are traceable in their evolution as corresponding to the interests, objectives, and resources of certain social groups. For SCOT, which emphasises the social nature of the work of construction, the notion of 'relevant social groups' is central: 'In deciding which problems are relevant, a crucial role is played by the social groups concerned with the artefact, and by the meanings which those groups give to the artefact: a problem is only defined as such, when there is a social group for which it constitutes a "problem"' (Pinch and Bijker, 1984: 414).

According to SCOT, technology in development can be better described if all possible social groups are identified and their interests captured. As the authors put it, 'some parts of the bicycle's development can be better explained by including a separate social group of feminine cycle-users' (ibid., 415). The approach suggested by Pinch and Bijker presupposes the availability of social groups for sociological analysis. It also assumes coherence inside a social group and unanimity with regard to the interpretation of an artefact: 'The use of the concept of "relevant social group" is quite straightforward. The term is used to denote institutions and organisations (such as the military or some specific industrial company), as well as organised or unorganised groups of individuals. The key requirement is that all members of a certain social group share the same set of meaning attached to a specific artefact. In deciding which social groups are relevant, the first question is whether the artefact has any meaning at all for the members of the social group under investigation. Obviously, the social group of 'consumers' or 'users' of the artefact fulfils this requirement' (Pinch and Bijker, 1984: 414). Resolution of conflicts and adoption of singular meanings of technology achieved by various social groups can be seen from the SCOT perspective as the stabilisation of a technological artefact as the latter achieves stable boundaries across the social worlds. In sum, the SCOT approach assumes that technology content is influenced by an 'external' technology context, and is capable of achieving a certain shape when the social processes around an artefact stabilise.

Actor-network theory is an attempt to further clarify the relationship between the content and the context of technologies. Against the idea of the context 'influencing' the content, sociologies of association (Latour, 1992) and translation (Callon, 1986) explore the mutually elaborated generation of technology content and context. The semiotic approach is introduced to bring the 'missing masses' of materiality into sociology (Latour, 1992). Socio-technical order is understood in ANT as a heterogeneous order acknowledging the (central) role of objects in holding the social order together (Latour, 1991). This, according to the ANT theorists, poses a major challenge to the sociological analyses of technology. The principle of generalised symmetry demands reconsideration of the traditional dichotomies pertinent to social scientific discourse. The semiotic approach based on the idea of the initial indeterminacy of actants thus contributes to a reconsideration of dichotomies such as of social/technical, technology content/context, production/consumption, inside/outside, micro/macro (Callon and Law, 1989; Latour, 1999a). The dichotomies are shown to be the outcomes of the actants' relations where, for instance, the 'outside' (France) is an effect of the activities 'inside' (Pasteur's lab) as in Latour (1999a).

In order to overcome the dichotomies entrenched in the sociological analyses, various provocative moves to shake up the analytic conventions have been proposed. Latour (1991) suggests a move from technology content and context to association and substitution. The relationship between social context and technical content is dealt with by suggesting a co-evolution relation between the two. To illustrate the point, Latour offers an analysis of how a hotel owner introduces metal weights in order to prevent customers from taking 'heavy' keys outside of the hotel, thus encouraging them to leave the keys at the reception desk. By using a diagram, Latour's analysis shows, in evolution, bundles of actants constituting association. As Latour explains, the socio-material associations do not 'retrace the displacement of an immutable statement within a context of use or application . . . it retraces a movement which is neither linguistic, nor social, nor technical, nor pragmatic . . . The diagram is thus used to keep track 'of successive changes undergone by customers, keys, hotels and hotel managers' (p. 103). Overall, Latour suggests that social relations can be more productively understood through the introduction of non-human actants into analysis as entities capable of acting: they offer 'a possibility of holding society together as a durable whole' (p. 103).

Akrich and Latour (1992/2000: 259) discuss how the introduction of semiotic actants helps to explain the construction of meaning through the co-construction of context and content: 'semiotics is the study of order building or path building and may be applied to settings, machines, bodies and programming languages as well as texts.' An important feature of this kind of semiotic approach is that it does not limit itself to signs: 'the key aspect of the semiotics of machines is its ability to move from signs to things and back' (p. 259). Akrich and Latour's *Convenient Vocabulary for the Semiotics of Human and Non-human Assemblies* (1992/2000) offers an analytical framework showing how the interactions between human and non-human elements can be seen as accomplished through textual series of displacements, or changing of the frames of reference.

As such, actor-network theorists seek to understand the nature of socio-technical *change* through radically reconsidering the question of *agency*.[2] The sociology of translation (Callon, 1986) seeks to further elaborate on how configurations of actants are established, being attentive to the linking processes through which the reconfigurations of actants are achieved. *Translation,* according to Callon and Law (1989), is what 'leads to the local generation of a distinction between the content and the context' (p. 58). For a researcher, this means identifying actants who produce a distinction between the technology and its social context (such actors may include non-humans) and for whom it matters how the content and the context are mutually influenced by each other. Sociologists of translation seek to avoid starting analysis from ascribing power to change socio-technical order to a particular actant, especially to humans, and instead look for processes leading to the emergence of agency (*intéressement,* enrolment, negotiation). For instance, in Callon's (1986) analysis of the 'domestication of the scallops and the fishermen of St Brieuc Bay' – informed by the principle of generalised symmetry – the scallops in St Brieuc Bay are spoken about as being 'willing' (or 'unwilling') to attach themselves to the collecting devices yielding to negotiations with researchers, hence acquiring agency in the process of translation.

Relevant to the market studies, Callon and Law (1989) assert that the ANT-informed sociology of translation needs to be further inspired by the principle of 'general agnosticism', which 'forbids distinction between technical and social, production and consumption' (p. 75). According to Callon and Law, it is important to retain the distinction between the content and the context, but in a different sense. The authors observe that the distinction is not clear-cut, and that its location and character cannot be legislated by the analyst. Analytical attention should be instead directed to how actors themselves establish the boundary between the technical and the social, or producers and consumers (p. 59). In line with this kind of argument, properties of the content and the context emerge in the traceable network of heterogeneous actants who/which create links between the dichotomies' parts.

From the actor-network perspectives, technology marketing can be usefully seen as a site of production of both markets and technologies. In other words, technology marketing is a nexus where agency and capacities of actants (corporations, technologies, markets) are negotiated, framed, made related, and networked together as a part of what is commonly called the innovation process. How can actor-network theory's radical flattening of the actants' capacities to introduce socio-technical change help us to address questions about technological innovation? In other words, how can we better understand technology in its (market) context, to use shorthand for the plethora of processes providing for the emergence of contents and contexts?

As above, ANT takes issue with the idea that the relationship between the content (technology) and its context (the market) has to be seen in the linear terms whereby the distinction is clear-cut, and technologies are simply waiting to be 'put on the market'. The actor-network approach does not a priori assume that technologies become successful as a result of especially favourable circumstances that could be unproblematically attributed to the 'market' situation, or 'demand', or clever 'design', or 'promotional strategies', or 'consumer interest'. To follow actor-network theorists' radical suggestion, for the studies of the market it is not helpful to introduce such assumptions in advance.[3] Furthermore, from this perspective 'the market' itself can usefully be seen as an actant in the discourses of economics, acquiring properties (such as 'laws') and acting as an independent entity available 'out there.' The role of 'the market' as a semiotic actant will be of particular interest to the further discussion.

A number of studies have already employed actor-network theory to unravel the nature of the relations between market constituencies. In one of his seminal works, Callon (1999: 186) contends that markets provide for new configurations of socio-technical 'imbroglios' that sociology of translation is best suited to analyse. In Barry and Slater (2002) Callon adds: 'Markets create new collective identities, that are not very well defined. It is impossible to take them into account without creating or setting up a space, that is a political space, in which these identities are discussed and confronted with each other' (p. 286). The actor-network approach suggests that the political space of the market is a *heterogeneous* space. In the market studies, a number of distinctive terms accommodating this analytic stance have been proposed and experimented with, such as 'hybrid forums' (Callon, 1998b; Neyland and Simakova, 2010); *agencements* (Beunza *et al.*, 2006); and 'sociology of the heterogeneous traffic'[4] (Grandclément-Chaffy, 2008). Cochoy (2009) develops object-oriented sociology of consumption practices as he analyses the introduction of the shopping cart in American grocery stores. The notion of the *heterogeneous engineer* was used to account for the activities of 'market-makers' (Callon, 1998a; Kjellberg, 2001; Lien, 1997; Araujo, 2007). A general idea of the actor-network approaches applied to the market thus appears to be the task of identifying and describing actants of 'variable geometry' (Latour, 1992) involved in the co-constitution (establishing, shifting, replaying) of market relations. This perspective usefully emphasises the relational nature of the market constituencies often labelled in summary terms as 'producer', 'consumer' and 'product'. Instead, it is suggested that the emergence and agency of these entities need to be understood within the heterogeneous arrangements of the market networks, where non-humans (shopping carts, price tags, labels, packaging) are shown to be participating in the ordering of the heterogeneous market spaces in their own right.

As it turns out, the market has presented a challenging case for ANT by provoking some thorny questions about agency and relationality. The question of agency comes to the fore in the attempts to now clarify the role of the *human subject* in market relations. As Callon (1998a) observes, the market phenomenon implies a set of relations where actants (human and non-human) are endowed with an asymmetrical agency, challenging the principle of the generalised symmetry of sociology of translation: 'The market is an institution which mixes humans and non-humans and controls their relations' (Callon, 1998a: 182). Controlling the relations between humans and non-humans is interpreted by Callon in terms of the separation between circulating non-human objects (goods) and human agents acting as decision-makers (Callon, 1998a). The ANT-inspired analyses of the market and various individual markets seem to agree that the human subject emerges as an 'event' of market relations. Markets, according to Callon and Muniesa (2005), present a convenient opportunity to observe and describe the construction of a special kind of actant, or 'calculative' agent, *homo economicus,* whose actions are construed through his or her ability to create and perform in the political spaces of the markets (Callon and Muniesa, 2005; Callon, 1998a).

In a more recent work of actor-network theorists on innovation (Akrich *et al.,* 2002a and b), the emphasis is on the role of human actors, whose activities include the practical resolution of conflicts and controversies understood as being specific to humans, such as distributing and reconciling mutual accusations, or trying to solve practical problems through building alliances. Human actants are rendered responsible for defining the relevant groups (consumers, markets, partners) to be recruited or dismissed as allies. In other words, it emerges that the actor-network approach to the market offers various versions of what accounts for the distribution of agency in market relations: the market itself? (Callon, 1998a); the collectives? (Akrich *et al.,* 2002a and b); the rational calculative agent? (Callon and Muniesa, 2005).

The emphasis on the role of humans in shaping market relations has continued to inform actor-network approaches.[5] According to Callon (Callon in Barry and Slater, 2002), if actor-network theory is to be employed as a theoretical foundation for the analyses of markets, it needs to be amended to reflect the strongly social focus of the practical activities composing markets. Callon (ibid.) calls for the development of a new vocabulary for ANT in relation to the market. The analyses of markets need to explore possibilities of producing a 'more dynamic' version of reconfiguring entities and networks of entities. Since the market is a complex process, the network metaphor may even not be applicable. The reason for this is the diversity of relations, modalities of coordination, or, in other words, all 'relations that are mobilized in order to create a basis where commercial transactions are possible' (ibid.). According to Callon, these processes are better accounted for through the new linking notions of *framing, attachment* and *detachment,* and *entanglement* and *disentanglement. Callon et al.* (2002) speak about the process of the 'qualification' of a good in terms of its 'singularisation', different 'stages' and 'devices' that 'ensure', afford, the fine-tuning of supply and demand. Fine (2003: 408), however, observes that 'disentanglement is a mystery'. He argues that the notion initially derives from ANT to define the relationships between the market entities more precisely, but that the nature of these new 'linking' terms is left unclear after the analytical dismissal of the heterogeneous network actants. Disentanglement of what, and from what? How are the entities participating in the market transaction distinguished? And how are we to treat actants' identities analytically?

As it follows, the emergence of the human subject as the principal actor in market relations provokes further questions about what counts as being *anthropological* about markets (Callon, 1998a: 50). As a premise for an anthropology of the market, the ANT-informed thinking contains assumptions of an independent existence of the market (or multiple markets) and its constituents that can be dissected and represented in analytical accounts. As such, empirical and, more precisely, ethnographic approaches are often suggested as a way forward for market studies (see next chapter for discussion). Some authors put it strongly that only social explanation can account for the complexity of markets. According to Miller (2002a), Callon's attempts to theorise the market are equivalent to 'looking at the bare bones of transactions, [and] hack[ing] off the flesh to show the relative solidity of the market principles inside' (p. 233). Mirowski and Nik-Khah (2006) argue that 'society' needs to be brought back into analyses of the market: the 'performativity' (Callon, 1998a) of markets as interplays of economic theories and economic markets needs analysis of *practices*. Anthropologists focussing on marketing and advertising in practice (Moeran, 2005; Lien, 1997; Moeran and Malefyt, 2003b) suggest that empirical analyses should focus on professional decision-making.

From the practice perspective, researchers have repeatedly emphasised the need to attend to the contingent nature of the market[6] as it acquires meanings in research and in practical deliberations. The market does not appear to be a stable, unified category. As Callon observes, 'the idea of the market as a unified category and institution is progressively disappearing' (Callon in Barry and Slater, 2002) because of different understandings of the organisations of concrete, specific markets (see Araujo *et al.*, 2010 for examples of such analyses). Some studies propose the idea of the market as a culturally bounded phenomenon emerging through contingent arrangements. Markets as embodiments of the producer–consumer relationship are shown to be outcomes of socio-historical processes whereby such relationships emerged in the cultural discourses. Agnew speaks of markets as situated phenomena, the historically evolving sets of bounded spaces and social relationships (Agnew, 1986: 18). For example, the development of merchant relations in seventeenth-century England entailed the adoption of the identities (or personae) of merchants and buyers, ready to perform negotiations. Some researchers also hint at the existence of 'hidden economies' on the margins of the market-based cultures exercised by some cultural groups (Grafton Small, 1999). Slater (2003) speaks of *marketisation* as sets of evolving relations adopted by cultures. In a similar vein, Abolafia (1998) suggests that an empirical approach to markets needs to be grounded in understanding markets as cultures, which are not fixed. In the institutionalised interactions, market culture is 'continuously reproduced through exchange relations that it is vulnerable to change' (p. 69). As Cochoy (2005) also shows, the work of establishing identities and responsibilities of the market constituents, for example, through standardisation, is always incomplete, and such identities and responsibilities are unstable.

In summary words, analytic representations of the market as actor networks usefully draw attention to the heterogeneity, instability, and complexity of market relations. They emphasise the importance of not taking for granted agency, categories, and relationality, which rather need to be understood in and through continuous recreation of socio-technical assemblages. Questions need to be asked, however, about how the understandings of the market categories, agency and relations are achieved in research, and in practice.[7] What are the interpretations of 'the market' as a phenomenon out there that inform academic writing? How are they constructed? If representations of networks depend on the network owner, namely the ANT analysts (as in Strathern, 1996), is it always clear what counts as a network, and for whom?[8] If a different description may provide a different distribution of agency of a market, one needs to stay alert to the possibility of *otherness* in the renditions of networks and relations (Lee and Brown, 1994). Is there an approach that takes into account the principle of generalised symmetry yet stays alive to the possibility of multiple interpretations of the capacities and roles of the entities? The next section examines the merits of the discursive approaches to market agency in science and technology studies and in the British version of the anthropology of the market.

The market as text

Another possible approach to the phenomenon of the market is to explore the merits of certain post-essentialist themes in science and technology studies and in anthropology. The discursive approaches inspire thinking of artefacts, of which the market is one, as textual phenomena. Textuality (studies of discourse, rhetoric) can be seen as another radical way of 'breaking down easy distinctions between form and content as well as showing the historical contingency and rhetorical orientation of the literary genres used in technoscience' (Ashmore *et al.*, 1995: 322). The textual metaphor suggested by Woolgar (1991a; Grint and Woolgar, 1997) promotes the understanding of technical artefacts as having a textual character. This embodies the position that the 'nature' of technology, as well as social arrangements, can be seen as isomorphic with their textual constitution. In science and technology studies, textuality relates to an anti-essentialist commitment to interpretivism. This approach highlights the importance of the discursively accomplished work of persuasion in establishing claims of technological capacities, and hence claims of agency. Post-essentialists emphasise that discourse should not be reduced to talk or to big claims with regard to technology: 'Discourse also includes structures of expectation, systems of categorisation, and modes of conventional practice' (Woolgar and Grint, 1991: 377). The post-essentialist metaphor is inspired by post-structuralist theorising of textuality and reader-response theory, although sources are not always provided. The discursive thought in STS broadly follows Foucault's argument about the relationship between power and knowledge in discourse. As such, it is a shift away from the 'knowing' or 'acting' subject, to the domain of contesting claims. In Foucault (1991: 28) it is proposed, for example, that 'it is not the activity of the subject of knowledge, useful or resistant to power, but power-knowledge, the processes and struggles that traverse it and of which it is made up, that determines the forms and possible domains of knowledge'. How can the market be understood from a discursive perspective as a domain of contested claims and practical action?

Some important observations emerged for me in what can be called the British tradition in the anthropology of the market. Some anthropologists (Miller, 2002; Dilley, 1992b; Carrier, 1997) usefully suggest that the market can be seen as discourse. This perspective suggests certain anti-essentialist reframings of what can be said about market agency. For Miller (2002a), the market can be seen as an ideological model rather than an empirical core to economic activity. As Dilley (1992a) puts it, markets are ascribed essence in economic models and societal discourses: 'As a displaced metaphor detached from its concrete referent, the term "market" has become a "pocket" whose contents are defined in relation to the uses to which it is put' (p. 3).

In this sense, it can be argued that a discursive approach to the market is not exactly about taking a market as a basis for economic transactions existing out there, nor about trying to locate markets in the material-geographical sense. According to Miller, studies of markets need to answer the question about how the agents use the frame of the market. Dilley (1992a) speaks of the market as a *plausible narrative* to frame sets of relations: 'The notion of the market is attractive, compelling and irresistible as a metaphor since it offers a ready-made analytical device to suggest flux in the face of structural constraint and closure. Not only that, but because of its double image, it can itself be construed as an agent of structure, collectivity and equilibrium' (p. 17). In other words, the market functioning as a metaphor is of interest to this approach.

By way of analogy, the market can be defined in terms of the discursive organisation of relations between producers and users of artefacts. One example of a debate in which the work of configuration of such relations through contesting knowledge claims was interrogated is the debate on the interactivity of social sciences and the production of socially relevant knowledge (Nowotny *et al.*, 2001; Woolgar, 2000b; Rappert, 1999; Shove and Rip, 2000). These recent studies of the rhetoric of user-relevant research and the role of the user in knowledge production suggest the possibility of looking at the role of the market (in the sense of market narratives) in the construction of relations between constituencies involved in commercial transactions. 'Markets', akin to 'users' in the studies above, can be seen as the discursive resources gaining or losing currency.

In other words, markets are best seen as sets of conventions of accounting for socio-material relations and attributions of agency whose currency needs to be examined. This means that descriptions of relationships between 'producer', 'consumer' and 'product' have to be scrutinised as *claims* that in principle can be challenged and contested. Market relations need to be sceptically approached as one possible way of organising the relationships between semiotic actants in the practical and analytical accounts. The analyst of the market is like an ethnographer who tries to understand the interplay of claims and categorisations with regard to market constituencies. As Woolgar (1988a) puts it, the analyst needs 'to resist the temptation to accept at face value the conventions that structure the text and the illusion of a world beyond the text which these conventions suggest. These conventions impose order upon a fluid (pre-textual) realm of actants and entities; they produce an ordered structure of categories, objects and subjects; they define distances and relationships between these entities; the moral order of rights and obligations – which of these entities can say and do what about whom' (p. 29).

The post-essentialist versions of discourse analysis elaborate a line of argument related to *attribution* of agency. Theorists representing semiotic approaches in STS agree that 'agency becomes a consequence of narration' (Latour, 1994: xiii), but the thesis is worked out differently. Acknowledging that attribution of agency is a long-standing problem in social theory, the post-essentialist discursive approach asks: do characteristics reside in, or are they attributed to, entities? (Woolgar, 1991a: 66). The metaphor 'technology as text' explored by Woolgar (1991a; Grint and Woolgar, 1997) shows the interpretive work the participants are engaged in while attributing and interpreting technological capacities. The work of interpretation involves any sanctioned procedures for representation constituting the moral order of representations, or any complex of relationships between entities. As Woolgar (1988c) shows, the moral order of representation may change with the introduction of a new entity. For instance, the introduction of a new item of apparatus in the scientific laboratory might be interpreted as having important consequences for the rights and responsibilities of existing pieces of apparatus enacted in the laboratory talk. Depending on the interpretive conventions, some entities are being ascribed the authority and capacity to act while others remain passive or receptive of action.

Post-essentialists explore how 'a text can be usefully understood as identifying, defining and configuring – in short, as performing – the sets of persons, social relationships and actions/responses which can be legitimately brought to bear in text' (Cooper and Woolgar, 1994). In a similar vein, an analysis of the market needs to focus on how those compelling narratives – which offer a distribution of agency for interpretation to readers, or users, of such narratives – work to organise human activities. How are various persons, groups, relationships and actions legitimately and credibly brought into the market narratives? How are these narratives written and interpreted? By whom? Or, in Cooper and Woolgar's (1994) words, how do the market narratives *perform communities*, as above? Rephrasing Grint and Woolgar (1997), a post-essentialist view of the market would contend that participants organise their actions depending on the properties they ascribe to a market. This anti-essentialist perspective provides for opening up a whole new set of questions. If the market is employed as a device to account for 'structure, collectivity and equilibrium' as in Dilley (1992a: 17), how and why does the notion get its currency? How do the relations embodied by the notion of a (single) market and its composing entities become produced, displayed and accepted as a description of the reality out there?

The questions about representations of markets posed in the final paragraph of the previous section can thus be recast in terms of the distribution of agency in the market narratives. The post-essentialist view of the market would contend that agency – such as the distinction, for example, between humans and non-humans, and hence, for example, attributions of intentionality or rational action – is sustained in textual practices. In Woolgar (1991a), Grint and Woolgar (1997) and Ashmore (1993), the problem of the distribution of agency between humans and non-humans is provocatively reversed. The critique addresses the rigid boundary between human and non-human actants based on what are assumed to be essential distinctions between the two categories (Grint and Woolgar, 1997: 10). The merits of this critique were explored by Ashmore (1993). Ashmore's narrative experiments are about producing behaviour modifications in human and non-human actants: a cat, a cat flap, and human cat 'owners'. He observes that a problem with the sociology of things is 'the perceived absurdity of the undertaking'. Experimenting with actor-network narratives provokes the suggestion that the stories granting agency to things require certain contexts to 'work'. Or, in other words, to seem plausible, to 'comfortably' (for the reader) distribute particular roles and statuses of actants, stories need to meet certain narrative conventions prescribing 'how exactly' non-human actants can or cannot influence the network configuration. Woolgar (1991a: 92) makes a similar point by simulating a letter written 'by a machine'. Descriptions of human intentionality are often perceived as other than metaphorical. And in some situations the ascription of agency to things does not seem implausible. But why, on other occasions, does the reader feel uncomfortable reading the text that plays with the agency conventions, or try to dig for the 'context' of this exercise?

From this perspective, how is the market construed as a plausible cultural narrative? Or would it be more useful to speak about multiple cultural narratives? Following Douglas (1982), Dilley (1992a) suggests that markets can be understood as *modes of accountability,* which embrace (at least) 'the nature and extent of object fetishism, the bases of control which exchange hides, the forms of agency and personhood represented in exchange' (p. 23). The notion of modes of accountability is employed by Dilley (1992a) to critique 'the fetishism of agency' and refers 'to the way a culture attributes and holds responsible specific forms of agency or aspects of social persons in their representations of exchange. These representations, of which the market is one, are predicated on specific constructions of personhood and notions of individual agency' (p. 24).

Dilley's explanation of the construction of agency in the cultures of trade and exchange is somewhat similar to MacKenzie's 'certainty trough' (MacKenzie, 1990). Dilley argues that construction of agency depends on alienability from the items traded: 'the greater the alienability from the items traded, the greater the extent to which notions of individual agency and aspects of the person are seen as instrumental in informing the ideology of exchange' (1992a: 24). In other words, Dilley's observation with regard to the market, along with a more general post-essentialist textual approach, is suggestive of the possibility of thinking of the market analytically as sets of narratives attributing agency, identities, responsibilities and capabilities to such actants as 'product', 'producer' and 'consumer'.

This approach is thus suggestive of the possibility of different descriptions of market relations displayed and interpreted in settings variously distant from the site of production of such market narratives. The academic, organisational, and wider societal narratives of marketing will be examined in more detail in the next chapter, as well as throughout the rest of the book.

For now, it is important to explore in what sense an analysis of the market relations built on the post-essentialist propositions would attend to questions of how notions about the character and capacity of different market entities, the relationships and connections between them, their relative boundedness, and the associated patterns of rights and responsibilities are achieved in market discourses. I argue that this implies analytical attention to interpretations accomplished by the actors engaged in the construction of agency, including the analyst. Technology marketing, as will be suggested below, is one such case offering the possibility of examining the construction of market narratives.

Technology marketing as a strategic case

Given the argument above, it is necessary to state at the outset that 'marketing' as it is used in this book is not necessarily understood in terms of one of the possible forms of 'market-making' (Araujo, 2007; Araujo *et al.*, 2010) activities. The latter approach emphasises a direct relatedness to, and contribution of, marketing as practice to some kind of 'market'. This kind of thinking introduces the preconception of a 'market' out there, which can be 'made': established, modified, influenced. Instead, following Dilley (1992a), I propose to see the 'market' as a metaphor carrying a compelling distribution of agency and power and being used in various (economic, societal, managerial) discourses. Similarly, 'marketing' is considered here as a label for a practical activity accounted for in various discourses of socio-technical order, often through the lens of the production–consumption dynamics. The question is rather to examine to what extent and in what sense 'the market' has currency as an element of the discourses of, in this case, technology marketing. And, the other way round, attention needs to be paid to when and how 'the market' is spoken about in terms of being an outcome of marketing.

Research on technology marketing can also help to shed light on questions about technology dissemination in the context of market relations. Furthermore, drawing on the existing scholarship in STS, such research can question, and re-examine, the assumptions about innovation and emerging technologies in the scholarly discourse. From STS perspectives on innovation, the linear (or diffusion) models adopted in some technology management literatures serve as a gloss for complex processes of innovative activities (e.g. Bijker and Law, 1992/2000; Brown *et al.*, 2000). The diffusion models – also entrenched as metaphors and reifications (Elzinga, 2004) in the policy discourse – tend to assume that technology *pre-exists* the process of innovation: 'the model of diffusion moves the technical object to the interior of a society which constitutes a more or less receptive environment' (Akrich *et al.*, 2002a: 205). Rather, STS authors argue that innovation is understood better as the 'interactive, time-dependent, process of sociotechnical bootstrapping' (Bijker and Law, 1992/2000). According to Akrich *et al.* (2002a), the main problem of the innovation management literature is the separation between the technological analysis of the object per se in terms of its intrinsic properties and the sociological analysis of the technology environment within which it spreads its effects. The task of this study is precisely to question the ways in which technological content and the circumstances of its production and reception are co-constituted in technology marketing.

This book will argue that while technology marketing can be seen as attempts to produce discourses allegedly capable of changing relationships between technology, producer and consumer, technology marketers can be seen as practical reasoners deliberating on the nature of socio-technical relations. As Woolgar (2000a) puts it, 'competing views about the effects of technology are not merely whimsical differences in technical understanding. They are instead heavily invested with usually implicit commitments to particular ways of ordering society. Technology – construed as a description of social arrangements – embodies deeply held ideas about the moral order' (p. 177). What exactly are the implicit commitments to particular ways of ordering society in technology marketing? In what ways do practitioners contest ideas about the moral order?[9] While marketers are engaged in the production of technology discourses, the researcher gets involved with and tries to understand attempts to produce 'multiple, often competing, views about ways of organising society' (p. 177). Assuming that hi-tech marketing is an exercise in social ordering, a hi-tech marketing department can be seen as a strategic ethnographic research site for the contemporary scholarship on innovation and socio-technical change.

An important idea this book develops is that marketing is about producing accounts of technologies, which are best seen in terms of the constitution of the relationships between market entities, rather than as a reflection of such relationships. In this sense, marketing can be seen as an element in the politics of representation whereby certain claims about technologies become more powerful, persuasive or actionable upon than others. Post-essentialist approaches suggest that we need to move away from a reliance on the content of (technology) claims through 'remaining agnostic about the contending representations, in order to bring out the ways in which some representations become more powerful – and hence acquire a stronger claim to "truth"' (Grint and Woolgar, 1997: 33). In relation to marketing, a central question to be asked in this book is: how do some representations of the socio-technical relations win out while others get refuted and dismissed?

In sum, the contention of this book is that technology marketing is of particular interest to science and technology studies in terms outlined in Bijker *et al.* (1987): 'Part of the task of the emerging field of technology studies is the identification of research sites at which the complexity of the seamless web is manageable but which at the same time serve to capture key aspects of technological development' (p. 191). Although science and technology studies have offered a number of theories of technological innovation, it is remarkable that technology marketing has been largely lacking ethnographic attention in STS so far. This book fills this gap by opening up the possibility of further investigating the anti-essentialist premises in STS. The next chapter continues this discussion by offering an approach to technology marketing as a situated cultural practice.

2 Marketing technologies

In theory and in practice

Marketing as a culture and as a cultural artefact

In this chapter I interrogate marketing as a cultural practice of knowledge production, raising questions about the nature of marketing theory and marketing practice. The chapter examines marketing in a variety of cultural, historical and sociological perspectives that help us to understand marketing as a cultural phenomenon, and technology marketing as a particular type of marketing. Both scholars and practitioners of marketing have been asking questions about its potential to establish itself as a valid social scientific discipline as well as a useful organisational specialism broadly concerned with understanding, and influencing, behaviour of social groups, such as consumers. As such, an empirical analysis of marketing – as sets of social science techniques, as well as folk theories – can shed light on the boundary institutional dynamics in the social science knowledge production, and the practical utility of such knowledge, as well as offer an insight into these issues at stake if thought about in the context of the production and circulation of valid social scientific knowledge in general.

A recent debate has emerged on the wave of the increasing recognition and appreciation of the constructivist approaches to knowledge production – as developed in the social studies of science – in the marketing scholarship. The controversy is framed in a way familiar to science studies scholars. Namely, through the contestation between the 'received' (normative, positivist) and constructivist views of marketing as a social science. As an introductory example, Hunt (1990) and Siegel (1988) defend scientific realism as the way to acquire objective knowledge about the world through model building and causal explanations against 'nihilistic' relativism. By analogy with the Popperian logical positivism seeking to discover the methods of science, it is possible, according to these authors, to formulate and employ the 'methods' of marketing, leading to an objective version of social reality. The argument seeks support with the received view of science claiming the 'obvious success of science over the last 400 years' in its 'pursuit of truth' (Hunt, 1990:13). Hunt urges marketing science to retain 'truth as an overriding objective of theory and research' (p. 2).

The received *positivist* view of marketing reinforced by the received view of science makes it difficult to think of marketing in different terms. However, as, for example, in Peter and Olson (1983), the *constructivist* critique of marketing knowledge recruits a different version of science. As Brown (1999) points out, marketing needs to explore possibilities of a different view of itself, through reflexively adopting critique that was developed in the social studies of science. Broadly speaking, Brown and others refer to the view of knowledge that suggests that individuals and social groups, through contesting different views, are actively engaged in the construction of artefacts and practices (Law, 1987). From this perspective, any science is neither a unitary set of methods and procedures nor a universal practice. What counts as 'science' varies over time (philosophically, historically and sociologically) and is elusive.

In other words, Brown suggests that scholars need to view marketing science as irredeemably social, inherently messy, and deeply affected by political, professional and personal interests. The debate on the status of marketing knowledge is remarkably similar to the one in the social sciences between positivist and interpretivist methodologies (Burrell and Morgan, 1979). Are marketing findings about consumer objective? (Laurent and Pras, 1999) Some authors contend that traditional marketing theory (especially Kotler's version of it) should be dismissed on the grounds of its positivist scientistic preconceptions about the nature of marketers' work. How is it possible to develop an approach to marketing that would take into account the realities[1] of marketing practice? (Brown, 1999; Grafton Small, 1999; Zwick and Cayla, eds, 2011). How can marketing be understood as a social science and an organisational practice though the lens of the constructivist critique?

Some ideas can be found in the STS literature, in anthropology, as well as in the increasingly visible body of constructivist empirical research in the marketing scholarship. One can begin thinking of marketing as a social process that takes place within a language community and hence responds to the prevalent values, beliefs[2] and expectations of that community. From the constructivist perspective, marketing is thus best approached as a fluid set of practices that need to be apprehended in their contingent, plural and differentiated contexts[3] (McFall, 2004). The STS approach to technology as a culture and as a cultural artefact (Hine, 2000; Jordan and Lynch, 1998) offers a useful heuristic device. From this perspective, marketing can be seen as a locus of practical activities of the professionals calling themselves 'marketers', as well as a part of a broader societal and organisational, managerial discourse. How is marketing, as a multifaceted cultural practice, locally construed as an agent of social ordering in various discourses?

One starting point for thinking of marketing as a culturally situated practice is imagining the possibility of certain cultures, or settings, where the marketing label did not get currency, or in terms of the *boundaries* of marketing. Brownlie *et al.* (1999a: 14) suggest that marketing discourse is inherent only to a society that has undergone a process of 'marketisation' through the historical stages of rejection and acceptance (see also Slater, 2003). Araujo argues that the concept of marketing culture has its boundaries, since marketing is practised only in the particular socio-cultural context of Western societies (Araujo, 1999). In the organisational context, marketing is also best approached as a situated practice.

For example, Workman (1993) shows that talking of a technological product in terms of the users' needs, which is a widespread characteristic feature of so-called marketing thinking, is not limited to members of an organisation's marketing department; it is also a topic of corporate shop-floor talk. However, a certain group gets compartmentalised as 'marketing' and sustains its (limited) authority to provide certain kinds of knowledge about users, often informally. Marketing can thus be seen as emerging from sets of social arrangements, as an institution or as a group whose participants come to identify their concerns and professional expertise as marketing, forming marketing as culture. Such local – cultural, organisational – marketing practices and conventions are of particular interest to the anthropological research informing the constructivist perspective.

In this regard, this book joins recent efforts (e.g. Brownlie *et al.*, 1999b; Araujo *et al.*, 2010; Brownlie and Saren, 1991) that critique the normative 'textbook' Kotlerian approach to marketing. This critique accomplishes the move from understanding marketing as a set of prescriptive rules and norms to understanding its use in organisations. In the ethnomethodological (Garfinkel, 1967) sense, normative concepts and rules such as the 'marketing mix' need to be understood as a part of reflexive activities of participants within organisations, through which rules and norms are interpreted and reinterpreted for the purposes at hand. In the managerial context, references to such rules and norms (e.g. assigning a specific role to marketing in a company) may occur as a part of strategic organisational discourse. Brownlie and Saren usefully suggest an understanding of marketing as 'a method of classification', or an ideology, or 'a way of thinking about business offering a framework for success' (ibid.: 36). However, such ideologies and methods of classification that accompany the marketing discourse are not stable.

Organisations, in turn, may or may not incorporate marketing as an element of their identity. Araujo *et al.* (2010) observe the disconnections, fluidity of the terms, and analogies by means of which marketing applies or does not apply to activities in organisations. Wensley (1990) observes that not every professional group happily adopts 'marketing' as a mode of societal or business identity. He shows that the marketing analogy, as a result of its recognised reliance on certain sets of expectations, responsibilities and power relations between (active, strategy-minded, or even aggressive) producers and (passive) consumers, does not suit certain groups wishing not to associate themselves with the image of a powerful producer.

This kind of approach – based on the recognition of boundaries of marketing knowledge – opens up a whole set of questions about the nature of corporate interactions, such as, for instance, the group performance at the intersection of marketing and other corporate specialisms, such as engineers, or sales (see, for example, Chapters 5 and 7); or the deliberations over the status of the 'the market' based on various ways of accounting for the consumer and the user in marketing and other corporate units (Licoppe and Simakova, 2007). It also promotes the possibility of looking at how marketing is spoken about in organisations, and at the emergence of different understandings of marketing in the corporate discourse. Applying Bittner's inversion in organisational studies (Bittner,

1965), one needs to ask: how do various (corporate, wider societal) discourses construe marketing? What are the common sense usages of 'marketing'? In the course of my research, I found it especially productive to ask: what does it take, and what does it mean, to become a member of the 'marketing' tribe through apprehending the language of a particular marketing setting?

Marketing power and marketing knowledge

Beginning the research project, I became concerned about the role and purpose of the renditions of marketing that emphasise the power of marketing to change cultural discourses. How can these accounts be addressed from an STS perspective advocating symmetry in the analyses of power relations, as in the previous chapter?

The associations of marketing with brainwashing, viral marketing, or spin – the everyday perceptions of marketing – often define it as a form of manipulation. In some sociological accounts, corporations, and marketing as a part of corporate cultures, appear as powerful societal agents who contribute to a redefinition of human discourses, practices and types of rationality.[4] In other words, marketers are seen as specialists occupied with creating discourses capable of imposing certain moral orders, or rights and obligations, with regard to artefacts. The sociology of consumption often blames marketers for imposing consumerism as the main ideology of capitalism through the possessing and applying of certain powerful tools that can affect human behaviour (Bocock, 1993; Slater, 1997; Lury, 1996; Klein, 2000). Marketers are negatively seen as agents capable of changing people's behaviour through the application of their skills.

Slater (1997) argues that organisations are becoming increasingly marketing-driven: 'advertising and marketing are no longer functions subordinate to production but are actually commanding discourses within firms' (p. 32). In such sociological discourses, marketing is seen as the driving force of the large-scale expansion of consumer culture, which is made possible 'by the integration of markets through marketing, using such new techniques as branding and packaging, national sales forces, advertising, point of sale materials and industrial design – all designed to unify product identity across socially and geographically dispersed markets' (1997: 14). In other words, the relationship between producers and consumers is sometimes portrayed in Foucauldian terms (Foucault, 1991) as 'the engine of a vast panoptic system of observation and social control by means of which it tracks, traces and seduces unknowing consumers into participation in its processes' (Willmott, 1999: 218).

The discourses portraying marketing as a powerful economic agent often rely on the producer–consumer dualism. Some scholars of marketing (such as those who take the 'critical marketing' approach) suggest that scholars should not take the dualism – as a reified set of attributes and boundaries – for granted[5] (Brownlie *et al.*, 1999a; Wensley, 1990). First, this dualism is understood not as neutral, but as already assuming certain power relations that, in principle, can be changed.[6] In the socio-political discourses of marketing, the relationship between producers and consumers is not seen as static. McFall (2004) makes a similar point: plural and multifaceted, the discourses of advertising are shown to have changed from the informational flow of descriptions of goods to the pervasive logic driving 'capitalist' or 'consumer' societies.

Although power imbalances can be negotiated and redressed in principle, the general view of marketing as a powerful institution persists. This is perceived by some (insiders of academic marketing?) as a worrying situation for marketing as a professional institution. Willmott (1999: 218) points at a possible crisis of consumers' perception of marketing, expressed as mistrust and suspicion on the part of consumers. He hopes that a 'more self-critical understanding of marketing expertise and its effects would improve the credibility and status of marketing theory and practice'.

Overall, the literatures attribute agency to marketing professionals in the producer–consumer relationship differently. Willmott (1999: 217) formulates what he calls 'a paradox of marketing': 'it exerts a growing influence upon processes of production and consumption in advanced capitalist societies, yet it is ascribed a comparatively low social and organizational status'. Willmott highlights shifts in prestige, or credibility, of marketing knowledge – linked, but not totally reducible to, marketing's reliance on scientism – leading to the situation when some, in academia as well as in industry, view marketing 'with scepticism and suspicion, if not distaste' (p. 206). Due to these perceptions, marketing has yet 'to achieve full respectability as an academic discipline or as a managerial specialism' (ibid.) In order to address the 'paradox' of marketing and to understand marketing agency, it is helpful perhaps to assume an attitude of analytical scepticism:[7] how and by whom are the claims of the status of marketing, or its societal or organisational power, sustained? Even if marketing is to be understood as a system of knowledge striving for control over societies and consumers, some studies of surveillance technologies (for example, Neyland, 2005) advocate a cautious attitude towards starting research with assumptions about the power of panoptic systems.

How is marketing performed as sets of academic and practical knowledges that became treated as a source of power to change cultural discourses? Marketing as an academic and professional discipline has developed what Wensley (1999) called the academic cultures of marketing. Numerous efforts have been made to consolidate the discipline and its practical activities through standardised patterns of marketing education and certified degrees (such as the Chartered Institute of Marketing in the UK), to establish marketing faculties in the universities and business schools, and to insert marketing into MBA curricula and management degrees. Marketers gather for academic and practical conferences worldwide and issue marketing journals. The two most influential groups of journals belong to the US and UK marketing traditions, the institutional history of which, as Wensley (1999: 81) pointed out, 'reflects a continual attempt to create institutional structures which integrate the practical and theoretical'. Forms of marketing socialisation less accessible to outsiders are practised behind corporate walls. Professional bodies coordinate activities of marketers through bulletins, professional mailing lists, websites, professional meetings and seminars. Marketing gurus publish books and give public lectures, often pursuing careers in both academia and consultancy.

Textbook marketing knowledge provides descriptions of certain 'methods' taught to and put into effect by professional marketers to influence the consumer. Marketing textbooks are primary examples of narratives construing marketing as a human activity and marketers as powerful agents of social change. Marketing is often portrayed as a social scientific endeavour seeking to understand how to control human behaviour through a set of rules and practical tools. The textbook marketing narratives traditionally establish 'consumers' as objects of knowledge and subjects of influence. One example is the early programmatic statements by Kotler, one of the best-selling authors of marketing textbooks. Although Kotler's largely 'imperialistic' portrayals of marketing have recently become subject to critique pointing at the boundaries of marketing knowledge (e.g. Brownlie and Saren, 1991), his books were largely influential in shaping marketing as a managerial discipline. Kotler (1972) introduces the marketer as a specialist who knows what it takes for someone to act. Marketing, as a 'category of human action', for Kotler (1972) is about individuals (marketers) influencing the acceptance (or rejection) of what he calls 'social objects' – any entity, or artefact, found in society, such as a product, service, organisation, person, place or idea (p. 49). As a programmatic stance for marketing practitioners and academics that is built on certain notions of human action, market and organisation, Kotler's earlier concept of marketing promoted the universalism of marketing knowledge through claiming marketing as a generic concept to be 'broadened' towards all kinds of social and commercial transactions. Kotler's (1972) approach informing the generic marketing textbooks stresses uniformity of marketing tasks and concerns that can be summarised and presented as axioms.

Perhaps the statements provided in the marketing textbooks contributed to the perceptions of marketing as a powerful institution. Other versions of marketing have been suggested but have not gained much currency. For example, Levitt's (1975) idea – oriented towards practitioners as well as scholars – that 'market orientation', or thinking in terms of a consumer, is not given but needs active work to establish itself in organisations did not get taken up as mainstream marketing thinking (Levitt, 1975; Brownlie and Saren, 1991).

The constructivist apprehensions of marketing – for example, debates on its historical and organisational aspects – may change the story of marketing power. Studies of marketing in practice provide a different, and more nuanced, picture of the role and power of marketers as creators of social order. Simply replaying the objective/subjective, art/science, producer/consumer dichotomies is insufficient for an understanding of the role of marketing as an agent of change. Echoing Levitt's manifesto (1975), studies such as Moore (1999), Workman (1993) and Elliott (1999) emphasise the practical need for marketing to be established as a part of organisational knowledge. A number of studies show that marketers are sometimes assigned only a 'limited role' (Workman, 1993) in organisations, and that marketers' attempts to interfere with existing patterns of organisational knowledge may create considerable tensions (Moore, 1999; Levitt, 1975; Workman, 1993; Eriksson, 1999). Ethnographies show how marketers enter into interprofessional competition with engineers (R&D) and need to demonstrate the generalisability of marketing expertise, or to learn to exercise their influence informally in organisational struggles for power.

Doyle (2003) pointed out that marketing competes with other business disciplines implemented in organisations, or, using Abrahamson's (1996) term, fads and fashions, such as Total Quality Management (TQM), Just-in-Time (JIT), Business Re-engineering (BRE), strategic alliances, and others. Marketing can also be seen as a construct that emerged through distinguishing marketing from other business disciplines, such as sales or engineering. Randles and Warde (2003) describe the boundary work accomplished to distinguish marketing knowledge from sales, or rather the 'scientific practice' of research from the 'informal knowledge' of customers obtained by salespeople in direct interactions. These arguments join the literature on the history of business concepts and consultancy tools (e.g. in Thrift, 1998: 169).

Analyses devoted to the socio-cultural dynamics of producer–consumer relationships show that the latter develop under certain regulatory regimes and accountability conditions. Randles and Warde (2003) show how marketing was engaged in contestations and alliances with social research in the fight for consumers' trust and willingness to participate in surveys. UK market researchers adopted a number of sociological techniques for involving respondents such as codes of practice and the adoption of confidentiality promises, which helped marketing to win consumers as respondents by pushing forward a democratic agenda of opinion polls and surveys. Miller and Rose (1996) demonstrate how the work of assembling the modern consumer involved building up the credibility of psychological knowledge by the Tavistock Institute of Human Relations in London. The authors discuss how in the beginning of the twentieth century the new psychological knowledges 'contested themselves up in complex ways with the technologies of advertising and marketing to make possible new kinds of relations that human beings can have with themselves and others through the medium of goods' (p. 3). Cochoy (2005) provides a historical analysis of how the requirement of traceability of industrial product affected the standardisation of the relationship between industrial organisations and consumers.

To summarise, I chose to approach marketing as a culture and as a cultural artefact as the basis for beginning to understand marketing in its cultural and organisational contexts. I suggested that marketing is best seen as a contingent set of practices performed in a language community. Addressing Willmott's (1999) concern of a more modest approach to marketing knowledge, one can say that a study of marketing needs to take into account the variability of accounts of marketing power and knowledge provided by different groups, insiders and outsiders: it is important to ask *whose* claims about marketing knowledge win out and how the participants manage (or not) to establish marketing as a useful source of expertise in the organisation.

Marketing as boundary work

Marketing has emerged – historically and culturally – as a set of contested claims. The cultural approaches to marketing dismiss attempts to locate the source of marketing influence in the normative marketing knowledge. Rather, this body of scholarship suggests that one needs to ask questions about how such 'influence' is achieved, in various socio-cultural and organisational contexts. What kinds of alternatives can be offered to shed light on the role of marketing in the production of cultural discourses and possibilities for change?

In science and technology studies, the language of *boundaries* has been employed to theorise the (purposeful) activity of introducing new entities (such as new scientific disciplines, technological development, objects or products) and to redefine currently dominating cultural discourses. The idea of political spaces as a contestation of boundaries, situatedness and locality of knowledge claims is important to the constructivist and relativist perspectives. As an STS sensibility, the notion reflects a relativist stance with regard to the construction of differences and similarities. For Haraway (1988), being analytically sensitive to boundaries helps to eschew the privileging of any insider's perspective, since all drawings of inside–outside boundaries can be seen as 'power moves, not moves towards the truth' (p. 576). From this feminist standpoint, knowledge is always situated and embodied, and is not a universal view created by the transcendental, all-embracing gaze of an observer: 'infinitive vision is an illusion, a god-trick' (p. 582). Boundaries reflect the partial perspectives of claimants, helping to theorise practical moves involved in the construction and uses of artefacts. STS authors argue that boundaries need not be understood as rigid demarcations (Mol and Law, 2005). Law (2002b) cautioned against the rigid distinction of inside/outside sometimes appearing in accounts that theorise socio-material relations through the notion of boundary: no particular boundary around an object should be privileged (p. 9). Instead, recognition of differences and similarities between constituencies should be treated as a continual achievement (Michael, 1998).

For the purposes of this book, marketing can be characterised as an activity purported to accomplish boundary work[8] related to the cultural ways of interpreting (apprehending, using) artefacts, such as goods. Marketers can be seen as social actors contributing to the 'social process of changes in the existing sets of identities, expectations, beliefs and language' (Woolgar, 1998: 444). In other words, marketing offers a convenient opportunity to study the dynamics of competing narratives in establishing certain moral orders of technology (Woolgar, 1991a). It can be said that marketers are engaged in the practical management of a boundary between an organisation and its 'outside' by attempting to make some technology narratives gain greater currency than others. With regard to the possible conceptualisation of marketing as boundary work, Callon argues that 'commercial transactions are boundary-shifting' (interview with Callon in Barry and Slater, 2002: 292). The practices of marketing and advertising are constituted by 'the project of destabilizing market boundaries and competitive relationships' (ibid.: 243). Prus (1989) suggests that marketers' performance can be described in terms of Goffman's 'drama of everyday life' metaphor, or as organising frontstage/backstage performance. If innovation (or putting a product on the market) is to be understood as a form of boundary transgression (Woolgar, 1998), how can the practical management of boundaries in market relations be analysed? To what extent can the practical management of boundaries be adopted as an approach to understanding marketing practices? And how can a study of marketing inform existing understandings of boundaries?

My research is especially inspired by the *discursive* approaches to boundaries, as a focus of practical activities, developed in science and technology studies. Examining how such practices aim to strategically redefine cultural discourses, some authors examine the ordering role of discourse. Shackley and Wynne (1996: 280), for example, introduce the notion of the 'boundary-ordering device' to account for the understandings achieved in the 'highly fluid institutional and epistemic sets of relations' through which communication about global climate change happens. The 'boundary-ordering devices' allow certain translation processes (the authors identify the following: reduction, management, transformation, condensation, scheduling into the future, and displacement) that convert uncertainty into a resource for symbolic action. The discourses 'allow the actors to define their interests, build alliances, map out futures, and construct identities rapidly and across many domains' (ibid.: 280).

Michael and Brown (2004) hold a less deterministic position, suggesting that boundary work is a means (not necessarily leading to a success) to accomplish persuasive objectives involved in the introduction of an innovative scientific claim. In their analysis, the discourses of a new technology of xenotransplantation are seen as instances of discursive boundary work accomplished through persuasion and the construction of the credibility of a spokesperson (Michael and Brown, 2004: 379). In the context of the public understanding of science, they suggest that new knowledge claims problematise existing 'lay' cultural assumptions, imposing new identities on the participants as supporters or rejecters of the new technique.

Woolgar's (1991a) 'configuring the user' argument is an example of boundary work accomplished by computer manufacturers. 'Configuring the users' of a technology implies identifying, enabling and constraining the users' actions with regard to the technology. The inside/outside boundary (of the company; of the machine) denotes the positions of insiders/outsiders with respect to a technological artefact. As in MacKenzie's (1990) 'certainty trough', the insiders and outsiders may exhibit different degrees of certainty with regard to technological capacity. The inclusion and exclusion of (imaginary; real) user communities into machine design *performs* communities of producers and users. This is accomplished through the interactive work of elaborating appropriate discursive constructs defining the machine, its users and uses, and technology content and context, or the moral order of technology.

For Rappert (2001: 562), boundaries constitute the focus of participants' practical activities in attempts to intervene. Questioning the 'appropriateness of particular narrative forms as a basis for intervention', Rappert seeks to understand how particular claims about the capacities of a technology (in his case of non-lethal weapons) are established. According to Rappert, to gain a better understanding of boundaries and intervention, it is necessary to 'develop an understanding of the interaction (or more forcefully the co-constitution) of "technology" with its "context"' (p. 571).

One way it can be done is to adhere to a post-essentialist line of analysis through dissecting 'the performative properties of particular narratives', as in, for example, Woolgar (1998). According to Woolgar (p. 444), the inclusion/exclusion of new actors into the network constituting a technology is achieved through the routinely accomplished discursive acts of maintaining membership in technology. Discussing the social glue that binds the technology networks, Woolgar writes: 'Through language and action, members of social networks routinely remind each other of their membership and of what counts as appropriate behaviour. Folk tales, stories, anecdotes and jokes deploy categories that display the basis for the network membership. In particular, jokes are powerful reminders of who is in and who is out of the network. With respect to technological innovations, jokes are the basis for adequate, member-like behaviour towards the technology' (p. 446).

Technology tales thus can be seen as boundary devices, the content of which can be dissected and whose functions can be analysed. Urban legends, according to Woolgar, represent a particularly stable narrative form enacting the boundaries and expressing the fear of foreignness and contamination with regard to new technologies. Technology narratives are thus said to be 'moral tales about the consequences of disrupting accepted social boundaries' and an 'index of cultural responses to new and potentially frightening social arrangements' (p. 450). Technology talk is shown to be an important element of the constitution of mutual relationships between the constituencies. Woolgar (1993a, also in Grint and Woolgar, 1997) discusses how members of a technology community perform boundaries between themselves and a community of users through the invocation of 'atrocity stories' as technology crosses organisational boundaries.

Interrogating the interpretive constraints

In his 'configuring the user' argument, Woolgar (1991a) proposes to explore the limits of the textual metaphor 'machine as text', which denotes the textual character of technology. As such, this proposition aims to interrogate one of the main issues accompanying the discursive approaches to boundary work: the problem of constraints imposed on interpretive action. As Grint and Woolgar (1997) put it, 'construing the machine as text encourages us to see that the nature of the artefact is its reading. But trying to escape technological determinism, in disassociating the upshot of reading and interpretation from any notion of the inherent quality of the text (what it actually says, what it actually means), we do not mean to suggest that any reading is possible (let alone that any reading is actually possible), although in principle this is the case' (p. 72).

My further line of inquiry was inspired by a particular treatment of texts as enablers or constraints for interpretation in the feminist studies, as well as by the post-essentialist tradition in science and technology studies. Post-essentialism follows an ethnomethodological feminist version of textual analysis by Dorothy Smith (1978), who suggests that the organisation of a text makes one or another reading differentially possible. For Smith, the important point is that the organisation of the text is isomorphic with the concepts we use to make sense of it. According to this school of textual analysis, the textual organisation provides certain 'instructions', which enable readers to make sense, for example, of content in terms of a conclusion stated at the outset of the text (see also Woolgar's analysis of the pulsar discovery account, 1981). The textuality of socio-technical relations can also be understood through paying attention to the roles of texts in organisational practices. Smith (2001) draws attention to the significance of organisational documents and texts as integral coordinators of what is made sense of, objectified – through these textual practices – as organisational activities. She suggests that textual analysis is a promising approach to exploring the ontologies of organisations, to capturing social organisations in people's doings, which are particular, local and ephemeral. Through the circulation of texts, these activities disappear in 'a universe of discursive objects' (p. 165), which do the work of actualisation and attribution of objective qualities to the entities employed in a text.

Anthropologists have studied how documents are created, reproduced and read in particular organisational settings and constitute local knowledges and practices (Riles, 2006). So documents can be analysed for their reproduction of social organisation and for participants' construction of rational behaviour. The particular technique of textual analysis offered by Smith is a form of an ethnographic reading of a text that also takes into account the local reading practices. The approach is reminiscent of Garfinkel's (1967) treatment of organisational documents as they take part in the construction of local organisational rationalities. The technique can be either applied to a single document, or extended to 'burrowing into organisational intertextuality' (Smith, 2001: 187), thus acknowledging that 'a text cannot be read in detachment from other texts that it addresses, refers to, presupposes, relies on and so on' (p. 187). Smith argues that by looking at how texts are recreated and read in an organisation and what kind of readership is involved, we can capture the coordinating function of texts in organisations, how people's work is coordinated by texts to accomplish organisational and institutional objectives. The documents are treated as data themselves, and can be analysed in order to find a set of rules or procedures for constructing (organisational) realities. Textual artefacts produced by marketers (such as advertisements and brochures) can be seen as such documents, discursive objects,[9] participating in the constitution of realities. For a study of marketing as an organisational practice, such attention to the coordinating role of texts seems a useful and informative approach, which forcefully captures the emergence of agents and agency, as well as the relations of accountability, in everyday marketing deliberations (cf. Woolgar and Simakova, 2003, for an analysis of a creative brief). In Chapter 4 of this book the reader can find a particular example of textual analysis of a weekly report based on the ethnographic reading of the document.

My primary concern, however, with the approaches seeking to explain social order based on the intrinsic properties of texts (or properties discovered through idiosyncratic analytical readings) is that they may have some limitations with regard to the study of marketing in practice. Such approaches assume that the *effects* of texts can be explained in terms of the intrinsic properties of such texts. To what extent is it useful to apply the techniques of textual analysis to marketing texts in order to understand how they work? And, anthropologically speaking, what kind of knowledge about textuality is produced when the analysis is informed by the content of a textual artefact? What can a further questioning of approaches to textuality tell us about the limitations of textual deterministic explanations?

A textual approach to advertising and marketing is not a particularly new idea, given a large body of scholarship in the semiotic tradition. McFall (2004) observes that research into advertising has predominantly been preoccupied with texts, growing into the 'enduring fascination not with advertis*ing* but with adver-tisements' (McFall, 2004: introduction). McFall critically asserts that in such studies of marketing or advertising, in general, textual approaches based on deconstruction of advertisements fail to address the institutions and practices of marketing and advertising that create and sustain those textual artefacts.

One example of a rather straightforward version of textual determinism is the normative marketing literature. The textual deterministic overtones of the market-ing communications textbook/'cookbook' style are obvious, and they serve to gloss the process of the creation of marketing texts.[10] These textbooks contain examples of 'good' and 'bad' brand components (e.g. logos, advertisements), assessing their effectiveness based on the analysis of their 'internal logics': 'the underlying logic is, for example, what appeals to consumer fears and will stimu-late audience involvement with a message and thereby promote acceptance of the message arguments' (Shimp, 2003: 304). Such statements and recommendations exhibit certain implicit assumptions about the nature of interpretive action, for example that the correspondence of the content of a message to a reader's reac-tion can be identified and realised in an advertisement. In other words, the success or failure of a narrative is portrayed in marketing textbooks as *predictable* and *formalisable.* But even if *some* narratives appear to provoke certain predefined reactions, researchers need to pay attention to how judgements and assessments of such effects and reactions are achieved in deliberations about, for example, the outcomes of an advertising campaign. The determinist approach cannot, for example, explain the *variety* of assessments of marketing and advertising campaigns, or conflicts between corporate clients and advertising agencies regarding the effects, or the outcomes, of a campaign.

But how easy is it to break from the deterministic explanatory tradition over-all? Post-essentialists try to eschew straightforward deterministic explanations by means of exploring the metaphor 'the machine as text'. However, the analysts also acknowledge difficulties with the approach taken. Woolgar and Cooper

(1999) offered self-criticisms regarding the replacement of technological determinism with textual determinism in their own version of textual analysis (also Grint and Woolgar, 1997). In other words, in the attempts to explain how some representations become more persuasive than others, the essentialism associated with the natural properties of real objects gets replaced by the determinism of social and political interests, or textual determinism, such as the 'pragmatic values' and 'rhetorical strategies' of the text. For example, comparing the form of Winner's Moses' Bridges story to an urban legend, Woolgar and Cooper say: 'although the focus (substance), the particular aspect of modernity at the centre of the story, might change, the form (structure) of the tale remains more constant' (Woolgar and Cooper, 1999: 441), thus rendering, retrospectively, the narrative *form* responsible for the success and currency of the story.

A possible route away from textual determinism can be found in Grint and Woolgar (1997). Theorising the moral order provided, but not determined, by a text, Grint and Woolgar emphasise the importance not so much of the textual features of a text, but of the *association* between text and reader:[11] '. . . the organization of texts hinges not so much on mundane features like the length of sentences, the amount of space devoted to different topics etc., but rather on *associations* made available within the text and between text and reader. Text, in other words, provides for a certain moral order, in which the reader is invited to join certain groups and dissociate herself from others' (Grint and Woolgar, 1997: 73, italics mine). The post-essentialist questions concerning the 'appropriateness of particular narrative forms as a basis for intervention' (Rappert, 2001: 562) thus need to address the issue of *association* between reader and text, which takes the question into the domain of the practical action of writing and reading, or interpreting, a text. Taking into account the discussion above, texts need to be understood as elements in a reader–text community (Woolgar, 1998; Smith, 2001), the question this book will try to address through an empirical study of marketing throughout.

The materiality of associations between text and reader constitutes another point of analytical concern. Marketing communications textbooks teach how to make marketing texts presentable to a consumer, readable (through design) and combinable with one another (Kapferer, 1997) in terms of visual or material appearance. In marketing cultures, these kinds of artefacts are assumed to travel socially and geographically as brochures, souvenirs, billboards, bus advertising, pop-ups or commercials. This normative stance – in the sense that a certain movement, or location, of an advertisement would ensure a desired response – also exhibits commitment to determinism, material determinism in this case. A similar kind of determinism can be observed in the science and technology studies literature. As I discussed in the previous chapter, Latour (1992/2000) suggests that materiality is what holds associations together. His notion of immutable mobiles suggests that certain *material* properties of texts may be responsible for their robustness, which involves the capabilities of textual artefacts to travel across social and geographical boundaries. Latour (1990) calls 'immutable mobiles' those visualised, printed and written artefacts created in order to mobilise a network of actants, or to change socio-technical arrangements: 'objects which have the properties of being mobile but also immutable, presentable, readable and combinable with one another' (p. 42). Such a definition does not encourage questioning *for whom* such objects have certain properties. But such questions, as I will discuss further in the book, arise in the domain of marketing practice. How helpful are the determinist material explanations of textual artefacts for the analysis of marketing practices?

Some scholars made attempts to overcome the determinist overtones of textual explanations through a greater attention to interpretive contingencies. Hine, in her study of Internet technologies (Hine, 2000), argues that the metaphor 'technology is text' acquires new analytic aspects when applied to the Internet. She argues that the focus of such studies should be on the situated processes of production and consumption of such texts, not only on textual analysis revealing the organisation of the elements of a text (Goodwin and Wolff, 1997: 142, cited in Hine, 2000: 36). The contingencies of the performative properties of a textual document in organisational sense-making are explored by Ashmore and Restrepo (2004), who point out the cultural boundaries of interpretive conventions. In some cultures, he contends, texts are not allowed to speak for themselves, thus requiring the (virtually endless) work of institutionalised authenticating procedures. Interpretive contingencies are offered as a way to avoid deterministic overtones in Latour's (1990: 42–47) concept of the immutable mobile. Coopmans (2006) argues that 'immutable mobility . . . only works by virtue of continuous maintenance work' (p. 6).

The use of historical contingencies is another attempt to avoid determinism with regard to texts and their effects. A move towards the contingent and historically negotiated nature of functional conventions of narratives can be found in Shapin (1984). In his analysis of Boyle's demonstration of the air-pump, Shapin argues that in the case of the air-pump, knowledge creation was equivalent to the creation of a scientific audience, or to multiplication of the witnessing experience through the creation and distribution of literary texts, or the pump's 'circumstance'. Shapin's historical analysis suggests that the ways inscriptions are devised and employed are matters of contestation and negotiation. Communities that decide on the properties of 'literary devices' are important. Shapin emphasises the following: 'it is important to understand two things about these ways of expounding scientific knowledge and its securing assent: that they are historical constructions and that there have been alternative practices. It is particularly important to understand this because of the problems of givenness and self-evidence that attend the institutionalisation and conventionalization of these practices' (p. 509).

Shapin tries to understand the process of constructing technological audiences through his analysis of the substance of particular narratives (acknowledging their historical contingency). This approach still preserves the textual determinist overtones. Revisiting Shapin and Schaffer's argument,[12] Woolgar and Coopmans (2006) observe that it would be interesting to know the kinds of accountability relations in which such particular narratives were produced. Why and how was the modesty of experimental science accepted as an appropriate discourse of witnessing creation? As Woolgar and Coopmans (2006: 17) observe, 'Shapin and Schaffer do comment that Boyle probably felt his own social standing needing down playing, lest readers think he was trading on his (relatively) noble station as a way of securing authority for his claims.'

In view of various claims made with regard to what accounts for interpretive constraints, and possible ways of avoiding textual and material determinism, I contend that the research on the performative properties of texts may benefit from an alternative approach. Rappert (2001: 584) suggests rethinking the terms of debates in STS. He claims that it is necessary to build an approach 'sensitive to the conditions under which interpretations are made'. This is close to the 'interpretive contingencies' propositions above. This, according to Rappert, may provoke new questions about the analytical matters of concern. For instance, in his own research on the properties of non-lethal weapons, Rappert suggests a shift in the debate towards analyses of how *practical resolutions of ambiguity* of technology help accomplish capacities of technologies. In other words, this suggests the possibility of studying the practical resolution of the material/discursive ambiguity of textual artefacts with regard to interpretive constraints. Such an approach would ask: Who bears the burden of interpreting and fixating a moral order provided for by a text? What constitutes the (writer)-text-reader community? What accounts for the distribution of interpretive action?

As such, I have sought a mode of research sensitive to the cultural forms of production and circulation of material texts in and by marketing, and have sought to stay alert to the contingencies of assessment of properties of texts. One line of this approach will be further elaborated upon in Chapter 5 through juxtaposing the perspectives on material texts in the material culture studies and in the post-essentialist STS approach. The starting point for such an approach is that marketers are themselves involved in deliberations regarding the performative properties of narratives, contending whether a statement (such as, for example, an *invitation*) is capable of constraining interpretation. In this regard, looking at how texts are recreated and read in marketing, and what kind of readership is involved, requires acquiring local knowledge of the contextual readings of the texts, equivalent to doing an organisational ethnography of texts (cf. Woolgar and Simakova, 2003). At the same time, as I discussed earlier in this chapter, marketing organisations watch and are being watched by some other communities (customers, shareholders, academics, wider societal concern groups, their peers, competitors) who make judgements about the power/properties of marketing texts. Various interpretive communities (Fish, 1980) can read different meanings into marketing texts, and these readings may differ considerably in their assessments of how texts (should) work. In other words, associations between reader and text need to be understood as emerging through continuous negotiations and assessments of the properties of such associations by various interpretive communities. In this sense, marketers as producers of narratives purported to accomplish boundary work are *accountable* to certain various audiences. We can ask, then, how exactly 'modes of accountability' (Dilley, 1992a) are established and sustained in market relations, and what the role of marketing is in this. Who assesses successes and failures of narratives produced by marketers, and how?

For a study of marketing in practice, I contend that it is not very useful to assume beforehand that there are certain given explanations available to us as analysts to account for the successes and failures of textual artefacts. A study of the performative properties of narratives needs to go beyond the exploration of rhetoric or textual organisation or the material properties of textual artefacts to engage with the effort of producers of texts. What are the folk means of achieving, in analytic terms, a robustness and stability of interpretations across audiences? What are the concerns and practical judgements of producers of texts in marketing as they try to achieve associations between readers and texts? The task of such a study, as in this book, will be to look at how participants in the marketing department assess the performative properties of narratives. This study of marketing in practice approaches texts as being parts of various cultures and conventions of textuality in the corporate world. Specifically, I will adopt the idea that texts are produced and read in various interpretive communities (Fish, 1980) whose members have different understandings and practical concerns about the organisation of textual practices.

Technology texts and their audiences

In this book I approach technology marketing as attempts to produce discourses capable of changing the relationships between technology constituencies through boundary work. As its main focus, this study of marketing in practice examines how 'the implicit commitments to particular ways of ordering society' (Woolgar, 2000a: 177) are contested in the organisation employing marketing. This book approaches technology marketers as practical reasoners deliberating on the nature of socio-technical relations. The cultural discourses produced by marketers introduce certain entities and relations between them (e.g. technologies and their users). In the ethnographic sense, these discourses need to be seen as continuous achievements. Some ideas regarding technology descriptions as accomplishments can be found in the science and technology studies literature (Woolgar, 2002b; Pinch *et al.*, 1992/2000; Myers 1991, 1993).

The STS version of discourse analysis has emphasised and studied the possibility of multiple accounts of a given technology. Controversies over capacities and impacts of a technology are one such topic of inquiry. As an important observation, some authors have argued that these contextual accounts of technology are established in relation to certain audiences. Pinch *et al.* (1992/2000) observe that different (economic, technical, implementational, as well as social scientific) aspects of technology vary depending on the audience: 'Technologies can be described and presented in texts for many different purposes, including that of sociological analysis. It is only by close attention to different discursive contexts in which these definitions are offered and an examination of the rhetoric of technology that we can begin to understand the full richness of its multifaceted and interpretative nature' (Pinch *et al.*, 1992/2000: 272). Myers (1991, 1993) offers an analysis of writing research proposals. He argues that writing a research rationale entails taking into account many competing audiences, so that the text becomes an assemblage of addresses to different readers. In the introduction to the *Virtual Society?* collection, Woolgar (2002b) deconstructs the research rationale to show in what ways 'the drama of potential technological impact', or its more cautious redraft, can be achieved in attempts to persuade and impress certain audiences of academic peers or funding bodies (p. 10).

A similar observation about the importance of audiences – imagined, constructed, addressed – was made in studies of advertising and marketing. Hennion *et al.* (1989) show the ways the consumer becomes inscribed in advertisements through the processes of incorporation of consumers into an object involving chains and series of intermediaries. Moeran (2005) examines practical deliberations concerning the construction of the images of audiences for the purposes of an advertising campaign. He argues that both putative consumers and brand owners are inscribed in branding proposals. Marketing represents a strategic site to better our understanding of the relationship between technology texts and their audiences. One can argue that the achievement of marketing texts in attempts to change accountability relations, or 'the existing sets of identities, expectations, beliefs and language' (Woolgar, 1998: 444), entails not only the practical management of boundaries between an organisation and its outside. Taking into account an earlier observation that knowledge of the audience in organisations is distributed and contested (Woolgar, 1991a; Licoppe and Simakova, 2007), marketers have to find practical ways of sustaining their expertise in organisations. How is technology marketing knowledge displayed and defended by the members of the marketing community? What do marketers do while they 'assemble their activities in anticipation of customer encounters'? (Prus, 1989).

By way of example, one of the purposes of this book is to address the issue of the construction of corporate public statements about a technology construed as new. Although the flow of communication between a corporation and its external constituencies is constant, some communicative events where encounters between the corporation and its audiences take place are compartmentalised and receive special status. Such events as 'a press release', 'a product launch' and 'a trade show' require preparations and must be formally approved and evaluated. I chose (or maybe it chose me to be one of the voices in its network) the case of an RFID technology, about which two interesting things can be said: first, at the moment of the study, this technology was not a notable part of the everyday discourse and was limited to certain labs and IT industries, with only a few visible instances of going public or attracting sociologists' attention;[13] and second, those industries were strategising about how to bring the technology to the worldwide business and consumer markets in the near future, expecting some awesome revenues. Chapters 6 and 7 in particular look at what happens inside a marketing department before the participants decide they are ready to launch a technological product.

The approach taken for such analysis is to examine, through participation, marketers' folk sociology and folk ethnography as they seek ways of telling stories about a technology on behalf of Virtual World. The term 'folk sociology' is not a negative label, but rather reflects certain ethnomethodological assumptions about the lack of a principled difference between the ways lay participants and professional sociologists make inferences about the world through accomplishing social structure, ordering and turn-taking (e.g. Sacks, 1992). Studies of marketing (Woolgar and Simakova, 2003; Moeran, 2005; Lien, 2003) suggest that marketers can be seen as interactants making claims about the likely readings of objects and texts. As was shown elsewhere (Woolgar and Simakova, 2003), folk-sociological analyses of the extent and attributes of likely recipients of/ respondents to the artefacts in question are an important element of marketers' everyday preoccupations. Knowledge of the consumer, or the user, is an outcome of contestations among members of an organisation who have various degrees of authority to speak on behalf of users (cf. Woolgar, 1991a, Grint and Woolgar, 1997; Workman, 1993).

Constructing and negotiating such 'objective' claims about the nature of recipients, or users, of technologies is a part of the organisational boundary work. Negotiations of knowledge claims on behalf of the user contribute to the management of the status of the insiders/outsiders achieved through knowing the machine from the inside/outside (Woolgar, 1991a). Lien's (1997) analysis shows the interactive nature of the construction of a product and its package in the marketing department of a Norwegian food company. The properties of mundane products such as pizza or poultry are construed through anticipations of consumers' reactions. The selected spokespersons in the organisation (an outsourced agency, the managers) contest each other's assumptions of the possible readings of the product. In Lien (2003), the focus is on the construction of an 'authentic' ethnic food for a Norwegian consumer. She shows how an 'Italian' pasta-based product emerges as an outcome of the interactive process in the marketing department. Lien discusses marketers' deliberations in terms of the construction of spatio-cultural constructs of 'authentic cuisines' through anticipations of possible readings of the constructed authenticity claims, to be inscribed in the packaging, by local consumers.

Moeran (2005) and Woolgar and Simakova (2003) analyse the accountability of marketers to the management board in an organisation, or to a brand owner. Elsewhere (Woolgar and Simakova, 2003), authors looked in detail at the production of a brochure for an academic institution and found that a particular brochure design appeared by virtue of anticipation of the reaction by (and the need to please) a benefactor, rather than that of potential audiences the new establishment wanted to attract, such as, for example, students. Moeran (2005) speaks of the *double* performance of authenticity. His observations suggest that marketers need to produce claims about the authenticity of consumers *and* claims of their ability to produce such knowledge. In other words, they need to authenticate their method, too, for the brand owner in order to win a bid for an advertising budget. He contends that the creation of an advertisement implies orientation, or the construction of an image of consumers as well as of those who order a campaign as potential interpreters of the campaign. This echoes Slater's point: 'When advertising and marketing agents devise marketing strategies they aim to produce definitions of objects that simultaneously accomplish two inter-linked goals: they must make sense in terms of relations of consumption and they must look capable of achieving profitable positions in relation to other products (relations of competition, the marketplace)' (Slater, 2002: 247). An ethnographic study of marketing professionals (Barrey *et al.*, 2000) also usefully indicates that marketers need to meet legal, administrative and the brand owner's requirements.

Marketers in the organisation may also have formal responsibilities and participate in performance assessments, as well as in accounting procedures providing for the construction of marketing as an accountable practice. In the marketing department, for example, the success of a marketing campaign can be measured through budget execution or other kinds of marketing metrics (Rust *et al.*, 2004). The accounting regimes in marketing departments are subject to change (Webster, 1992). Overall, Schudson's (1984) characterisation of marketing and advertising as forms of 'uneasy persuasion' remains apt.

To sum up, I suggest that intervention in the cultural technological discourses by marketers needs to be seen as the practices associated with the creation of persuasive technology narratives. However, how can the approach taken help to address the questions about the materiality of market relations, as I discussed in Chapter 1? I borrow the notion of *articulation* from Dilley (1999a) as a useful way of thinking about marketing as the construction of narratives with regard to a technological artefact. Dilley[14] (1999a: 37) observes that interpretation and contextualisation involve making connections. From the perspective of the anthropological critique of the content/context relationship, Dilley usefully suggests a shift from context to *articulation*:[15] what is articulated is a particular mode of knowledge and a set of relevant connections. Seeing marketing as attempts to introduce certain 'modes of accountability', in Dilley's words, implies a type of 'discursive formation or form of articulation which connects particular attributes of things, in that case, objects, exchange relations and exchange partners' (ibid.). As a form of boundary transgression, articulation is thus the process of creating connections, which has, according to Dilley, double meaning: 'it has the sense of "to utter," "to speak forth," "to articulate," as well as the sense of connecting two parts, namely articulation as linkage' (ibid.). Articulation helps us to think about technology marketing storytelling as the production of a 'discursive formation . . . which connects particular attributes of things, in that case, objects, exchange relations and exchange partners' (Dilley, 1999a: 37).

In other words, such an approach helps us to think about how the *accountability* of particular objects is achieved by marketers: how is a product rendered accountable in and through marketing practices? How are these attempts to create narrative articulating particular objects, or technologies, carried out in marketing practice? How are the interactional scenes and the interactants' identities construed and managed? How are certain interpretations rendered privileged? On the one hand, marketing can be seen as a practical activity performing certain accountability relations. The emphasis on *performing* accountability relations, the work of strategising about what accountability relations vis-à-vis marketed artefacts might be and how to create those, is one possible sense of accountability in relation to marketing. In this sense, marketing practice can be examined as *the practical management* of accountability relations, the practical work of recognising relevant audiences and creating narratives providing for certain interpretations. On the other hand, marketing can be seen as *being performed in* certain accountability relations, which involves the work of accounting *for* marketing. This may include accountability procedures, authentication of marketing knowledge, maintaining membership in the marketing community and, last but not least, being (or not being) accountable to the ethnographer, too.

As a corollary of the discussion above, in this book I will develop the idea that marketing in practice can be characterised as the construction of stories that can be told to various audiences both inside and outside of an organisation. I introduce the concept of *tellable stories* to characterise bounded attempts in articulation, or the establishing of new accountability relations. This chapter offers an ethnographic study of participants' deliberations related to the *tellability* of a narrative, the birth of a tellable story, through a particular example of product 'launch' (which is a participants' metaphor). Note that this approach is different from the way Sacks (1992) uses the term 'tellability' in relation to the properties of conversational items. Sacks writes: 'For some sorts of items we can pretty much say that their total currency turns on being tellable. What makes an item a good piece of gossip is its tellable character' (Sacks, 1992: 776). For Sacks, tellability appears to be an inherent feature of a language item, whereas my analysis focuses on participants' accomplishment of the tellability of stories they produce. In other words, I suggest that the ways that stories are rendered tellable need to be approached as outcomes of contestations of marketing knowledge.

This approach to the production of narratives in marketing in terms of tellable stories differs, in two important ways, from some other schools' analyses of narrative forms (Linstead, 1999; Czarniawska, 1997), which emphasise the primacy of narratives in social ordering and organisational life. First, my analysis focuses specifically on technology narratives and aims to address questions posed in science and technology studies, specifically the question of interpretive constraints in this chapter. Second, narratives here are approached as ongoing accomplishments involving the performance of a marketing community, whereas narratives in Linstead (1999) and Czarniawska (1997) are understood in terms of the content of a marketing text, its structure, as in Tsoukas and Hatch (2001), who argue that narrative analyses focus on studying narrative structure (e.g. a sequence of events, or a plot; motives and temporality). This study explores the merits of shifting away from analysis of the rhetoric of marketing texts. Instead, it asks questions: How do copywriters construct a plot? How do they make decisions about the structure of a narrative, and attributions of certain properties to a story? What in the actions of marketers makes a story tellable?

3   Inside corporations

An ethnographic approach

Corporation as a field site

'Marketing Life' as a project

Ethnographic studies in STS have enjoyed the particular status of forging our understanding of the 'inner workings' of science and engineering. In some sense, the task of writing a book titled, for example, 'Marketing Life', by analogy with 'Laboratory Life' (Latour and Woolgar, 1979/1986), should not be any different from doing ethnography on a lab bench. It turns out, however, that conducting research on and with corporations may entail asking certain questions about the ways corporate ethnography is carried out. To what extent, and in what sense, are corporations 'transparent' and accessible for an anthropologist? What does it take for an ethnographer to achieve meaningful interactions with participants?

In this chapter I offer some reflections on conducting corporate ethnography. I pose a spectrum of questions about the ethnographer's dilemmas, choices and strategies. These reflections are not only accounts of the practicalities of research. They also explore ways of asking further questions about the new places of knowledge, such as corporations. From this perspective, access and ethnographic movements inside the setting become a rich source of interactive occasions that serve as the fabric for continuing exchange with the field. These interactions also provide insight into the language and the cultural practices of exchange (of expertise, of information, of resources) in the setting. In particular, analysis of these movements casts light on the questions of marketing theory and marketing knowledge discussed in the previous chapter by putting them into the empirical interactional context inside an organisation. Additionally, the corporate settings perform a set of relations between the ethnographer and the participants that involve local, situated assessments of mutual relevance, obligations and understanding. These are, in particular, the relations of utility, of non-disclosure, and of what can be called ethnographic mobility. How to manage these relations with the field practically is a matter of everyday concern, which I address in this chapter.

In traditional anthropology, when coming to an exotic tribe, the anthropologist tries to establish rapport, select informants, transcribe texts, take genealogies, map fields, keep a diary and, finally, produce a report. The ethnographic report would thus offer an account of a particular culture in a manner that Richard Geertz (1973), borrowing a notion from Gilbert Ryle, calls 'thick description'. By this is meant a very detailed, 'intelligible' description of the events studied by the ethnographer, including observational notes, background information and records of actual social interactions. According to Geertz, the production of 'thick description' entails observation and interpretation of interactions among participants in a setting, in an attempt to understand how they themselves interpret other participants' behaviours and artefacts. This book, and this chapter in particular, is a kind of such a report purported to produce an intelligible description of marketing practices by a participant observer negotiating access to and conducting research in, and with, a marketing organisation.

Where are technology marketers, and who are they?

The definition of a potential research site as 'marketing' (and later as 'technology marketing') immediately raised for me the question of where marketing is performed and who marketers are. Some existing studies of marketing and advertising (e.g. Mocran and Malefyt, 2003b; Lien, 1997; Abolafia, 1998) adopt participant observation as a way of engaging with a marketing setting. Finding and joining a technology marketing tribe is a part of the ethnographic research. Selection of a field site can be characterised as a practical accomplishment emerging from interactions between the ethnographer and representatives of the marketing profession. These interactions interestingly reveal what kinds of preconceptions about marketing were held by both me and the representatives of marketing. Before finally selecting Virtual World as a marketing setting, I considered a number of choices. I studied the database of Oxford Business Alumni, and identified some potential contacts. Several opportunities occurred through meetings with marketing executives who came to the business school to meet marketing academics in search of useful insights into marketing knowledge. A few colleagues, including my academic supervisor and an MBA placement officer at the business school, helped me to explore access opportunities. Discussing possibilities, ethnographic assumptions about good marketing sites were articulated, assessed, accepted or rejected. Representatives of companies understood what it means to do marketing and to adopt an ethnographer into their company in different ways.

Moerman's (1965) examination of the demarcation of ethnic/professional entities is very apposite here. The uses of labels (for members and non-members) need to be understood as claims to membership in a community, signalling 'unity among those who do the labelling'; although the fact that different usages may occur indicates that not all participants recognise the same features as distinctive for ethnic or professional classification. Making my ethnographic choices, I had to consider what an appropriate use of the 'marketing' label would be as I was going to join, and associate my research trajectory with, a particular professional community. A giant tobacco company wanted to explore new ways of incorporating smoking into consumers' lifestyles. I had doubts about the 'utility' of this kind of research if I joined in and contributed. Other marketing projects seemed either too limited in terms of my potential involvement with marketing practice or too difficult to follow because of their geographical location. Following a self-employed marketing consultant in London would entail extensive travel. An engagement with a university spin-off did not seem to provide enough diversity of marketing activities, being focused exclusively on 'pricing', as the executive explained. In his view, doing marketing meant data-mining, conducting Internet research and compiling price lists. A leader of a newly established local market-ing consultancy asked me whether I could provide any academic insight that would help him to market his own company. Joining his organisation would be the equivalent of setting up my own marketing business. As I was searching for a company to join, it always seemed to me that the right kind of marketing for me was being done somewhere else.

Virtual World, a major world corporation, occurred as a possible field site as the result of some Oxford networking. The enthusiasm of Terry, one of Virtual World's managers, to adopt an ethnographer, as well as my anticipation of a diversity of marketing activities, contributed to my decision to pursue the offer to join the company. I could not get a clear answer from Terry regarding his own role at Virtual World. He said he was in marketing, here and there, often travel-ling locally and internationally. He could attend a meeting in Banbury, near Oxford, one day and fly to Munich the next. Terry had earned his undergraduate degree in natural sciences from one of the most prestigious Oxford colleges, Christ Church. He still maintained connections with the university through his alumni activities and occasional visits to the business school workshops open to the public. He said he had a general interest in new developments in the areas of management studies, and in marketing in particular. He was surprised to hear that Steve Woolgar had been nominated the Chair of Marketing at the business school. He had always thought that 'the kind of sociology Steve was doing' (he wanted to learn more about it) and management studies were wide apart. He thought it was an exciting development anyway, and wanted to use this opportu-nity to help conduct research on marketing in practice.

Some hi-tech marketing/management literatures present technology marketers as a distinctive species of marketing professionals. Hi-tech marketing is some-times portrayed as a heroic, difficult[1] endeavour (Kosnik, 1990: 120). It is said that one needs to *do* hi-tech marketing in order to appreciate how difficult it is. The difference will arise immediately as 'the difference between reading a biography of Michelangelo and setting out to paint your own Sistine Chapel' (Kosnik, 1990: 145). Within the corporation, such assumptions constituted the very identity of the technology marketing group projected to outsiders. Statements of the 'differ-ence' of technology marketing, and its 'difficulty', were utilised to establish the identity of technology marketers in interactions with the ethnographer. My first impressions of technology marketing conveyed to me in conversations with Terry and through the first ethnographic engagements were of technology marketing as a potential 'hard case'. The 'difficult' nature of technology marketing was used by the participants as a membership device. Terry's proposition that I was entering the study of a special kind of marketing sounded intriguing. Terry said he was surprised at meeting a female doctoral student, not even an MBA, who was interested in getting her hands dirty with everyday hi-tech marketing realities. The perception of the activity as a difficult, heroic one, possessing some yet-unrealised strategic potential for the corporation, was conveyed to me later as well, during my encounters with the field participants.

In the first encounters, marketing managers explained to me that perhaps theirs would be a different, much harder type of marketing than what I had been doing previously in my professional life. They referred to my diploma in marketing and my work experience, which included a few years with a small advertising agency and a couple of years of public relations for an intergovernmental science foundation. This, the gatekeepers observed, was useful experience, but perhaps not very suitable for the tasks they were doing. The initial meetings with corporate gatekeepers contributed to my perception of hi-tech marketing as a masculine, macho-like activity. I remember having an intense sense of my own exoticism to the setting. The feeling, however, changed soon after I realised that most of the marketing managers I was introduced to when I started working with the 'vertical' marketing team were females. The 'difficulty' and 'specificity' of technology marketing dissipated as participant observation continued. Some women made successful careers, too. JoanneW[2] was appointed the head of 'corporate marketing'. The 'difficulty' of the profession was undermined by a female marketing manager's remark that she was happy to come to the office to escape for a few hours from her household duties and the demanding task of being a mother of three. The rewards of doing marketing for the global hi-tech corporation included first-class international travel and a decent salary, which, as the participants observed, made work pressures bearable. The 'difficulty' of 'doing' technology marketing thus featured as a discursive element of distinguishing between the insiders and the outsiders of that specific kind of marketing.

The 'difficulty' of technology marketing was also contested in conversations with my line manager, who generally believed that marketing was not 'rocket science'. The apparent messiness and tribulations of the everyday practice were perceived as an exception, rather than the rule, and were attributed to the messy character of a large organisation. These various possible ways of accounting for marketing are an important feature of corporate life. As such, I will discuss the marketing practice as it was accounted for through contested claims and in organisational disputes so as to acknowledge its contingencies and to avoid reducing the practice to the rigid frameworks of strategies and planned actions. The participants can of course perceive the latter to be the appropriate way to talk marketing on some occasions, especially when potential readership is imagined. What we, as ethnographers, are used to thinking of as being a 'thick description' of an organisation looked like an exaggeratedly detailed narrative to the marketing manager, who upon glancing through a chapter of my thesis, assumed that emphasising the everyday routines, troubles and overall 'difficulties' of the marketing life would not provide for an interpretation of tasks I described as *successfully* accomplished. For others, however, especially those in more senior positions, recognition of the messiness of the activities in various corporate marketing departments served as the basis for endorsing more and newer systems of accounting and assessment across the corporation. As such, some of them acknowledged my dissertation to be an honest account of marketing as practised on the ground. Descriptions of the everyday corporate life sounded almost like a trivial thing to write that would not add much to the practitioners' knowledge of the organisation. The worthwhile result of such study (in line with certain ideas about the format of academic research) would discuss implications for marketing, not simply convey everyday details. However, for this study it was important to recognise and keep alive questions about the circumstances of such assessments of what counts as useful organisational knowledge. What is marketing well done, and who defines it, and who are the audiences for such evaluations? This was as an open interpretive matter, as participants, together with myself as ethnographer and a participant, proposed and assessed various versions of the normative, the practical, and the achievable marketing knowledge. I will pay attention to such episodes throughout the book.

Being associated with technology marketing as a researcher also made visible certain wider boundary assumptions about this activity. Some of these assumptions were articulated by my academic colleagues and friends. As a reaction to my new engagement with 'a large corporation similar to IBM, Intel and the like', as I introduced it, I was often asked if I wanted to get a job at Virtual World afterwards. Managers repeatedly noted that some of the tasks I did for the company would look good on my CV. Some of PhD researchers I met were open about their intent to work for the companies they were studying. Stories were exchanged about how well they were treated by the corporations, who sent them to travel internationally. They wondered, was I at least being paid for the assistance I provided?[3] If the company did not pay me, did it mean I belonged to an academic institution that could afford, or that had the resources and reputation to engage in, a relationship with a company of this calibre and to indulge in this kind of *disinterested* research? Consequently, as an ethnographer studying a big techno business, I needed to deal with (identify with or contest) the socially cultivated sense of belonging to the powerful/affluent ones. My association with the corporation was generally perceived as not easily achievable, but as desirable, as a direct way to secure a prosperous future.[4]

The impression of the affluence of my subjects, notably the gatekeepers, was immediate. Terry gave me a lift from Oxford to one of our first meetings with top managers. On a rainy February day I was at his recently refurbished house in North Oxford, from where we took off softly in his silvery Mercedes packed with gadgets. The forty-five-minute ride was fast, easy and pleasant, which was perhaps the only instance of an effortless journey in the course of my fieldwork while I was commuting using public transport. This also contrasted vividly with our very first trip to Virtual World with Steve Woolgar, when we were invited for an introductory meeting. Presenting the research as a study under Steve Woolgar's supervision was an important part of access negotiation. The gatekeepers sought a bigger picture of the interests behind the ethnography, having learned from Terry that Steve was one of the early ethnographers of science. Having little knowledge about the discipline, the managers found the idea of having an observer in the organisation to be odd. During a series of introductory meetings, the ethnography of marketing was endorsed and accepted through portraying and acknowledging it as having roots in an unconventional, yet existing scholarly tradition now adopted by the Oxford business school. The research was presented as having roots in a more general anthropology of modern cultures. Steve Woolgar mentioned that he had spent some time working and conducting a similar kind of study in a company developing software, and added that recently he had become interested in research on marketing in practice. The presentation of the study was the reason why, a few days before the Mercedes ride, Steve and I were driving to Virtual World for a meeting equipped with a map of the area sent to us by Terry. The arrival story inadvertently marked the identities of the academics and practitioners. In a small town, as we were already approaching Virtual World, the car suddenly got stuck in the midst of traffic while stopping at a crossroads. Steve realised he had filled his old car, which he had chosen to use for the day, with the wrong kind of fuel. We pushed the car to a roundabout shoulder, called a rescue service, and left it until the end of our meeting at Virtual World. Terry, very much amused by the episode, arrived promptly upon our plea to pick up the distracted and impractical academics.[5]

The EMEA[6] premises of Virtual World were located in a place called 'South Park' in West London, an area mixing residential neighbourhoods with blue-chip giants. Upon arranging a visit, a visitor to South Park received motoring directions, a gesture that assumes he or she would come by car, a means I did not have. Terry and his colleagues were audibly proud of the corporate offices while showing us around. From a transparent lift the whole spacious open area inside the building, as well as its glass ceiling, was visible. Introducing us to the place, my hosts drew our attention to the classy architecture, the spaciousness of the suggestively called 'Wireless' canteen, the luxury food options in the canteens and the cafeteria, and the free availability of fresh fruit and soft drinks, generously supplied to little kitchens in every section of the building. An even lusher office located in the City area of London was also mentioned.

The first meeting with MikeR, the VP of Marketing at that moment, took place in a transparent cubicle, just after Mike briefed representatives of 'Ogilvy', as Terry explained. As I recognised, the agency briefed was Ogilvy and Mather, the world's largest advertising chain, which bears the name of its founder and the author of the (in)famous *Confessions of an Advertising Man,* David Ogilvy. The meeting with 'Ogilvy' took five minutes longer and, with apologies, Mike invited us in. He was friendly, chivalrous and assertive. After introductions, Mike went to a whiteboard and drew an organisational chart of the corporation showing marketing's place in it. As I learned later, drawing an organisational chart was a necessary feature of every introductory meeting I had with managers. Did I ever see the same diagram twice? The organisational structures allowed for a light touch of carelessness in presentation styles. 'Geographies', or countries in the 'theatres', were easily lost; managers admitted apologetically that they were not really sure whether they had correctly depicted marketing's place in the corporation or relationships between various groups in drawing their charts. In a casual manner, Mike, too, was 'not exactly sure' whether the company had thirty or thirty-five thousand employees, or whether its annual income was 4.5 or 5 billion dollars. He informed us that the company offices were established in almost all geographical regions of the world, including the Americas, Asia-Pacific, Europe, Africa and the Middle East. The corporate 'global' headquarters were located in the Silicon Valley area, whereas we were sitting in the EMEA, or Europe, Middle East and Africa, headquarters. Having been in the hi-tech business for almost twenty years, the company was one of the biggest and most successful corporations in the world, earning its revenue selling IT-related products and solutions. Mike spoke proudly about the scale and successes of the corporation, but with a note of concern: you can imagine what it takes to manage such a giant. Seeing us off, Mike, signalling perhaps that I was among those who could be adopted into the 'family', mentioned that his Italian wife's name was Elena, too.

Once I entered Virtual World, the ethnographic study took almost seventeen months, with the last five months spent being a 'virtual ethnographer' (more on this later in this chapter). My ethnographic engagement with the field was neither linear nor uniformly saturated with events. I persisted in visiting the field up to four (sometimes five) days a week, occasionally visiting other sites in the Greater London area. This did not mean, however, that I was busy there working full-time all the time. The ethnographic life ranged from uneventful days or weeks to storms of activity. There were moments, especially in the first few months, when I felt totally incapable of establishing any meaningful contact with my subjects and was haunted by a 'get me out of here' feeling. Later I created somewhat closer relationships with the team members, although none grew into personal friendships.

Marketing knowledge and the rhetoric of access

One of the notable features of the access negotiations was the articulation of preconceptions about mutual relevance, utility, and the nature of marketing and ethnographic knowledge in interactions. These negotiations not only provided insight into the ways of apprehending marketing in the corporation by participants. For the ethnography, these interactions did the same kind of discursive work helping to establish my presence in the company in meaningful ways. As a set of social science research methodologies, it is important for the ethnography to be alert to how the meaning of this kind of research becomes constituted in interactions with the field. The ethnography and marketing had to be configured as being compatible, and as having the potential to benefit from each other as the research continued. The main way by which this field relationship was configured was via the discursive framing of ethnography as having potential to bridge the 'gap' between marketing theory and marketing practice. This framing is sometimes also used in the academic literature (e.g. Brownlie *et al.*, 1999a; Dibb and

Stern, 1999; Brownlie and Saren, 1991; Rossiter, 2002). The 'gap' is explained by these authors as a poor current understanding of 'how marketing is actually done'. The discourse of a 'gap', as well as the need for research into how marketing is done in practice, successfully constituted the rhetoric of access to Virtual World.[7]

In technology marketing, the rhetoric of the 'gap' between marketing theory and marketing practice relates to Levitt's (1975) earlier observation that industrial corporations are not the keenest adopters of marketing thinking, or of 'market orientation'. Levitt's pointing at difficulties with establishing marketing in organisations was not quite taken up as mainstream marketing thinking, which is said to be dominated by universalist, generic representations of marketing (Brownlie and Saren, 1991). Thinking in terms of the consumer, rather than in terms of a product, was portrayed as an achievement for hi-tech industries, as something that hi-tech industries still need to learn to appreciate (Levitt, 1975; Moore, 1999; Workman, 1993). These authors argue that marketers in such organisations do not take leadership positions and can only influence product development to a limited extent. In other words, they contend that marketing academic literature does not appreciate the difficulties of *implementing* marketing thinking.

My attempts to access Virtual World coincided with an upsurge in corporate deliberations on the role of marketing. One of the reasons why the study on marketing in practice was welcomed, and encouraged, by the practitioners, was a perceived upsetting difference between what one could read in marketing textbooks and what was really happening on the corporate floor. In the managers' opinion, technology marketing relied on a kind of literature different from traditional marketing management manuals. Moore's (1999) book *Crossing the Chasm* was introduced to me as the 'hi-tech marketing bible'. The managers not only insisted that they adopted many practical tips from the book, but also described their main preoccupation as 'crossing the chasm'.[8] I could hear repercussions of Levitt's (1975) 'Marketing Myopia' in the discussions of the unfortunate reality of Virtual World that was still a very much technology-driven company, very product-centred and dominated by the engineering culture. The marketing managers saw marketing as a mature and resourceful discipline that could potentially serve as a source of strategic insights for the corporation. In reality, they said, marketers felt deprived of their potential, being subsumed under the much more powerful group of sales managers (see Chapter 5 for discussion).

The objectives of the ethnographic study thus aligned well with top managers' need to understand how various marketing teams worked at Virtual World. This allowed me a glimpse into corporate plans for the reorganisation of marketing, which, supposedly, had to be accomplished on the ground of a thorough analysis of existing marketing activities. The initiative, called 'marketing enablement', came to the EMEA from the US headquarters, where, according to the managers, a similar initiative had already been implemented successfully. The ultimate goal of the project was to become a world-class marketing organisation. According to the view that substantiated the need for change, marketing disciplines within the corporation were poorly defined, and job descriptions were extremely vague and often overlapping. There was no prescribed career path for marketing profession-als, and understanding of the role of marketing among the employees was very poor. In order to achieve this goal, it was crucial to know what was going on in marketing. This is, presumably, where the researcher could help.

Additional access discussions further highlighted the corporate views on the nature of marketing and its role in the organisation, and the same for ethnogra-phy. Some assumptions questioned the very possibility of achieving knowledge of how marketing works in a big corporation where various interests seemed to rule the organisational life. Some found it rather humorous that I wanted to learn about how marketing works in practice at Virtual World. This was exactly what they wanted to know themselves! Did I understand, they asked, that it was impos-sible? Even those in top management do not understand how this company works. An oft-repeated saying maintained that everyone in this corporation feels as if they are playing on several chessboards at the same time, and before you realise you are in the game, you learn you are mated! Everyone wanted to know what was going on in other parts of the organisation. Even my location with 'vertical' marketing turned out to have some strategic purpose for Terry, who wanted to gain access to that part of the company.

Importantly, the negotiations also performed ideas about what kind of academic audiences are relevant for ethnographic research on marketing. The study was conceived of as a means to establish a better relationship with the academic community and to increase the visibility of marketing practice at Virtual World. Terry was known as someone who 'owned the relationship with Oxford' because of his previous and present connections. He also suggested that the research would complement the two existing initiatives with Oxford. The corporation already sponsored a professorial chair and had hosted an MBA team doing project development a year earlier. It appears that adopting an ethnographer was seen by the managers as a means to achieve representation of the corporation to some audiences (at least within a certain imagined academic community). Viewing the research as an addition to their own effort to enhance corporate reputation, the marketers hoped that the study could potentially become one of Virtual World's tellable stories (see Chapter 6).

Thinking of my involvement, the managers suggested I could be useful initially as a disinterested project participant, coordinating the marketing reorganisation between US and EMEA managers. The initiative was not uncontroversial, as a result of some kind of lack of trust between the human resources departments in the regions, with the US managers officially running the initiative; as well as because of criticisms of a lack of understanding of the European cultural specifics by the US counterparts. The corporate belief in EMEA was that in smaller coun-tries marketing life was different from how it was in the United States. In smaller European or Middle East countries, for example, one marketing manager can carry on a number of diverse tasks because offices and budgets are considerably smaller. In order to establish a legitimate cause for a change in the organisation of marketing in Virtual World, the corporate management felt they had to exam-ine such regional practices first.

As I was preparing to interview marketing employees, and beginning to accumulate documents relevant to the 'marketing enablement', I also started helping the 'vertical' marketing team (see Chapter 4). Within a few weeks, reaching managers involved in the 'marketing enablement' initiative suddenly became difficult. The managers replied that they 'were not in the loop', they did not know what was going on, and they were not sure it would be appropriate to send me documents or to invite me for a conference call. In addition, my line manager reminded me that my non-disclosure agreement had not yet been signed, and my participation in marketing enablement somehow faded away. The plans for the role of the ethnographer were reconsidered, and the initial idea dissolved as I continued with the 'vertical' marketing team, and then with RFID marketing.

Inscribing ethnography in a non-disclosure agreement

Another instantiation of the mutual articulation of the nature of marketing knowledge and of ethnography was the negotiation of a non-disclosure agreement with Virtual World. A non-disclosure agreement (NDA) is a document routinely employed by some organisations that care about protecting their identity and proprietary information, and in commercial settings in particular. NDAs can be signed with employees, external consultants or business analysts to prevent undue release of relevant information. An NDA can be seen as a discursive resource employed to manage the accountability relations in and of the corporation. Seen as a textual device employed to perform corporate audiences, the production of an NDA at times requires special resources, such as procedures, lawyers, NDA templates, and time to accomplish the routine. The NDA negotiated for this study entailed figuring out the nature of research and the appropriate form of the document. Several options for NDAs, such as one used for MBA research, a standard corporate purchase agreement, as well as an NDA signed for a similar kind of study with another company, were proposed and dismissed. Signing an NDA is a form of framing the research discursively whereby the roles and responsibilities of participants engaged in proposing and hosting the research are negotiated.

While NDAs are negotiated routinely in business settings, there is no standard assumption about what such practice may mean for the production of ethnographic analysis. Little has been written of these practices in academic literature,[9] but the situated nature of the negotiated importance of an NDA for participants in ethnographic research has been highlighted. Chapman points to the importance of formal barriers in negotiating the ethnographer's access to a business setting associated with disclosure (Chapman, 2001: 31). Moeran (2005), on the contrary, reports the ease of his joining an advertising agency in Japan, and the willingness of participants to become publicly known as subjects of his research. The same can be said about non-disclosure in other settings at the university–industry boundary. While some respondents may prefer their names to be concealed, for others the incentive for joining a study is to make their personal opinion known via research.

Whatever the rationale for signing an agreement, if such an agreement needs to be signed, the practicalities may involve identifying relevant signees and authorities (individuals or units within an organisation) to put the agreement into place. As such, it may or may not become a (temporary) obstacle to gaining access, or, on the contrary, the process itself may contribute to maintaining a relationship between the researcher and the corporation. Turned into an analytic problem, an NDA can be seen as a document that circulates in and between organisations, and that sets up a certain moral order by introducing entities and the relations between them. It may also set practical limits and raise questions regarding the research assumptions about and the practical ways of writing up what counts as an acceptable portrayal of corporate practices, and of describing a technology in question when the researcher needs to deal with proprietary information.

In this study, the agreement was eventually signed between my university's legal office and a corporate marketing unit, with the involvement of corporate and university lawyers beforehand. Neither side admitted experience with inscribing this kind of research into the document; hence in numerous discussions the process revealed many hidden assumptions about the roles, expectations and desirable outcomes of such an agreement. This initial set-up entailed a long thread of email and phone negotiations, with the delay in the agreement being signed used inside the corporation to regulate my access to certain intranet resources and meetings, albeit accompanied by an overall friendly attitude towards my presence. The agreement needed to specify the meaning of ethnographic research, and to state whether the study would yield any potential contribution to corporate activities and provide tangible outcomes. The corporate managers and lawyers initially perceived the study in terms similar to those of an MBA project that would produce certain corporate deliverables, such as, for example, a business plan or the launch of a new business project. The company would also retain the rights to use the final report (as the dissertation was initially perceived) for its business purposes. On the university side, the general idea was that the practical contribution of the project should not exceed menial help, with the outcome being a doctoral thesis and academic publications. Attempts were made to frame the ethnography in terms of a 'collaboration agreement' (such as those used for spin-offs) or as a 'consultancy' as a compromise on the university side that would go along with the proposed corporate language. But since the research was unpaid in order to keep any possible influence at bay, the suggestion was not accepted on the university side. Neither did the research fit the format of a 'standard CDA' (which stands for confidential disclosure agreement) as used to cover initial interactions between university and industrial representatives, because no 'disclosure' as such was to take place.

Compared with non-disclosure agreements that I had to sign for access to other corporations afterwards, signing the NDA with Virtual World seems a somewhat inflated case of lengthy negotiations, but one in which many of the assumptions about acceptable research framings came to the fore. Over the course of a month the number of actors engaged in tossing the agreement back and forth on both sides increased. The emails in the business school circulated between Steve Woolgar (who was acting as the director of research and as my academic supervisor), the research projects manager, the director of administration, the MBA placement officer, the DPhil student who had signed the agreement the year before and, finally, me. At Virtual World, three managers, a corporate lawyer and I were engaged in negotiating the agreement. As the number of people increased, the document preparations became even messier. It did not become any clearer who exactly should negotiate the contents of the agreement. Should the academic supervisor talk to the corporate lawyer? Should a university lawyer be invited to talk to the managers? Furthermore, who should actually sign it (the ethnographer? the business school? who at Virtual World? who at the school?)? Each of the actors becoming involved had to delve into the complexity of the exchange produced earlier. The exchange replayed the familiar theme of the different speeds of action on the corporate and university sides, with reminders sent to the university rendering the agreement a 'pressing matter'. In the end, the outcome and speed depended on contingent circumstances such as suddenly running into the people involved in the negotiation and mentioning a word about the state of the art of the matter. The agreement between the university and the corporation was signed at the end of May 2004, four months after the starting day in February when I received my badge and laptop. The university negotiated the upper limit of the liability from an 'onerous' £100,000 down to £5,000, but still felt it would be too much of a burden for the ethnographer to be personally responsible. The researcher's responsibility diminished as the university became the major actant in the text of the agreement 'providing a student' for the corporation.

As a conversational resource employed to settle an inter-organisational matter, the non-disclosure agreement shows in what ways making sense of ethnography depended on pre-existing definitions of what academic research was about. It also implied figuring out and stabilising the emerging meaning of 'ethnography' *de novo*. Representatives of legal, academic, administrative and marketing communities were engaged in actively interpreting the meaning of ethnography and the possible relationship between ethnographer and corporation. Through negotiations of responsibilities and authorities of actants ('the Student', 'the Company') and accountability relations between individuals (who should talk to whom? who should sign the agreement?), the document stabilised as a set of agents and audiences particular to the research on marketing knowledge. The NDA can be seen as a practical means to anticipate and to capture the situated work of narrating technologies for various audiences inside and outside of the corporation. Equally, it raised analytic and practical questions for this study about the status of technology in its renditions to academic audiences.

In this respect, the ethnographic writing is an example of such achieved descriptions of a technology leaving a corporation.[10] Capturing the situated work of narrating technologies inside the corporation, this study simultaneously raises questions about the status of technology in its renditions to academic audiences. An earlier era in STS was once aptly characterised as 'the golden age' of science studies, opening up a 'window of opportunity' for access to scientific content.[11] Such access was reflected in the programmatic thrust to examine technical content in the making, in order to show how things could have been otherwise. The situation is different when research is conducted under a non-disclosure agreement. Rather than directing analytic attention to the 'technical content', the restrictions sensitise us to questions about *what counts as* technical content and for whom.

Corporate ethnography and the conditions of non-disclosure in some sense run counter to academic expectations of analyses of technology being able to freely report any possible detail of technology in the making, as well as of practices employed. This preconception does not seem to be sensitive enough to the distribution of such knowledge in socio-technical relations. Nor does it exhibit appreciation of the conditions of ethnographic inquiry in settings where anonymity and non-disclosure are routinely negotiated, and where the very possibility of letting certain accounts of technology in/out are a matter of negotiation of terms, such as it will be discussed in especially Chapters 6 and 7. In other words, the traditional approach leaves underanalysed the practical (participants', analyst's) ways of achieving technology content, or, in other words, of going about leaving a technology unpacked for some while opening its content up for others. This analysis is strongly suggestive of the idea that answers to the question of 'what is the technology like?' are highly contingent and are a matter of contestation. What we do deal with are achieved (sufficient, acceptable, conventional, adopted for the purposes at hand) technology descriptions.

Achieving anonymity (of participants, company, technology) is one of the instances of negotiated technology descriptions. The ethnographer has to simultaneously render technology to academic audiences and to fulfil her non-disclosure obligations. As such this condition informed, but certainly did not dictate, the ways in which access was gained and accounts of the technology were produced for the readers of this book. Negotiating conventions of disclosure of (technical) content in attempts at intervention and ordering, such as a launch, appear to be a practice neglected in STS. However, such practice sheds light on the performance of accountability relations around technology. By producing greater insight into the accountability work in and of technology marketing, I seek to explore distribution of technical knowledge. The approach taken here promotes sensitivity to the instances when the very portrayal of what technology is like in relation to its various (anticipated) readings becomes subject to practical questioning and negotiating. To conclude, a working suggestion might be that the current moment, when scholars' attention is increasingly drawn to activities behind corporate walls, might be better characterised as 'the age of non-disclosure'. This assumes different possibilities, practices and conventions of accounting for socio-technical ordering in science and technology studies. How does the ethnographic attempt at holding the field accountable, as in this book, change our expectations of what counts as analytically acceptable analyses of a given technology? How successful can STS writings be 'without' rather than as a result of attending to technical content?

Marketing practice: a place for ethnography

Another topic that informed a place for ethnography (and more precisely for ethnographer) in the marketing department was utility. Ethnography and marketing are sometimes interconnected through the discourse of the utility of ethnography for marketing (Winick, 1961; Arnould and Wallendorf, 1994; Ryder, 2004; Sherry, 1995; McGrath, 1989; Elliott and Jankel-Elliott, 2003). The practical contribution of anthropology to marketing strategies, policymaking and consumer studies is seen in these works as a major and unquestionable value of the discipline to marketing. The adoption of ethnography, however, may become subject to organisational politics (Moeran, 2005; Brownlie *et al.*, 1999a; Moeran and Malefyt, 2003a). In a marketing department that decides to take ethnography on board, new sets of professional relations may develop. Moeran and Malefyt (2003a: 18), for instance, emphasise that ethnography may be used to establish the primacy of certain (qualitative) marketing strategies in a corporation over others. What were the ways in which utility became a part of the conversation between ethnography and marketing at Virtual World?

As above, the meanings of marketing knowledge and ethnography proved to be mutually constitutive in negotiations of access and of a non-disclosure agreement. I began participant observation while the NDA was still in negotiations. The general notions of ethnographic research as performed by both the NDA-in-the-making and by the expectations of the purpose of my study articulated in conversations with gatekeepers had to be reinterpreted, by both managers and myself, and translated into the appropriate modes of my everyday presence in the company. As described above, the initial agreement with gatekeepers assumed the ethnographic study would contribute to better visibility for Virtual World in academic circles. This proposition seemed to contradict the pressure to sign the non-disclosure agreement, constant reminders about the confidential nature of some documents, and reluctance to invite me into some meetings. This, as I will discuss below, entailed a number of fluid arrangements, the decisions about which had to be made *ad hoc* as I engaged in more and more tasks.[12]

What does it mean for an anthropologist to pass for a skilful technology marketer? My 'line manager' observed in our farewell conversation that I 'did well'. He meant that I was able to establish myself in the complexity of corporate relations, and to find my own way through in what everyone perceived as a fairly chaotic environment. The word 'career' is not simply a metaphor accounting for changes of locations and teams within the company. In participants' eyes my movements between different marketing groups were understood as 'career moves' from the lower-status 'organising' work I did with the 'vertical' marketing team to an invitation extended by the Head of Corporate Marketing to contribute to the work of a highly respected 'public sector' team. The latter, as it was suggested by a marketing manager, would definitely look good on my CV (had I found it useful to disclose the company name). Perceived as a 'promotion', my joining RFID marketing yielded the major portion of ethnographic observations. It appeared to some that there was even some kind of logic in my accumulating 'relevant' experience so as to provide for further movements and, so to speak, to climb the corporate ladder.

Ethnographic methodologies

Conducting ethnography with a large IT corporation, where the use of information and communication technologies (ICT) was encouraged among employees, not surprisingly involved elements of what Hine (2000) called 'virtual ethnography'. Becoming a member of the corporation, and a contributor to its marketing activities, entailed becoming proficient in the use of technologies employed in marketing rituals, such as, for instance, conference calls and the corporate intranet. In an interrelated manner, corporate talk featured themes of location and mobility, thus prompting questions about ethnographic mobility and multi-sited ethnography. The participant observation was taken seriously by the managers as something that needed to be properly arranged within the company from day one. Settling me in entailed a number of administrative tasks, such as making me a 'badged employee', which involved assigning me a magnetic badge that would allow me to enter the buildings; providing me with a corporate laptop to access the corporate intranet and email; and finding a desk for me; as well as preparing a nondisclosure agreement. Calculating the costs involved in hosting a researcher was done, too. The corporation agreed to pay my travel expenses to commute by bus, and my installation in the company meant some work for the human resources managers and other administrative staff. This made me a legitimate, albeit odd, insider whose presence was established through corporate structures, including an entry in the corporate intranet address book accompanied by my photo, which I had to have taken during the first week. These, together with the ethnographic task of managing face-to-face interactions, provided basis for the ways I began to collect my ethnographic data.

Ethnography and virtual access devices

As Hine (2000) and Beaulieu (2004) observe, in the age of information and communication technologies, ethnographic stories of gaining access to the field are sometimes presented as arrival stories describing the first encounters with such technologies (for example, an Internet website). The ethnographers' accounts of their first 'witnessing' the field and encountering 'the object' of study through making sense of the technologies in the first instance sets the initial place of the ethnographer, the reader, and the field (Pratt, 1987, cited in Beaulieu, 2004). Such encounters may also call into question the initial conceptions about the field as well as the meaning, and the purpose, of ethnography. Beaulieu (2010) discusses how a laboratory website became an access issue bearing on the construction of what counts as adequate initial information about the field, shaping the ethnographer's trajectory in the lab. Dealing with mediated market discourses may also entail our rethinking of how we make sense of the interrelation between markets and technologies, and what these interrelations mean for the ethnographic enterprise. As in Pollner (2002), the research at the intersection of the market and the Internet – for example, an Internet investment community – helps to reconsider the merits of the analytic language used to describe the particular setting, such as networked society, or 'self-fulfilling prophecy' in his case study.

In another episode of my arrival story, information and communication technologies became an obligatory element of my access to the corporation, occupying me on my first day on the company premises. Within about two weeks after meeting the gatekeepers, I arrived at the company to gear myself up for the fieldwork. The first thing to do was to meet my line manager, who took me to an IT office in order to receive a laptop configured to provide me with access to the Internet and to some parts of the corporate intranet. I received a large suitcase containing what I thought to be a pretty smart laptop, and its accessories.

Having received the laptop, I spent a considerable amount of time trouble-shooting, or 'raising cases with TRC', a technical support service, before I became a competent user of the technologies. By the end of the first month of my ethnography I was configured up to the level of being a user of IP voicemail, having wireless access to the Internet and intranet inside the company premises, and having access to the most general level of the corporate intranet and the corporate members' directory. The level of my electronic access was closely related to the status of my non-disclosure agreement, and arrangements changed as the agreement was signed. Remote access, for example, remained unavailable to me until the non-disclosure agreement was signed, since it was perceived as endangering corporate information protection. As I became more involved with activities in the field, the attributes of my membership changed, such as the possibility of being 'conferenced in', while other options, such as being able to set up a conference call myself, did not become available to me.

In the course of my participant observation I gradually realised that I have become a user of a number of information and communications technologies through my fieldwork engagements. The multiple social boundaries of communication technologies became especially visible in a company that produces a wide range of connectivity tools and encourages the internal deployment of many different kinds of technologies. It was not uncommon to receive invitations to and to attend staff meetings, such as an activities update or a new-product introduction, being conducted by phone for participants in different countries.

Virtual ethnography problematises the role of ICT in and for ethnographic research. In recent methodological discussions, ethnographic embeddedness is understood from the perspective of the researcher's engagement with a culture, or of a community using information and communication technologies. Hine (2000) advocates a reflexive approach to Internet research understood in terms of the importance for the ethnographer to become a competent user of the Internet, as well as in terms of the researcher's attention to interactions with participants encountered in the field: 'The processes through which field sites are found and materials collected become ethnographic materials in themselves' (Hine, 2000:

55). Presenting her own ethnographic experience, Hine (2000) describes her attempts to develop a network of 'virtual' informants while following Louise Woodward's case.[13]

Technologies of communication subsequently emerged as the means/object of ethnography. How do technologies bear on the inclusion of an ethnographer in a community of ICT users? How do technologies become a noticeable part of access negotiations? Instead of quite commonly construing technologies as 'tools' or 'research sites', the question rather needs to be asked of how usages of information technologies are made observable and accountable in the course of research. A related question also concerns the ways of learning the conventions for using ICT. Those may not always be available to a researcher who needs to work on recognising and learning where to find and how to use technologies adopted in an organisation. Making sense of such technologies turned out to be closely intertwined with travel arrangements, hence bearing on the modes of ethnographic presence.

Organising my travel was as important as arranging my access to corporate electronic resources, in an interdependable way. One of the reasons to commute to the office from the very beginning was the need to keep up with conference calls, as well as to gain access to the intranet, which was initially only possible at the office. In order to be able to access it from other places, one needed a remote access, which I obtained only after my NDA was signed. Conference calls were an important feature of corporate life in the global corporation. As an initiatory rite, a conference call was usually organised at the beginning of a project as an introductory meeting for more than two participants often scattered across different locations and countries. My first conference call experience was rather awkward. Conference calling assumes certain communicative conventions (e.g. who begins, how to take turns, how to quit, how to join late), of which I was not aware. I was also not confident about how to present myself as a researcher. A competent user needs to be a member of the corporation (or be invited by one) in order to access a virtual meeting place. A personal invitation to a conference call sent by email as an Outlook Calendar entry contains a call ID number and a telephone number, which the corporation (sometimes) pays for. A conference call organiser needs to 'set up a bridge' through a dedicated intranet webpage, access to which I never obtained and had to ask the managers I worked with to help me with when I had to set up a call. Additionally, as I worked on projects, such features of conference calling as 'conferencing in' on a mobile phone became applicable to me. In order to be 'conferenced in', and thus receive a free incoming call on a mobile, one needs to ask another call participant who uses an IP phone from the office to dial his or her number, and to perform some hard-to-learn manipulation with phone keys. Since it takes time and requires some extra knowledge of technology, 'conferencing in' was considered a favour. Thus, becoming a more proficient conference caller was equivalent to organising my relationships with my 'colleagues' both in Virtual World and in the business school too, where I could use the equipment. Thus, one observation that I would like to highlight is that the use of information technologies in the corporation was construed as an element of membership.

Multi-sited ethnography?

If a study of marketing in practice is to be conceived of by analogy with laboratory studies (Latour and Woolgar, 1979/1986; Knorr Cetina, 1981; Latour, 1987; Lynch, 1985), what are the bounded ethnographic locations equivalent to the lab? Does a 'marketing department' have the same sense of situatedness as a 'laboratory'? This discussion is particularly pertinent to this study of a global corporation.

The corporation owned several locations around London, one of which was in the City, London's financial district. I usually came to work at the corporate headquarters in West London, and occasionally to another office in Reading, when I began working with an engineering team. I also paid visits to some external-to-the-company locations, such as the RFID Expo (see Chapter 7) in an industrial area between London and Reading, and a market research studio in the City of London, where focus groups for a new product that I followed were conducted. I also changed my workplace in the office, migrating with the 'advanced technologies' team from Building A to Building C in South Park, and worked wirelessly from unusual places such as a cafeteria. Some authors (Marcus, 1995; Hine, 2005) have discussed the notion of multi-sited ethnography. In the sociology of technology, multi-sitedness, or moving purposefully beyond the bounded spaces to which traditional ethnographers were confined (e.g. 'beyond the bounds of individual laboratories'), was shown to be an insightful way of doing research and exploring new ways of developing theory and contributing to practice (Hine, 2005). An example of such an approach is also De Laet and Mol's (2000) account of the bush pump and its fluid boundaries, which the ethnographers could follow as they travelled. This, according to the authors, was possible because they suspended their judgement of the appropriateness of various sites and instead engaged with the situations they found. The strategy also relates to an early actor-network theory methodological suggestion to follow the actors themselves (Latour, 1987).

How can one account for the multiplicity of locations, which yet belonged to a single ethnographic journey following activities in an organisational entity such as the corporation? Would the notion of multi-sited ethnography suitably account for my ethnographic moves? What constitutes multi-sitedness? What makes an ethnographer mobile? To what extent would it be useful to construct the study as an effort to enumerate and describe multiple possible network(s) of actants and enactments? How would an ethnographer go about trying to provide an exhaustive account of contexts constituting a technological product, such as in the studies accounting for multiple ontologies (Mol, 2002)?

A 'mobile ethnographer' is an outcome of the social interactions in which an ethnographer is immersed. For example, in the first two or three months my connections inside the company were rather chaotic before I became associated with more or less well-defined projects and individual managers. This demanded that I constantly 'monitor' the emails I was receiving, which I could only do from the office, having no remote access. It took me almost five months to become a configured user of remote access through negotiating non-disclosure and technical issues with managers and technical support. My further involvement with the 'organising' activities (Chapter 4) demanded even greater attention to the contents of my inbox. Even when remote access was in place, I think I hardly used my membership in the 'virtual organisation' fully, realising that I could make much more of my fieldwork if I came to the office.

Installing myself as an ethnographer in South Park meant, for me, becoming an efficient commuter. Finding efficient ways of getting to and from the company occupied my thoughts for the first couple of months as I learned to make connections between Oxford–Heathrow buses, the Tube, and the corporate courtesy shuttle bus running between Hutton Cross station, Terminal 4, and South Park. I found myself spending four to five hours on average in public transport commuting to and from the company on each of three to four days a week, sometimes five. I chose to catch an early 6:30 a.m. bus to shorten my commute. I learned to complain about traffic on the M25.[14] Catching a shuttle bus was an experience of its own kind, since (no, I mean it, really!) traffic around Heathrow and on the M25 made timetables unreliable. I also discovered local bus routes passing by the business area, and learned to exit at Heathrow Central Station, not Terminal 4, to take the Tube for one station and catch the shuttle bus at Hutton Cross to avoid delays in the 'crossing area' in Heathrow where planes crossed the road as they taxied from one hangar to another. It was easy to recognise the business crowd early in the morning at Hutton Cross, waiting for the minibus running late, some people carrying their badges ready to show to the driver or, on a cold winter morning, hastily finishing their coffee. Customer representatives could be recognised by their disorientation when identifying the exact location of the shuttle bus stop. They also usually carried a small wheeled suitcase. They jumped on the bus at Terminal 4. In the bus, a CNN TV channel or a London radio station was always on, so passengers could watch or listen to the news or to music. The IBM, Oracle and Sun employees exited earlier, and finally the bus made a circle in front of Virtual World's buildings A, B and C, letting the passengers off.

If the reader thinks I've indulged myself in writing about the commute, I was not the only member of the corporation obsessed with travel arrangements. Commuters' stories and travel experiences were a part of corporate small talk. Information about road situations in the area and on the M25 was circulated through a corporate mailing list. A taxi service was available and was pretty busy during the day. Mentions of the 'M25 standing still' and delays on the Piccadilly Line could be heard in the cafeteria. Conversations about airports and coping with jetlag after a transatlantic flight were constantly exchanged. The marketing managers I worked with disappeared from time to time while travelling to one or more EMEA countries or to the United States. International travel possibilities were one of the attractions of the marketing job in this global corporation.

The definitions and uses of multi-sitedness turn out to be local and partial. Ethnography is about tracing connections and complex engagements taking an ethnographer across the sites. These local encounters with the field are constitutive of the phenomenon of study (Law, 2004). However, the constitution of boundaries as engagement with various communities in the field is what deserves special attention. On the one hand, changing teams within the company can be seen as changing ethnographic sites: social relations as well as foci of marketing activities changed as I moved to different teams. At the same time, the very travel to another team or project retained some linkages with previous sets of relations, too. The moves contributed to the construction of my identity within the organisation. Engagements with different teams were a part of my 'career' and were referred to as such by participants. It can be equally said that the multiplicity of sites occurred during my ethnography within a single organisation. A difficulty occurs if I try to describe my ethnographic visits to an external location such as RFID Expo as a multi-sited study. As a researcher, I engaged with a different setting. As a participant, I was a representative of Virtual World. The company considered the site to be an extension of its own presence through the building of a trade show booth.

Another perspective on multi-sitedness arises from the recognition that participants themselves are engaged in the practical management of boundaries. One of the technology marketing notions one learns on becoming an insider is that of the 'ecosystem'. While outsiders' view of corporations such as Virtual World may be that corporations are stand-alone, bounded entities, insiders constantly accomplish boundary work, engaging in strategic alliances, partnering, competition, joint projects, co-sponsorships, co-branding and co-design in one area, while recognising other corporations as competitors to avoid in others. The notion of an 'ecosystem' helps to organise participants' discourse of boundary work as managers try to figure out whom they need to side with and whom to avoid at all costs in relation to a technological product. Thus, the multiplicity and separatedness of entities (or sites) or their unity appears to be a matter of practical management, which involves moving between these different entities. This work is institutionalised in some marketing or business development jobs responsible for partnering and building relations with other corporations and within business alliances.

Data gathering and organising

The constitution of ethnographic locations is thus an important feature of ethnography. The ways in which boundaries are constructed and experienced in ethnographic engagements bears on the contents of the ethnographic narrative, its audiences and the circumstances of its narration. The collection and organisation of fieldwork materials is such an exercise in managing research boundaries, and in assessing opportunities and limitations. How was this ethnographic description of marketing practice achieved? The main materials gathered during my participant observations were emails, interviews, observations and notes made during meetings, working notes as reflections of everyday tasks, and instructions given to me by the managers. I was also asked on a few occasions to prepare reports for other projects and separate tasks I was helping with. I also maintained a field diary, especially in the first few months. In addition, I kept an archive of electronic and hard copies of various documents, promotional materials, drafts and design proposals for texts, imagery and video.

Having an email address at VirtualWorld.com resulted in more than three thousand emails and more than fifteen hundred sent items by the end of my field-work. This amount of electronic correspondence reflects my email exchanges with managers, emails sent to other companies on behalf of Virtual World, and invitations to meetings. The contents of my inbox also constitute me as a member of a broader set of relations inside the company, in terms of the kinds of general announcements, mailing-list items and meeting reminders I received. Some mailing lists were automatically set up to include every new email account created for newcomers on the 'corporate' and 'marketing' levels. I learned about other mailing lists related to certain products (such as RFID), or events, or trainings, from marketing managers and asked them to subscribe me where possible.

Interviews with members of the organisation and some external participants (such as the RFID Expo Director and his colleagues) were another way of gathering data. There were reasons both for and against setting up formal interviews. On the one hand, an interview was at times the only means to reach an executive whom I wanted to ask to comment on a certain issue. On the other hand, one of the reasons against setting up a formal interview via a cold email was that an informative talk occurred much more easily when I was introduced to someone as a member of the project who could legitimately show interest in the roles and responsibilities of the people involved. In addition, the attitude of talking to an academic in an interview provoked a conversational register that was more intensely packed with textbook expressions. Usually, the time allowed for the interviews was short. Twenty to thirty minutes was the average slot I could obtain for an interview, often on the phone. Interviews mainly took the form of managers 'lecturing' me about what they assumed I wanted to know. In interviews, I could sometimes recognise 'PR' talk translating the corporate discourse, that could be found on the website, to me.

Brownlie (1997) is generally pessimistic about the possibility of producing a 'truthful' ethnographic account of marketing: the sensitivity of his subjects to the disclosure of the details of their activities turns into their public relations exercise in relation to the ethnographer: 'I was dealing with appearances. My ethnography was his [company boss's] public relations exercise, his impression management test' (p. 270). In other words, the subjects have to pass as marketers, and they know how to do it. In this sense, an ethnographer will never gain access to 'what's really going on' in marketing practice. As Brownlie (p. 278) observes, 'many marketing managers are now fluent in the techno-speak of marketing academia and can easily talk to researchers using this vocabulary when they think it appropriate to do so.' One can ask whether impression management of this kind can be sustained in the course of a long-term participant observation – my experience rather speaks about a mix of attitudes and attempts to play with the researcher's identity, such as trying to impress me with marketing techno-speak on some occasions, downplaying my status as a researcher on others, or not considering it to be relevant to a task at hand. However, what these observations raise is a question about the variability of corporate accounts.

Discourse analysts (Gilbert and Mulkay, 1984; Potter and Wetherell, 1997) argue that the reliance on informants' accounts removed from their everyday working environment does not take into account the relationship between the construction of discourse and the particular ends to which it is put. Gilbert and Mulkay (1984) called the way the accounts are put together in different contexts 'interpretive repertoires'. According to the authors, interpretative repertoires (such as PR talk) are not stable discourses belonging to participants. They shift and change from context to context, and therefore participants' accounts should be studied as they are used for particular purposes. In other words, it is important to be aware not only of the occasional nature of discourse, but also of the strategic use of discourse and the ongoing recognition of interviewing conventions by ethnographer and participants.

Most of the managers were very confident talking to me. They were skilled in public performance since they presented for the corporate TV, in meetings, and sometimes as company representatives for mass media. Some of them also expected me to adopt the role of professional journalist-like interviewer, with a prepared set of questions, clear ideas of what I wanted to hear, and perhaps even to be an aggressive interrogator, as they were prepared to defend their position against attacks. One need only watch a few interviews with corporate executives in the business news to get an idea. The embarrassment that occurred when my questions and reactions did not meet such expectations was a regular feature of such meetings. The tension eased sometimes since I showed no intention to discredit the company.[15] Unlike ethnographic encounters, corporate interviews given to the media are often not spontaneous occasions to provide information. Interviews given by top executives or corporate spokespersons are one of the ways the corporate world establishes its relationships with its publics. In the drive to build up and protect the corporate reputation this ritual is one of the most sensitive towards the construction of a spokesperson's performance. Business interviews as seen on TV or heard on the radio are usually far from being a spontaneous encounter of a curious interviewer and an interviewee. The work of preparation behind the scenes involves a careful selection of wording and gestures. The conversational exchange is often rehearsed and pre-recorded, and sometimes influenced by the powerful corporate interviewee. In other words, an interview is always an interview for some kind of public, an attempt to show 'us saying this' to achieve certain interpretations in the audience.

The participants also held different expectations about the outcome of my work. As above, some of them expected the study to get into the marketing textbooks as an example of good marketing practice. Others were concerned about whether the marketing they do shows them in a good light. These expectations shaped my discussions with marketers, the degree of openness they showed and their willingness to let me into their world. The assumptions about potential audiences of the study influenced the way I received and was denied access to the organisational materials. I did not succeed in establishing myself in the company as someone freely allowed to make either audio or video recordings, having recorded only a few meetings. However, I found it helpful to make audio recordings where I could, and these occasions happened more often as I became immersed in the fieldwork. The accountability of the setting to the ethnographer, or the possibility of soliciting and receiving accounts of marketing activities, was the upshot of interactions, mutual adjustment of communicative conventions, and organisation of communicative spaces. To maintain an ethnographic presence in the field was equivalent to becoming a routine member of communicative engagements, learning what it means to do so, and introducing new conventions in the encounters, such as the use of a voice recorder and note-taking. In other words, rendering the ethnographic setting accountable entailed work by both ethnographer and participants to initiate and to maintain the interactions.

Discussion

While the previous chapters offered an approach to technology marketing mostly based on the examination of literatures, this chapter began looking at the constitution of marketing knowledge in ethnographic interactions. Negotiating access entailed a particularly rich set of deliberations about the nature of both marketing and ethnographic research, rendering the two mutually constitutive. The analysis also raised questions about the possibility and analytic utility of understanding ethnography as a 'truthful' representation of marketing in practice, which I will return to in the chapters to follow. Rather, in this chapter I tried to show in what sense various devices were employed in the negotiations that made knowledge about how marketing works in practice an element connecting corporate and scholarly activities. The examples included the rhetoric of a 'gap' between theory and practice, and discussions about the anticipated utility of ethnography for marketing and about what constitutes an acceptable form of research under a non-disclosure agreement. In all these episodes, different points of view about what marketing is about, and which elements of access became necessary to join the marketing organisation, were advanced and negotiated.

Learning about how marketing works in practice was thus a matter of negotiating the accountability of the marketing setting to the ethnographer, through creating possibilities of witnessing or interrogating 'marketing'. The choice of the field site itself was an interactional accomplishment revealing preconceptions about the nature of marketing practice on both researcher's and practitioners' sides. Such possibilities also involved figuring out the practical and the technical means to establish membership in the organisation that relied on certain conventions of travel and the use of communication devices.

In other words, the nature (content, research questions and opportunities for access) of this study as a *project* was continually shaped in interactions. Some directions, seen initially as a useful starting point (such as the 'marketing enablement' project) were taken, and then abandoned, while new opportunities emerged. Staying with the corporation was equivalent to managing numerous connections and relations along the way, remaining flexible in terms of the content and the duration of the fieldwork, and at times taking responsibility for certain tasks in order to ensure the continuing availability of ethnographic materials. All of that allowed for establishing a malleable space for ethnography inside the corporation, balancing various degrees of involvement, affiliations to corporate projects and, finally, the possibility of letting the ethnographic account out to readers. The next chapter continues the empirical account of the ethnographic work through an analysis of becoming a neophyte marketer as I joined a 'vertical' marketing team.

4 Becoming a neophyte marketer

Vertical marketing and accountability

This chapter offers an analysis of joining a so-called vertical marketing department at Virtual World as an apprentice marketer. What does it take, and what does it mean, to become a competent member of a marketing department? How are the practices of vertical marketing made sense of in the organisation? From an ethnomethodological perspective, marketing practice is constituted in and through *accounts* produced and exchanged in the cultures employing the language of marketing. As in Chapter 1, if markets can be understood as 'sets of accountability' (Dilley, 1992a), this chapter further asks what kinds of sets of accountability vertical marketing performs. How are vertical markets and marketers held accountable through contingent exchanges and assessment routines? How is their agency constructed? Becoming a member of a marketing department means, in the first instance, learning the ways of accounting for marketing as everyday practice.

The accountability of vertical marketing can be understood in at least two senses. First, in the Garfinkelian (1967) sense, accountability can be seen as a constitutive feature of a marketing setting, as the ways in which marketing professionals account for their activities in their everyday talk and actions. Second, accountability can be seen in terms of specific accountability procedures, such as evaluation, assessment and measurement, both inside a corporation and in a wider societal context. Accountability measures (accounting systems, reports) can be implemented in order to assess the contribution of, for example, a marketing department, or an individual manager, to corporate performance (Rust *et al.*, 2004; Webster, 1992). Assessments of a societal impact of marketing practice are often put in the context of the ethics debate and may become a matter of academic and public concern (Willmott, 1999; Neyland and Simakova, 2009). Moeran and Malefyt (2003a: 15) contend that the very marketing action becomes visible by virtue of an evaluation of marketing effort.

Accounting for marketing practice happens on different, formal and informal, occasions. The nature of tasks can be discussed by marketing team members out of earshot of senior managers; through regular accounting routine such as reports; in corporate discussions about what should be done to improve the outputs of marketing; as well as by top managers deliberating on the merits of introducing new accountability procedures. Similar to access negotiation, ethnographic participation in the everyday work of a marketing department serves as a source of observations about the everyday conversational uses of the term *marketing*. What counts as marketing skills and marketing knowledge in the marketing department? What are the working hierarchies of the marketing expertise? What kinds of marketing images are projected to the outside, and what are the less known aspects of the marketing profession?

In the academic literature, 'vertical' marketing is an example of an attempt to introduce a form of marketing management as a 'solution' to organisational problems that goes in and out of fashion (see Chapter 1 for discussion). Vertical marketing has been discussed in academic literature as an innovative initiative that emerged in the 1960s as yet another attempt to draw corporate attention to customer problems. The first mentions of vertical marketing can be found in the late 1960s and early 1970s. In 1968 a symposium dedicated to vertical marketing gathered at North Western University in the United States. Vertical marketing was introduced in Europe in the academic marketing literature in the beginning of the 1970s, with the announcement of Bucklin's (1970) edited book *Vertical Marketing Systems*. The book was presented to the European marketing scene in 1971 by the editors of the *European Journal of Marketing*.

This marketing approach was described as a novel way to build corporate expertise in understanding distributors' and consumers' problems (Carpenter, 1995). Vertical marketing has also been described as a means to repair the 'loss of some sensitivity to the consumer' (Moyer, 1975: 8), especially in what are considered maturing retail industries. Such corporate initiative also aimed to establish stable long-term relationships between a wholesaler and a group of retailers (Dawson and Shaw, 1989). Establishing vertical marketing as a way to improve corporate performance, some authors account for its success in terms of the implementation of a new type of relations between product, producer and consumer. Unlike the traditional view of corporate behaviour in which 'the same' product is sold to all customers, vertical marketing assumes that each product will be matched with a special set of customers, or vertical markets. Etgar (1976: 12, fn. 1) defines vertical marketing as 'a set of establishments which are concerned with the production and distribution of a specific product or of related groups of products'.[1]

In the 1990s vertical marketing received attention from marketing academics and professionals as a 'better management method' (Robbins *et al.*, 1992) purported to increase corporate performance. However, while some authors proclaimed the birth of a new marketing specialisation, others expressed scepticism about the novelty of the approach. Carpenter (1995) anticipated 'the rise of the vertical marketing manager' and reports an increase in headhunting for vertical marketing managers. On the other hand, some authors saw vertical marketing as simply a redefinition of existing marketing activities. Pearson (1998: 36) drew practitioners' attention to the fact that they already do vertical marketing – their customer databases perhaps contain 'a number of clients in one particular market, whether it's biotechnology, insurance, education or health care'.

Vertical marketing as a professional occupation introduces the idea of a specialist who is able to solve organisational conflicts between wholesalers and retailers, or problems associated with the management of distribution channels, especially in IT industries, where corporations rarely work with end customers directly. The expertise of a vertical marketing manager would thus be related to his or her ability to identify specific vertical markets, to discover customers' problems and to establish relationships with customers, helping distributors to narrow their selling strategies. Such a specialist would have to find ways to align the thinking of the managerial corporate structures in terms of channels of distribution that construe the interests of particular retailers as essentially the same, with the particular interests of retailers who claim they have to deal with their local customers.

Vertical marketing assumes reconfigurations of accountability relations within organisations implementing vertical marketing, as well as between wholesaler and distribution channels. Etgar (1976) points out that the introduction of vertical marketing systems in organisations immediately raised questions about how to assess the efficiency of the new marketing function. Moyer (1975) observes that vertical marketing specialists were perceived as competitors to existing leadership hierarchies in corporations. The emergence of vertical marketing systems entailed boundary work: 'Who should lead this extracorporate organization?' (Little, 1970) Similarly, the introduction of this new configuration of relations between wholesaler and retailers also initiated the search for identity in retailers, who sometimes were unenthusiastic about full vertical integration, wishing not to be classified as belonging to one particular market but to save some degree of autonomy (Dawson and Shaw, 1989). Producers uniting under a vertical marketing system also had to find agreement on new leadership structures (Etgar, 1976). In other words, the advent of vertical marketing provoked attempts to reconfigure relations between product, producer and customer in terms of the formation of identities and a reconfiguration of responsibilities.

As it follows, marketing as a general term (as, for example, it is often used in the academic literature) can acquire some specific meanings, becoming a narrow practical and organisational category. Similar to the boundary work around 'technology marketing' discussed in Chapter 3, labels attached to marketing departments inside organisations may denote a type of marketing within the more general marketing discipline. The labelling may bear on the particular ways participants construe their practices as being distinct, (more) efficient, or innovative. Joining a marketing department as a novice represents a particularly apt case for examining the everyday uses of the terms *market* and *marketing*. The everyday talk in a marketing department is a rich source of observations about the pragmatic interconnections between markets and marketing. The practice-based approach to markets and marketing (cf. Araujo *et al.*, 2010) argues that these notions have been reified in the economic discourse, leaving assumptions about the empirical nature of markets and marketing uninterrogated,[2] and that the practical interconnections between the two need empirical scrutiny. As a part of its main task to examine everyday interactions in the vertical marketing department, this chapter looks at some examples of such interconnections.

The materials analysed in this section also provide for a convenient opportunity to rethink the idea of the market as a network in terms of accountability relations. Organising activities in marketing, using the actor-network language (Callon, 1999), can be understood in terms of managing semiotic networks comprising technologies. To remind the reader briefly, the actor-network semiotic approach is associated with Latour's introduction of the notion of the actant in *Science in Action* (Latour, 1987) and Callon's study of the domestication of scallops in St Brieuc Bay (Callon, 1986). It generally relates to the debates on the nature of technology content and context, in which artefacts are understood as sets of contingent negotiations between human and non-human network actants.

While the proposition to understand the market as a heterogeneous network has been actively taken up in some recent analyses of markets and marketing (Callon, 1998b; Kjellberg, 2001; Lien, 1997; Araujo, 2007; also see Chapter 1 of this book for discussion), the contention of this book is that more attention is needed to what the practical management of the market as network involves. It seems that the recent 'amendments' to the ANT vocabulary suggested by Callon (Callon in Barry and Slater, 2002), the moves towards 'after ANT' (Law and Hassard, 1999), as well as the language of *agencements* (e.g. Callon, 2005), using Deleuzian vocabulary, all redefined the actor network in such a way that the semiotic origins of ANT are now somehow lost, giving prominence instead to materiality. However, in a post-essentialist spirit, this chapter revisits the earlier semiotic sense of the actor network, which, in my view, is cognate to the discursive approach to the market this chapter elaborates through an analysis of marketing accountabilities. My intention is to show that precisely by keeping alive the notion of semiotic networks of actants, the market as network may still hold as a viable metaphor for a post-essentialist anthropology of the market. The renewed focus on language also builds on earlier anti-essentialist critiques of ANT (Lee and Brown, 1994; Strathern, 1996; Collins and Yearley, 1992; Grint and Woolgar, 1997), generally stressing the importance of possible multiple interpretations of relations composing a network. As the analysis below will show, in participants' accounts of marketing activities semiotic networks are created and cut, as well as ownership attributed and contested (Strathern, 1996). Descriptions of networks are displayed, evaluated, accepted as good enough or rejected, being an open interpretive matter in the marketing department. How are markets-as-networks accounted for? How can the practical management of markets-as-networks be understood in terms of accountability in the marketing department? The task of the following section, which looks at these questions in detail, is not to show how exactly vertical marketing was assessed and evaluated. The point is rather to demonstrate that 'vertical marketing' is understood and constituted differently through different sets of accountability relations in the organisation. This contention will be explored in the next sections through an ethnographic analysis of becoming a neophyte marketer and taking part in the corporate accountability rituals.

Becoming a neophyte marketer

The remainder of the chapter offers an ethnographic discussion of how participants make sense of what is going on in a vertical marketing department. One of the central premises of ethnography is that the researcher must work on making things strange in the field (Geertz, 2000; Woolgar, 1988c). However, strangeness is a double-edged sword for participant observation: being totally estranged may make it difficult to build a relationship with the field and gain access to the everyday details of marketers' activities. An ethnographer of a modern setting is never an absolute novice to the activity: 'research never starts from scratch; it always relies on common-sense knowledge to one degree or another' (Hammersley and Atkinson, 2002: 64). The ethnographic task required to make this particular kind of marketing activity look strange was not straightforward. These activities are infused with the seemingly mundane sense of such common practices as, for example, 'events', or 'organising', or 'invitations' – not least because these terms permeate our own academic culture of organising workshops, conferences and seminars through categorising, choosing relevant participants and sending out invitations. And, indeed, in what sense do we term these 'organising activities' and assess their utility? What do we call an event if understood as a native category? One of the ways of doing this, as in this and in the following chapters, is to approach organising ethnographically as a *documentary* practice.

Joining the company as a participant observer meant that I had to assume the work of figuring out what kind of a role the ethnographer could adopt and what kinds of contributions could be expected in exchange for access to the organisation. My professional experience in marketing, announced in an email sent widely to a corporate marketing team, was discussed with my line managers. My initial letter to gatekeepers, which suggested menial tasks corresponding to what I thought might pass as a menial job for marketing, was re-examined in terms of the departmental realities. The proposed help with photocopying or secretarial assistance was rejected straight away as irrelevant to the paperless office, where managers were self-sufficient and did not have secretaries. Perhaps, they mentioned, I was a little bit overqualified for the photocopying job, if such occurred, and perhaps I had something more to offer from my professional experience. My experience in public relations (for an international science fund) could not be immediately put to work because the fieldwork did not seem to provide a reasonable frame for engaging with the PR team, whose task was to establish long-term relationships with the press. In my case this seemed neither possible nor appropriate, since I was admitted to the organisation initially only for a six-month term, and my non-disclosure agreement had not yet been signed. Therefore, it was decided that I could not become a full-blown representative of the corporation to the outside world. Rather, what appeared more valuable as a professional experience was my ability to coordinate the production of 'marcom'[3] materials as well as my general familiarity with marketing routines. No particular tasks were assigned to me at first, and the managers adopting me suggested that we play it by ear in order to find where my expertise could be useful.

The sudden difficulty of figuring out what was going on in the marketing department and where I could help was my first and strongest ethnographic impression. Although my letter of introduction and CV had been sent to an extended marketing team, I had very little knowledge of who was who in the marketing department, only gradually expanding my acquaintance with managers during the course of my fieldwork. When Alex, the team leader, showed me to my desk, not even a few gazes detached from monitors. I spent my first day in the field calling technical support to learn how to listen to my voicemail on the IP phone and to connect to the corporate intranet wirelessly. I also went to wo(a) nder around for a while, found a cafeteria and a canteen, got lost in labyrinths of corridors and desks, and found my way back. People were busy walking up and down the stairs, pouring coffee from machines, queuing in the canteen, sitting at their desks, and talking on mobile phones in the walkways. Meetings were held in larger rooms with transparent walls. Some people were carrying small suit-cases as if they were on a short trip. Later a marketing manager explained to me that those travellers were customers who visited the company. For this reason, the corporation was known as having a 'wheely culture'. Nobody seemed to notice my presence, and my queries about how to get to the vertical marketing team did not provoke any questions in response while people were helpfully giving me directions. They seemed to be used to having unfamiliar faces around.

I did not exchange a single remark for months with some of the managers who shared the office, until we were introduced to each other either in the course of a project, in a corporate marketing meeting, or while just having lunch together with a manager who knew both of us. I was trying to understand what the managers I encountered were doing, how that could be translated into the language of marketing that I knew, and also to convey to the managers a sense of ethnography when asked about my own occupation. The idea of having a researcher on the team was not unanimously embraced (some perceived me as an observer imposed by senior management), so the meaning of ethnography remained a grey area throughout my stay. This eventually proved to be a productive ambiguity that allowed for various moves in the corporation as answers were mutually elaborated in discussions with my line manager's strategically vague question, 'Are you achieving what you are trying to achieve?'

Some activities seemed to be more interesting, or relevant, or intense from a participant observer's point of view. But if something I was interested in happened, an invitation to take part did not always follow. The beginnings and the ends of marketing activities were initially difficult to observe. A manager in the United States whom I wanted to interview about an advertising campaign went on holiday suddenly. A TV crew had just returned from a shooting session, but they had not known that I was interested in their assignment. This feeling of a constant effort to catch up with activities was shared by the marketing managers, too. A manager who had just started with the team discovered seventy emails in her inbox on the first day from colleagues she did not know. Working on projects later, sometimes I had to surprise managers with an approaching dead-line they had forgotten about or even remind them that they were 'in the loop'.

In the overall pursuit to catch up with events in the marketing department (or to avoid being overwhelmed, too), demonstrating 'busy-ness' was a noticeable feature of the shop-floor talk – people went to the canteen 'to grab a sandwich and have it in a meeting', 'for a quick coffee'. Some complained they did not have time to have lunch at all. Things turned out not to be so extremely pressing later on, but learning the local ways of handling the conversations about the workload became a useful part of staying connected.

Not being able to engage in the small talk firmly grounded in the local culture of projecting busy-ness, and hence missing ethnographic opportunities, initially made me severely doubt my own social skills. Not that it was a cultural shock compared with academic life at Oxford – in the end, the research turned out to be a rather intense exercise that disconnected me from the joys of the social life at Oxford considerably, as I was spending my days at the company. Rather, office life presupposed certain notions of what counts as being busy that one had to be able to understand in order to become a proper member. Also, as I realised later, some invitations were much understated. Discerning the subtleties of the way of conversing was a way to get involved. A British manager would say, for example, that they had a meeting and I could come if I wanted to, but I didn't have to if, as she was sure, I had other things to do. Hearing this, I was not sure whether the manager was only being polite and, in fact, did not want me to join the meeting. As a novice marketer (and ethnographer, too?), I had to judge daily the appropriateness of my presence at meetings or in conference calls. In the beginning, I felt more comfortable just following the flow of projects I was accepted to participate in, not intruding in the work of others. And luckily, in the end, there were plenty of cases where my help was appreciated.

Similarly, some definitions related to my presence framed in terms of mutual benefit emerged. A compromise on my role was construed by the managers in terms of being a vertical marketing *apprentice*. The novelty of vertical marketing in the organisation contributed to this. Some of the marketing activities, such as 'community building' through databasing and news bulletins, were rendered innovative marketing practices that would be 'good for me to learn' if I wanted to participate in a good marketing practice. Other activities (e.g. working with designers, or sending promotional materials out) were presented to me as more typical marketing routines that, presumably, I was familiar with by virtue of my previous experience. This assumption was different from the one employed in the access negotiations, and perhaps construed the PhD at the business school as a kind of professional-school experience rather than academic social science research. The notion that I came into the corporation to *learn* from marketing managers what it means to be a marketer became finally entrenched in the rites of passage from one team to another. Notably, the discussions about what kinds of activities in the vertical marketing department might be relevant to my research highlighted the local hierarchies of marketing tasks and their professional career value.

At Virtual World I could not observe any consistency in the marketing managers' backgrounds. The corporation did not offer any special training for marketers.

Some marketing managers attended professional marketing trainings outside of the company, while others were hired having an undergraduate degree in history, English, or business. Some managers (usually higher ranked) had a master's degree in marketing or communications. While some managers were hired into the corporation after years spent in marketing at other companies, engineers wishing to switch career paths were also recruited into the marketing department.

My presence at the company was made accountable through the formal procedures of signing a non-disclosure agreement, and through introduction and farewell letters sent by email. I was asked to write a letter of introduction (and attach my CV to it), as well as a letter summarising my achievements in the course of my ethnography at the end of my fieldwork. After thirteen months, in March 2005, I stopped visiting the company premises but continued to communicate with managers via email and conference calls in the virtual ethnography (Hine, 2000) mode. At that moment, I was asked by my line manager to write an end-of-year report, which I composed as a thank-you letter to the extended marketing team, many members of which I had not met in person. The striking difference between the letter of introduction and the final report was the degree of practical detail. The first communication contained a request to help me gain access to the everyday tasks and situations in which 'discussions and practical actions happen (planning sessions, brainstorms, working meetings, negotiations, document preparation, etc.)'. The end-of-year report used the local marketing language that I learned in the course of my ethnography. The note listed teams I worked with and enumerated extensively the activities I took part in, such as 'product launches', 'product development', 'project management', 'campaign execution', 'content production' and a few notable corporate meetings and projects.

My first task (not mentioned in the end-of-year report) was to put a few hundred brochures into envelopes and then into boxes to be delivered to a post room. The manager I shared the job with found it appropriate to apologise that my first contribution (and a part of her job) should be so lowly, saying that this was, nevertheless, a good example of 'what marketing is about'.[4] The menial tasks involved mainly collating sales managers' current information needs through electronic surveys, plenty of copying and pasting while preparing slides or creating databases, printing and photocopying, sending out emails to tens and sometimes hundreds of people, and collecting responses, adding up even more names. I was also often asked to post boxes with brochures or banners using the post-room facility. After a few months the post room manager knew me well and no longer required me to fill in a complicated online order form, but allowed me to bring him a postage order on a yellow sticky note. While laboriously sorting and posting brochures was not seen as a particularly glamorous job, the notions of new skills that could allegedly contribute to my professional growth involved copywriting and project management. Later, attempts were made to construe my input as an 'independent opinion'. Twice I was asked to help with a competitive analysis and an end-user-experience report based on website trials. Those quasi-ethnographic tasks were meant to provide practical suggestions. The managers who delegated the tasks to me had been unsuccessful in trying to voice their concerns about the website's usability. My reports, which indicated difficulties with the use of the interface, were interpreted as confirming their own positions and were presented as an independent opinion to their senior managers to show why audiences had been reluctant to use the system.[5]

The distinctions between the marketing skills one would like to be able to demonstrate (to a researcher, to an employer) and those the marketing managers would prefer not to include in descriptions of their profession were made recurrently. Marketing jokes are particularly revealing of the difference between glossy textbook portrayals of marketing and the contingencies of everyday tasks. By analogy with scientific jokes (cf. Gilbert and Mulkay, 1984), marketing humour attempts to reconcile competing interpretive repertoires. A CV describing marketing achievements in terms of 'strategic planning' and other sparkly expressions could be laughed at as being ridiculously pompous on other occasions. After hauling upstairs and unpacking a heavy banner from the storage room, a novice intern also taking a course in marketing at university would wonder whether what he learned at the uni had anything to do with what real marketing was about. Making claims (by the ethnographer as well as by participants) about what counts as marketing knowledge, such as, for example, distinguishing between commonly recognised professional knowledge, specialist expertise, and tasks with which anyone can help, was an important feature of interactions in the field. An important aspect of these interactions is the distinction between the knowledges that can (not) or should (not) be projected to the outside (depending on whether the ethnographer is seen as a reporter to civilisation or as a professional marketer). Was it by chance that I became associated with the vertical marketing team in the first place? The vertical marketing team was promoting itself within the organisation as an innovative marketing group, distinguishing itself from 'corporate marketing', which, it was said, did not want to innovate. The signs of success were visible: the executive supervising vertical marketing was named a corporate 'marketing champion', a successful leader of a new generation of marketers setting examples of good marketing practice.

The 'vertical' markets

The team of vertical marketers consisted of three young women in their late twenties to early thirties: Sara, Charlotte and Carrie. On meeting me, they noticed that I 'was really good at studying full time' since I was still in academia at the same age as them. Carrie had earned her bachelor's degree in commerce and had worked since then. Sara had a few years' gap since her undergraduate years, and now was taking a professional training course with the Chartered Institute of Marketing, which occupied only a few hours a week. Carrie was the most recently hired member of the team; she had joined shortly before me. Born Greek, she moved to London from Sydney, where she had lived since her early childhood. She wanted to have some London experience for a while, she explained. International travel as a reward for working for a global corporation was one of the attractions of her new job, and she seemed excited when her projects could result in a business trip. Charlotte was Polish by origin, but lived and worked in Germany. At least once every quarter she came to see her vertical marketing counterparts in the UK for a day or two, staying in one of the hotels near Heathrow airport.

Each of the vertical marketing managers was responsible for a vertical market or two. Being responsible for a vertical market meant engaging in and attempting to organise relations between the corporation and its end customers through communications with the sales managers working with those end customers. A vertical marketing manager would create marcom materials and display those in special 'vertical' intranet portals aimed at the sales managers (see the next chapter for further discussion).

The language of the vertical reflected the forms of relations between the product, the consumer and the customer. It also introduced boundaries between marketing teams within the corporation. Classification of the markets depended not on the nature of technological solutions, but rather on the potential customer groups the corporation was targeting. Virtual World's products and services were presented in terms of similar technology solution packages to be adapted for the needs of specific enterprises classified by their industry affiliation: 'transportation', 'manufacturing', 'retail', 'automotive', 'hospitality' and 'financial services'. Manufacturing, automotive and financial services were stable categories. Transportation and hospitality were related through a similar set of customer concerns that the solutions would help to solve. The two verticals shared a budget, and finally merged under the supervision of one of the vertical marketing managers. Some specific customer groups were not referred to as vertical markets at all. Pauline, a 'public sector' marketing manager, occupied a desk next to the vertical marketing team's office space in an adjacent row over a narrow aisle. However, she did not belong to the vertical marketing team since her audiences (primarily governments and schools) were not considered a vertical market. Our first work-related conversation took place more than a year after I joined Virtual World, when I started (as a sign of my 'promotion') helping the 'public sector' team with copywriting. The so-called horizontal marketing teams were seen as competitors in budget pitches. By definition (given to me by the marketing managers) the marcom materials produced for horizontal markets did not contain special propositions for singular industries. As a matter of local judgement and classification of markets out there, a new product usually began as horizontal (undifferentiated markets) and then became 'verticalised' as value propositions were created for identified vertical markets.

Each vertical marketing manager liaised with a group of 'subject-matter' experts – business development managers responsible for the production of technology value propositions for vertical markets. The experts also had authority to approve marcom materials created by the vertical marketing managers and were invited to speak at technology seminars for specific verticals. For example, Nick was an expert in 'airports', working for the 'transportation' vertical. He was presented to me as someone who best understood the 'careabouts'[6] of airport managers. This means that he was able to create a technology value proposition for airports, or to portray technological capabilities in such a way that they would match the concerns of airport managers.

'Organising' as a documentary practice

As one of its daily occupations, the vertical marketing team was engaged in creating encounters between customers and Virtual World's representatives. This was accomplished through the organising of special events: seminars, workshops, trade shows and conferences devoted to the presentation of Virtual World's products. Some events were held by the corporation, while for others Virtual World acted as a co-organiser. It was suggested that event management was the right activity for me to participate in if I wanted to 'get my hands dirty' with vertical marketing, and I began to be assigned little tasks from the vertical marketing managers related to 'organising'.

Vertical marketing occupied me for almost eight months, from February until late September 2004, and the perception of my affiliation with the team changed throughout the fieldwork. This activity was not recognised as a 'proper' part of my fieldwork by the marketing managers. A number of circumstances contributed to this perception. First, as I described in Chapter 3, working with the vertical marketing team was meant to occupy me only temporarily until I became involved with the 'marketing enablement' project. Second, organising (or 'event management') was not regarded as a particularly exciting marketing task by the managers themselves. It did not entail much interaction with top management, nor could it be described in terms of strategising. Usually, a decision to carry out an event was not a vertical marketing manager's own initiative, nor could she witness or enjoy the results of the preparatory work she had done. Organising an event in Germany from her office in the UK did not necessarily mean that the manager would travel to Germany – the finishing touch of welcoming and hosting people was often delegated to the local team in the country or to an outsourced hospitality provider. Travelling to an event (even if it entailed a considerable amount of work shepherding people around and verifying that the transportation, catering and speakers' arrangements were in place) was seen as a treat. After helping out with the organisation of a seminar in Germany, I was offered a chance to go to Germany 'as a bonus'. That, of course, meant helping with logistics (bringing executive delegates to and from a restaurant), but as a reward I could stay in a luxury hotel and be reimbursed for first-class travel expenses.[7]

According to the managers, helping out with organising did not require any thorough understanding of the specifics of Virtual World's marketing, and I would be able to grasp the basics quickly. Thus, this was perceived as a suitable temporary occupation for me. During the period February through October 2004 I felt that if I wanted to stay connected to my field, I had to be present in the office as much as I could. The fairy tale of the 'virtual organisation' dissipated quickly as I started helping with real projects. I had to be available for all those tasks I described above. Meetings and conference calls took place in the meeting rooms, representatives of advertising agencies as a rule came to see the marketing managers, not vice versa. The managers I worked with most closely usually showed up in the office between 8:30 and 9 a.m. They left the office after 6:00 or 7:00 in the evening, sometimes later, since calls with their counterparts in the United States had to take into account the time difference and were often scheduled for the evening hours. Occasionally, the managers were not in, saying they were working from home or in the City office, or had meetings outside the company premises, or went away for an international trip.

Despite the view of organising as an 'invisible' and 'unimportant' marketing activity, in retrospect I realise that this period from February to September contributed greatly to my socialisation with the company. The ways in which my ethnography developed after August 2004 were influenced by the connections I made during the first months. The tasks I took part in then helped my introductions to other marketing teams and activities later. Those eight months yielded at least half my emails and notes. During that time I mostly helped Carrie, the marketing manager who began with Virtual World just a few days before I joined. As a newcomer to the department, Carrie was made responsible for two vertical markets: 'transportation' and 'retail', and was glad to have a helper. Her workload progressively increased as hospitality merged with transportation. This was supplemented with a temporary responsibility for financial services, too, when Sara left for another marketing group.

Carrie's responsibilities to a large extent included organising corporate seminars and conferences for business executives. This implied selecting a venue, preparing the content and the programme of an event, producing marcom materials (brochures, CDs, invitations) and collating lists of invitees. The last task was often done in collaboration with sales managers. Carrie asked them to provide the right contacts in their accounts to be invited, and then to deliver and to check the reception of the invitations to reinforce an executive's determination to come to the event. As above, organising was not a glorious job in the hierarchy of marketing tasks. This messy and fleeting activity goes almost unnoticed as a marketing manager sits in front of her laptop holding a phone between her shoulder and her ear, at the same time checking the dozens of emails she has received during a single day, and surrounded by her quarterly marketing plans, creative agency briefs, and invoices, yellow sticky notes, and the boxes of brochures and CDs she needs to send to event locations. Depending very much on the responses of the other people involved, the work of organising is about one's ability to get other people to do things for the project, to be constantly aware of their reactions, and to move on promptly as soon as a response is received. Finding ('chasing') an executive speaker for a briefing before a conference depended not so much on the marketing manager's own schedule as on the speaker's. His or her PA[8] needed to be reminded, and his or her (late) response needed to be constantly monitored, since as soon as the marketing manager gets it she is ready to move on, filling in other people's schedules.

The moments of attention that the marketing managers devoted to me or their requests for help were rather irregular, and followed the rhythm of the marketing department. The tasks I performed sometimes fell on me like rain, and were followed by free hours and days when I had plenty of time to check my email, write notes, read papers, or browse the corporate intranet. Sometimes I sent emails to the marketing managers, or asked them if they had anything I could help with. For the managers, it was a matter of situated judgement whether something could be delegated to me or not. I recall (as my field diary prompts me) that while doing organising I had the recurrent thought that I should really start doing proper ethnography tomorrow, to become more organised. I found it difficult to keep track of my activities while doing event management, and my working notes and calendar entries almost replaced my field diary, at least for the initial period. Willing to help me in return, Carrie shared the feeling, assuming that more explanations of the nature of the tasks she was doing could be provided. She promised repeatedly that someday 'we would sit down and talk about this stuff properly'.

A storm of activities usually started with Carrie briefing me on her tasks and figuring out where exactly I could help her. Sometimes there was a bunch of tasks related to a single event; at other times it was just a single errand such as arranging for brochures to be posted or checking the availability of promotional materials with another marketing manager or a creative agency. My notes of those meetings consist of pages of notebook sheets with layers of yellow sticky notes helping me to keep track of the events and steps to be taken. Carrie also had a notebook in which she wrote down her tasks and her brief notes from meetings and conference calls.

Looking through my archives, I now realise that as a 'marketing project manager' I came into contact with a considerable number of people sending out invitations to dozens of 'hi-touch'[9] corporate executives. The mailing databases representing vertical markets were collected and verified for some events, and were assessed in terms of relevance (e.g. status, geographical location) of customer representatives through consultations with experts or sales managers. Defining relevant groups of sales managers to be involved in interactions with those vertical markets was a matter of contestation too. When consulted about what industries they worked with, sales managers often admitted they could not or did not wish to identify with only one vertical, trying to keep their reach broad. They pointed at difficulties with categorising industries in terms of the classifications adopted in the vertical marketing department. Often they preferred to be included in several verticals, to retain a degree of flexibility in approaching a range of enterprises, claiming a broader scope of their expertise and connections, or, on the contrary, to be able to define their customer accounts in multiple ways. These idiosyncrasies and *ad hoc* requests resulted in a considerable amount of time being spent accommodating various categories of customers, locations and sales managers' preferences into the organising work. Organising usefully points at, and helps to illuminate, some analytical questions in relation to the *management* of vertical markets. How is this practice constituted and assessed as a useful contribution to the vertical marketing department's work? How are relevant (human and non-human) market categories produced and managed? In order to better understand the role of organising, in the next section I will discuss this activity through the lens of organisational reporting.

Accountability in and of vertical marketing

If I were asked to name one of the most notable features of my fieldwork, at least in the beginning of my ethnography with vertical marketing, it would be the sense of uncertainty about my own contribution, or the value of my help. My own insecurities about the value of my contribution to an individual manager's tasks or to the team's performance reflected a general participant's concern about how marketing practice can be assessed. The tension was associated with the discrepancy between tasks making sense in general and the lack of knowledge of local routines making the process seem slow. By way of example, I was asked to coordinate the production of marcom materials with creative agencies. The sense of working with a creative agency on brochure production was familiar to me from my professional experience. However, the activities were embedded in the local knowledge of people and procedures that I had to learn. Obtaining budget approval for an event ('raising a PO'[10]) meant that I needed to become familiar with other teams and services, such as finance officers. My attempts to establish direct working connections with the finance person, who was somewhat openly wary of my role as a researcher, did not prove very successful. I doubted whether I was of any real help to Carrie: my questions multiplied the number of emails she had to deal with. She had to remember to copy me on her emails and to send me invitations for conference calls. She could have, it seemed, sorted out some of the issues much more quickly if she had been doing the task herself.

The vertical marketing team's activities were embedded in accountability routines in the company. This involved various reporting procedures. Carrie's organising activities were of interest not only to her line manager, to her immediate colleagues and to me as an ethnographer, but also to some other members of Virtual World who were concerned with the worth of her contribution. And those assessors held different views about the nature of her marketing work.

What counted as marketing work was subject to definitions and assessments in attempts to measure and evaluate corporate performance. The deliberations on how marketing could be measured and assessed implied continuous redefinitions of what counts as 'doing marketing' in the organisation. In other words, assembling marketing as subject to evaluation (Power, 2003) entailed articulating definitions of marketing. It needs to be noted that the ethnographic encounters with accountability procedures and systems were fairly haphazard and depended on the ethnographer's access to the 'centres of measurement',[11] which I continued to discover as long as my fieldwork lasted. As mentioned (in Chapter 3), one such initiative was the 'marketing enablement' programme, which I never joined. To learn about the new VP of Marketing's views of marketing metrics, I had to ask my line manager to endorse my request for an interview. An encounter with a manager responsible for a marketing performance assessment system was facilitated with the help of the corporate marketing leader, when I started working with a corporate marketing team. The manager who was responsible for designing marketing metrics was difficult to reach for further updates. From my perspective, as a marketing project manager I received regular reminders about a report deadline, and invitations to training courses devoted to a reporting procedure or a measurement technique. These assessment procedures seemed to come from different places in the organisation, whose positions sometimes did not coincide. This view, perhaps, would not be popular as an official discourse in the corporation that relies on the language of the linearity and coherence of management.

The above suggests that accountability may rather be thought of not in terms of structures, but of rituals (cf. Power, 1999; Grint and Woolgar, 1997: 24[12]). Marketers are held accountable through certain procedures (such as corporate meetings, reports), for which certain preparatory work needs to be accomplished. Different reports are written for certain deadlines and presented on special occasions to dedicated audiences (accountants, line managers, colleagues and competing teams, the executive board, outside observers). To illustrate the idea of accountability rituals as the practical management of semiotic networks in vertical marketing, I look at two fieldwork episodes. First, my input into the vertical marketing team's weekly report. And second, an attempt to introduce 'marketing metrics' to measure marketing performance as an organisational function.

The weekly report

The activities providing for the construction of vertical markets were made visible in the marketing department through a weekly report. As above, I was mainly helping Carrie (transportation and retail). Occasionally, Sara (financial services) and Charlotte (automotive and manufacturing) sent me their requests for help. This shared function earned me the special title of 'cross-vertical support', suggested by Alex, my line manager and the vertical marketing team leader. A few months after the beginning of my fieldwork I was invited by Alex to submit my own weekly reports because I had begun working on some of the 'live projects'.

The analysis of the weekly report employs a certain version of textual analysis (Smith, 1978, 2001; Woolgar, 1981) in order to understand how the report performs certain organisational relations and provides for recognisable distribution of accountability. This kind of analysis highlights the situated nature of marketing knowledge, the experience of successful and unsuccessful practical attempts to contribute to and to interfere with certain work situations, as well as an understanding of everyday exchanges and comments on what counts as activities 'going in the right direction'. What are those 'things', 'matters of concern' that can go right or wrong in the vertical marketing department?

The following email was received by the ethnographer (Elena) from her line manager (Alex) on 14 April 2004:

1   Elena
2   Now that you are working on some live projects, pls send me a
3   weekly update on Fridays
4   Format
5   – top 3 or 4 accomplishments (this week)

6 – top 3 or 4 projects (next week)
7 – any issues or roadblocks
8 Thx
9 Alex

The reporting format represents an example of how marketing is made sense of in the organisation. The participants accomplish descriptions and analyses of marketing practice, making a number of assumptions about the nature of marketing work, its potential outcomes, teamwork coordination, and the team's contribution to organisational performance. For a novice like me, facing the task of writing my own report prompted a number of questions about what would count as an adequate description of the marketing activities I was involved in. The report suggests that a certain kind of *format* (4) had to be applied. Being able to formulate 'accomplishments', 'projects' and 'roadblocks' shows one's proficiency in the marketing language, the ability to demonstrate locally accepted conventions of adequate contribution.

Each statement in the report can be seen as a network of semiotic actants constitutive of the market. The analysis below is intended to illustrate in what sense 'cutting the networks' (Strathern, 1996) of actants in the descriptions of marketing projects implied anticipation of what would count as a 'good enough' description of activities by readers of such a report.

(a) Accomplishments (5)

Having received the email above, I had to figure out what could count as an appropriate description of the tasks I had been doing during the week. The problem I faced the first time I had to submit the report was what level of detail to include. Should I provide contact information for everyone I'd got in touch with during the week? What exactly were my 'top 3 or 4 projects' or 'accomplishments'? How should I select an 'accomplishment' from the flow of tasks? In order to do this I meticulously browsed my weekly emails and my calendar and wrote the following:

> SONA customer forum, Paris: promo materials (pop-up banners; Retail brochures, videos) agreed and found; Virtual World reps contacted (Pete Harris); shipping to/from under discussion (have to contact Paris office)
> (Elena to Alex, 16 April 2004)

The report was accepted by Alex ('very good'). Reading the report compiled by Alex the following week (EMEA Enterprise Vertical Marketing Operations Update, W/E 16 April 2004) from the other marketing managers' inputs, I found out that I'd got the reporting style right. The other managers sometimes used brief statements such as:

> Internet community set up;

more elaborate descriptions containing names, places and actions:

> Met with John Stone to commence discussions on demo layout and look and feel;

or added some more details on the content of a meeting, for instance:

> Transportation partners and ABC Europe: Developed Virtual World's messaging that should go into a white paper (with Robert Smith). Met with ForMax to discuss joint marketing initiatives with them and our transportation partners for ABC. Made plans with RTF to do joint marketing (external to formax's [sic] plan) prior to ABC plus developed ideas for promotions at the ABC event.

The report statements are akin to Garfinkel's (1967, in Chapter 6, '"Good" organisational reasons for "bad" clinical records') example of medical records. Garfinkel points out that organisational documents are necessarily indefinite records and portrayals of organisational affairs. Their interpretation is an essential everyday participants' accomplishment. The production and reading of a report's inputs assumes participants' skills in contextualising such statements, relating those to known activities or to past reports. The items listed can also appear to a reader to be incomplete, and to demand further clarifications. One Friday I was reminded that I was late with the report, and the items on my 'accomplishments' list shrank to projects' titles only because I was too exhausted to refresh my memories about what had been done during the week. This was also accepted as a good-enough description – the format of the report, it appeared, was flexible with regard to the details of the marketing activities and tolerance towards grammatical forms and spelling used. The casualness of the communication style is also reflected in the adopted short form of politeness, for example, *thx* (8), *pls* (2).

(b) Time frame (5, 6)

The language of accounting for organising in marketing involves certain time frames: 'this week', 'next week' (5, 6). The marketing managers were aware that certain changes could occur right before a project deadline. As Carrie observed, 'I prefer not to say "this project is finished" until the very last moment – this agenda, for example, can change any minute.' The vertical marketers, including myself, had to be reminded to send their 'weekly updates on Fridays' (2–3) to Alex. Alex spent some time each week bidding for resources for his team. Having the updates from the managers on time helped him coordinate the resources (time, budget) allocated to the team by the other assessors of marketing practice in the organisation (see next section for further discussion).

(c) Issues and roadblocks (7)

The description of a running project is a task demanding careful judgement of whether things 'go well' or 'go wrong'. The marketers tended not to initiate any kind of an immediate inquiry into the details of organising unless things were defined as 'going wrong'. The project reporting is largely a means to convey to management that 'there is nothing to worry about at the moment'. Assessing situations and finding remedies for 'things going wrong' were ongoing achievements. Identifying problems and solving those constituted the matter of everyday conversations. Helping out with an organising project meant providing occasional updates for Carrie. I was terribly concerned not to inadvertently mess things up, often relying on Carrie's intuition about whether I had to wait or rush things. At the same time, Carrie felt I had to be in control when she delegated part of a project to me. Carrie was not always happy to dig deep into the details of the project, being occupied with her other doings: 'What exactly do we need to catch up with? You know, I've got all these things [meaning other things, her things, as she pointed at her desk] to finish before I leave at 1p.m.' . . . 'I am leaving it with you.'

Keeping organising under control also meant that at certain moments 'things' needed to be reviewed in order to shed light on what kinds of wrong steps had been taken and what kinds of remedies could be applied. In a situation defined as an emergency, or a failure, a whole thread of emails could be forwarded to Carrie in order to provide her with evidence of 'why things went wrong'. Marketers, as I noticed, were very suspicious of assertions that a project was running smoothly. At the same time, there was pressure to show that certain projects had been accomplished, deadlines had been met. Judgements had to be made about whether an item was to be mentioned as an accomplishment or a roadblock, without multiplying problems in the need of a remedy.

The metaphor of 'roadblocks' (7) requested by the report format assumes a certain direction and possibly a destination, as well as the sudden (anticipation of) disruption of the following of a path. Issues and roadblocks were often associated with unwillingness or refusal of individuals, things or situations to supply their input into an organising effort. A number of reasons could be evoked to explain why certain deadlines were difficult to meet: people being slow in replying, technologies breaking down, speakers changing their plans at the very last moment, delays in taking materials through Customs. Gilbert and Mulkay (1984) discussed in detail how scientists used a special kind of discourse to account for action not as generic responses to the realities of the natural world, but as the activities and judgements of specific individuals acting on the basis of their personal inclinations and particular social positions. The contingent discourse, as they call it, was also employed by the marketing managers. In marketing, personalities were often blamed for abusing the perceived-as-adequate, normal, order of communication. The contingent remarks formed a part of shop-floor talk, which was often not meant to reach an observer's ears, unless the observer had been involved with the process very closely and had a chance to also become exposed to this kind of personal interaction trespassing the boundaries of the normal order of communication, and could provide a moment of commiseration.

> Sorry to hear about his reaction . . . Nation Z can be very rude!
> How can they [sales] allow themselves behaving [*sic*] like this?!
> Y's been ignoring my voicemail all week last week . . . I had to call him at 10p.m. yesterday! He switched his mobile off.
> This guy's driving me mad – he is so unreliable. We need somebody else to take care of the stand, otherwise we'll lose it.

The terms 'issues' and 'roadblocks' (7) assume a certain further context ('issues'), or direction, purpose, destination ('roadblocks'), of the marketing activities. Those were articulated and redefined in the report and the following conversations with the line manager. Thinking of difficult situations occurring during the week, I could not help mentioning certain individuals and groups whose opinion or behaviour was important to achieving closure of projects (Elena to Alex, 23 April 2004):

1.   Nick cancelled his participation – we had to find a Virtual World rep and are now looking for a person responsible for shipping the banners back (Paris office).
2.   Derek Peck changed his brief for the Hotel Bon Voyage, which increased the cost from 0 to 1,000; looking for budget.
3.   Need to find a new hotel for Retail training, Berlin, because everybody says the Sunny Day is ugly; The Star Hotel is too expensive (the Fair days in Berlin).

As my experience of writing the weekly reports shows, the choice between what counts as an 'achievement' or a 'roadblock' was always a trade-off, depending on whether I wanted Alex or Carrie to interfere and help, or whether I anticipated a remedy to the situation to occur the following week. When a project element was rendered a 'roadblock', Alex needed to know more details about it:

> Elena
> I dont [*sic*] understand the issue – what did you need from Derek?
> (Alex to Elena, 23 April 2004)

A discussion with Alex followed in which I explained the initial agreement with Derek. Derek's proposed changes led, according to the creative agency manager, to an increase in the cost of the brochure production. I conveyed to Alex Carrie's budget request and a financial quote from the agency. The budget increase was not accepted. Alex's work now was to persuade Derek to look for other sources of funding or to return to the initial brief.

My detailed analysis of the reporting and of the doubts and uncertainties accompanying it is intended to illustrate the nature of the practical management of markets as semiotic networks. An important point I wish to make is that the semiotic networks of actants in the marketing discourse were constantly managed through their stabilisation, unblackboxing, the adding of new actants, and the establishing of connections between those, as in the examples above. Marketers are aware that the networks they coordinate may expand or shrink suddenly. This fluidity (or indexicality) of networks and the possibility of keeping networks under control are apprehended through the language of *manageable* relationships between the network elements. Accounting for networks in the marketing department involves the attribution of responsibilities for achieving 'adequate' composition of a network's elements, and recognition and appraisals of successful (or unsuccessful) closures in organising. The *manageability* of the flux of events (and my subjects were marketing *managers*), as well as of relations between elements of a network refers, in marketing, to an assumption of the possibility of providing an account of successes and failures of, in this case, organising.

The construction of marketing as an accountable practice implies the recognition of the relationships (duties and responsibilities) of the actors involved, as well as situated production of the accounts. Depending on whether a situation was perceived to need remedy, further details about it were invoked and responsibilities attributed. The practical management of semiotic networks in marketing is achieved through descriptions that are produced and accepted as good enough by writers and readers of, in this particular case, the weekly report.

What does marketing do? A local response

Virtual World marketers did not use the language of actor-network theory, nor did they speak about vertical marketing in terms of the practical management of semiotic actants in relations of accountability. This is one of the possible and analytically compelling ways of rendering marketing. What is worth further attention is that in the corporation there was no single set of descriptive rules as applied to marketing practice. The language deployed to account for the nature and effects of marketing was a matter of local contestation, employing various notions of agency, scientific objectivity and accountability relations performed in and by marketing. The successful performance of Virtual World had not always been accounted for in terms of 'clever marketing'. The decade of Virtual World's phenomenal success and its growth into a global corporation was generally attributed to the 'Internet firestorm', when customers sought to buy products from Virtual World without much effort on the part of marketing.[13] The emergence of marketing as a corporate discipline, together with the politics around new EMEA top management, prompted rethinking of its role in the corporation.

As Munro and Mouritsen discuss (1996), accountability and technologies of managing are closely intertwined in the attempts to produce and sustain local accounts of organisational practices. At Virtual World, situated attempts to produce definitions of marketing and to inquire into the nature of marketing practice were continually made. The weekly report was one among many efforts in the corporation to improve marketing performance through gathering information about what was going on in the marketing departments. During my time with the company, an organisational effort was made to render marketing practice measurable through the application of certain kinds of metrics. This initiative provoked mixed reactions among both the developers and the future subjects of the assessment. The discussions in which I participated involved deliberations about the nature of marketing practice, and its amenability to measurement. Perceived by most of the managers as a novelty for this corporation, the measurement initiative stimulated a search for acceptable metrics and expertise. Assembling an organisational discipline – such as marketing – as subject to assessment (Power, 2003) implied identifying and bringing in resources (knowledges and managers capable of implementing the change) both inside and outside of the corporation. The ways marketing was defined for the purpose of these initiatives bore on the construction of accountability practices in the organisation. Conversely, once an accountability scheme was suggested, it would be used by participants to make statements about the ways marketing should be done.

Dedicated managers were forming 'centres of assessment' (by analogy with 'centres of calculation' in Latour, 1987), accumulating measurement resources and tools. The initiatives to reform marketing purported not only to define what marketing is, but also to understand who marketing is. The flow of marketing professionals who had to be socialised into and trained in the new accountability system that assumed a certain punctuality in reporting and quantitative criteria was a point of special concern. Since the corporation offered only a few permanent positions in marketing, most of the marketing managers were on temporary contracts. People were constantly searching for better contracts and could leave Virtual World on very short notice. Giving at least one month's notice before leaving the company was promoted as a good practice facilitating the timely replacement of employees. With the perceived very high fluidity of the marketing workforce, the corporate discourse encouraged career development plans within Virtual World and commended those who stayed with the company for longer terms. Gifts – such as a shopping voucher at La Samaritaine in Paris, worth a few hundred pounds – awaited those who stayed with the corporation for ten years. Staying for five years was a superb achievement, for which an employee was congratulated. In February 2005, hearing me say that I had stayed with Virtual World for a whole year, people usually appreciated that. Carrie, who started with Virtual World at approximately the same time I did, left for Australia after one year. She explained that she was 'leaving the party at its high', being overwhelmed with the increasing workload and having had enough of a London experience.

The difficulty of grasping connections and differences between various marketing activities was often admitted in conversations as a trivial feature of corporate life. But this was not an official way of talking marketing. Good marketing practice, according to the official view, had to be readily available to a novice to apprehend and to make sense of. The messiness of everyday practice was instead presented by senior management as a part of their rationale for organisational change and the implementation of a new accountability system.

With the new EMEA marketing leadership came the idea of constructing a clearer vision for European marketing, so that the above-mentioned 'marketing enablement' initiative would become the first step towards better marketing based on a new accounting system.

In deliberations about what is and what is not to be made accountable, marketing as practice was construed differently. The boundary between marketing and non-marketing was also drawn in a variety of ways. The need for a new kind of accountability was built in relation to another group in the corporation: the sales force. The new measurement initiative would also reflect the contribution of marketing to corporate financial performance. The ideas about the value of marketing for profit-making turned out to be different if assessed from the position of sales. Instead of apprehending marketing as an independent organisational function that holds expertise in assessing the value of marketing programmes, sales-oriented marketing would become the subject of assessment not by peers but by the group perceived as somewhat antagonistic.[14] A marketing programme, as a rule, included a set of marcom materials (e.g. advertisements, value propositions) as well as content and scenarios for business technology workshops. Under the new assessment regime, the programmes had to be evaluated in terms of 'lead[15] generation', a parameter that was rendered measurable in terms of eventual deal estimates (ROI)[16] adopted in the sales department.

Making marketing work accountable to another group within the organisation was not a particularly new proposition. For example, the vertical marketing team competed with other, not verticalised, marketing groups for resources and recognition of their way of doing marketing. Quarterly meetings were intended to evaluate marketing programmes by regional marketing managers in the EMEA regions, or 'countries'. The 'countries' marketing managers expressed their own concerns about whether a marketing programme presented by the central office offered good selling tools to approach regional customers with. The vertical marketing team had to pitch their programmes in front of the regional marketing managers, who evaluated the offers and voted for the best ones. Even without the involvement of a different organisational group, the evaluation rituals proved to be controversial. This practice generated a number of concerns: Who is in a better position to determine the quality and the performative potential of the marcom programmes? The managers in the countries trying to meet the concerns of and persuade their regional customers? Or the central organisation, having a better sense of the content of technological solutions and drawing on the experience of their counterparts in the United States and other countries worldwide?

Being accountable to sales rather than to peers was perceived as an undesirable measure by some marketing managers, thus provoking discontent and efforts to redress the situation. In attempts to produce the new accountability system, and to find arguments for and against such a measure, local knowledge about existing scientific tools and marketing metrics for measuring marketing performance, as well as best practices, was assembled. This included a search in the academic journal database that I was asked to help with. This exercise pursued the goal of constructing a persuasive basis for retaining judgement within the marketing corporate discipline on some 'scientific' grounds. The idea of measuring market-ing in terms of return on investment was confronted with the assumed possibility of offering some alternative 'objective' measurement tools rather than relying on what was perceived as 'subjective' sales assessments. The alternative measures would employ quantitative or qualitative techniques, such as, for example, meas-uring a show in terms of 'footfall',[17] or assessing a web page's usability. Sonya, a marketing manager responsible for designing the accountability criteria, was trying to understand whether marketing activities could be characterised in terms of their intrinsic *purpose*, not their outcome for lead generation, as proposed by the VP of Marketing. Lead generation, as she insisted, was not necessarily the main outcome, or purpose, of marketing activities. As an illustration of her thinking (representative of the 'anti-sales' attitude), such results of a marketing effort as 'awareness' or 'loyalty' cannot be linked to lead generation, since being 'loyal' (attending corporate seminars) was not seen as a direct stimulus for a deal with the company, which would eventually bring financial results.

According to Sonya, some marketing activities are not even intended to stimu-late any visible response in the audience. In the case of new products, for instance, messages are sent out in order to create 'awareness', rather than to stimulate 'action'. To Sonya, some marketing activities were measurable, while others were not. Can the creation, the writing, of marketing text be defined in terms of its contribution to corporate revenue? The following distinction between what counts as 'doing' marketing (or 'execution') and 'just writing' was made:

> [Content creation means, for example] writing brochures, putting stuff on the website. I think it just cannot be measured. You just write it, publish it, and it can be used over and over and over again, in millions of different ways (you can use brochures at expos, or can just send them away). While execu-tions actually mean *doing*. You actually *do* stuff.
>
> (Sonya, 21 September 2004)

Agreeing that, in general, some marketing messages and activities may lead to deals, Sonya hesitates to say that the power of marcom messages can be specified at the outset. The anticipation of possible leads may also not come true:

> If we want to attract an audience of a thousand, is it good? Even if the task is to generate a hundred leads out of these thousand, how can we be sure not all those hundred leads will be rubbish?
>
> (ibid.)

Hence the ambiguity of the effect of marketing action (including questioning what the very action is), and hence of its amenability to measurement according to the metrics applied to sales, was perceived as residing in both the content of the marketing texts as well as in the circumstances of their production and use (distribution, reading, interpretation). The assessment and measurement of marketing would render the interpretive action amenable to evaluation by different competing criteria.

Textual artefacts thus emerged as an integral part of the organisational debate on the role of marketing. Apart from corporate managerial attempts to make the marketing effort accountable, questions about the content, purpose and effect of marcom materials were a matter of everyday work in the vertical department. The question of whether marketing texts played a particular role in the encounters between the corporation and customers was an important matter also bearing on the corporate identity of marketers within the organisation. Being a matter of practitioners' deliberations, the role of material texts in social ordering is also an important analytic question, which will be discussed in the next chapter.

Discussion

In science and technology studies, agency was rendered one of the pressing issues with regard to understanding the market, and socio-technical relations in general. The actor-network approach offers the possibility of stepping away from the a priori distinction between the entities engaged in market relations. This flattening of the distinction between product, producer and customer offered by the sociology of translation was discussed in Chapter 1 as a helpful step towards the post-essentialist anthropology of the market. As Callon (1998a) observes, the market implies a set of relations in which actants (human and non-human) are endowed with an asymmetrical agency. This, according to Callon, challenges the idea of the generalised symmetry of the sociology of translation. Markets, according to Callon, strongly suggest the emergence of actors who have objectives and goals (Callon, 1998a). This chapter set out to explore a post-essentialist way of thinking about market relations in terms of the accountability and attribution of agency. How can markets as networks of semiotic actants be rethought in terms of the attribution of agency? In Dilley's (1992a) words, the accounts of marketing management I discussed can be understood in terms of 'the way a culture attributes and holds responsible specific forms of agency' (Dilley, 1992: 24).

The analysis of vertical marketing in practice offers an understanding of markets as networks of semiotic actants that pays special attention to the accountability relations in which these networks are performed. What deserves further thought, however, is the diversity of ways in which agency emerges in market relations in the practical deliberations. According to textbook marketing, market relations can be changed if certain sets of skills are applied. The figure of a 'marketing manager' entails the distinction between markets as manageable objects as if those existed 'out there' and an individual (manager) engaged in managing markets. Indeed, the examination of accountability in and of vertical marketing speaks in favour of the construction of a vertical marketing manager as an individual capable of changing accountability relations vis-à-vis a technological product.

From the ethnographic perspective, the distribution of agency is neither stable nor fixed in the organisational marketing discourse. Becoming one such 'manager', or a good member of the 'vertical' marketing team, one learns how to attribute agency and distribute action and accountability. To show that the markets were managed well, one needed to be proficient in the 'vertical' marketing language, to be able to demonstrate locally accepted conventions of adequate contribution, such as problem solving. The inputs into the weekly report illustrate the point that vertical markets as semiotic networks and the ways they were practically managed were created and displayed for the purposes of reporting. This entailed recognition and portrayal of the everyday flow of activities in terms suggested by the weekly report format. The 'manageable' networks appear to be the upshot of assigning responsibility and holding accountable marketing managers, who were expected to provide accounts of their everyday occupations in terms of their purposeful effort.

How *well* does this kind of attribution of agency to marketing managers hold? And who decides? Too much or too little emphasis on the active problem-solving individual agent can be interpreted in favour of or against the value of marketing in organisations. On the one hand, in the example of the weekly reporting, the conventions of accounting for marketing management assumed individual marketing agency and individual responsibility. The 'problems' with markets were accounted for in terms of individuals who contributed to or hindered market management, which required continuous negotiations of actions (as well as of silences). As in the case of the attempt at making marketing accountable to sales in the first instance, deliberations on the nature of marketing show that attributing capacity to change social arrangements to marketers is a matter of practical judgement implicating other communities. What exactly is being attributed to marketing managers as their capacity to manage markets? What is the role of material texts, or marcom materials, in constituting 'good' marketing practice? This question will be further examined in the next chapter, which looks at marketing texts as discursive objects.

5 Marketing texts as discursive objects, or do texts speak for themselves?

Technology as text or text as technology?

The recent research at the intersection of STS and economic sociology has drawn scholars' attention to the material forms of social ordering in economic practices (for recent collections, see Pinch and Swedberg, 2008; Callon *et al.*, 2007). Marketing is a site rich with practices devoted to the creation and dissemination of material artefacts that allegedly help to facilitate economic exchange. The professional identity of marketers is often built on claimed abilities to produce texts with predefined effects, or on the capacity to provide for parameters of social action through the imposing of interpretive constraints. In a more general context, copywriters, artists, designers (the 'creatives') earn their living by establishing themselves as professionals possessing special skills indispensable to the producing of texts purported to achieve certain ends. Marketers, as a broadly defined professional group, stand behind such inscribed objects as billboards, banners, flyers, furry toys, pens, T-shirts, lighters, mouse pads and balloons carrying, for instance, a company logo. As in the previous chapter, at Virtual World, marketers were busy preparing and sending so-called marcom[1] materials ('emails', 'brochures', 'banners') to prospective customers in the course of 'organising'. In the context of the proposed post-essentialist textual metaphor of the market, it can be argued that marketing texts participate in the creation of the moral order of technology. This is achieved through ascription of properties to actants participating in market relations, and narrating relations between them. As such, textual artefacts offer for interpretation certain rights, obligations, expectations and possibilities, and thus play a role in establishing what Dilley called 'modes of accountability' (Dilley, 1992a) in market relations around a technology.

As in previous chapters, marketers can be seen as practical reasoners exchanging claims and engaging in practices regarding the nature of social order and of ways of influencing it. Marketing in practice is an apt case to revise some analytic approaches to textual artefacts and their role in social ordering. Before offering some ethnographic observations, this chapter will introduce some elements of a debate on the materiality/discursivity in STS and in the material culture studies in order to illuminate what is at stake in this debate for the study of technology marketing in practice.[2] To what extent can the two approaches provide an analytical framework for the empirical study of textual artefacts in marketing? What would organisational archaeology of textual artefacts need to pay special attention to?

Post-essentialist thought in STS has examined the metaphor 'technology as text' (Woolgar, 1991a). The material metaphor with regard to text – text as technology – is a prominent feature of the material culture discourse. Material culture studies offer the metaphor to explain literacy (Ong, 1982/2002; Tilley, 1991), seeing writing as a craft requiring special inscription tools. It appears that post-essentialism and material culture studies came to embrace metaphors that employ the same terms, but in which meaning transfer works in the opposite directions. What is the relationship between discursivity and materiality in the marketing practice? Before inviting Carrie, a vertical marketing manager, to illuminate the debate, two responses – from the material culture studies and from the post-essentialist tradition in STS – are offered to inform the discussion, as well as a background to the boundary work between sales and marketing at Virtual World.

First response: the material culture studies

Studies in material culture associated with the disciplines of archaeology and anthropology show contending approaches to the relationship between material world and text. The materialist tradition promotes the idea of looking at the *materiality* of the written word, as it is 'inscribed in a solid medium, . . . collected in volumes' (Ingold, 2002: 337). The written word, in other words, is understood in material culture studies as a material artefact. Although a post-structuralist[3] response to the materialist thinking in archaeology – claiming the pre-eminence of *textual, descriptive* practices in our understanding of material culture – has been introduced in, for example, Tilley (1990b), it became a matter of debate.

Criticising the logocentric attitude towards material culture, Miller (1987) insists on keeping alive the division between material objects ('artefacts *per se*') and language. Miller argues that academic studies dominated by language cannot appreciate adequately the 'humility', or 'subtle significance', of objects for human culture: 'If, however, the social properties of objects are not as "evident" as they are visible, this very factor may actually be, in part, responsible for our inability to appreciate the significance of the objects. This, in turn, might account for our difficulty in dealing with the object through academic studies dominated by language' (p. 100).

Material culture studies, in other words, attempt to approach texts as material artefacts built into material culture and manipulated through material practices. Ong's argument on the distinction between orality and literacy is largely based on the 'text as technology' metaphor. He discusses the artificiality of writing, arguing that writing calls 'for the use of tools and other equipment: styli or brushes or pens, carefully prepared surfaces such as paper, animal skins, strips of wood, as well as inks or paints, and much more' (Ong, 1982/2002: 81). The scribal culture is, according to Ong (ibid.: 99), material culture due to the physical properties of writing materials. While writing, as a process of 'technologising the word', emerged in the human culture with, first of all, the invention of early inscription tools, the invention of print 'suggests that words are things far more than writing ever did' (p. 116). Compared with the transient, evanescent nature of oral statements, texts, as the 'efficient reducers of sounds to space', 'are thing-like, immobilized in visual space' (p. 98). As Ong puts it, 'all script represents words as in some way things, quiescent objects, immobile marks for assimilation by vision' (p. 90).

Some anthropologists suggest that the substantial difference between language and material objects should be retained if we want to understand written texts. From this point of view, such material signifiers ('material texts') as an urban sign could be approached by analogy, for example, with the built environment (Rappoport, 2002: 473) as it regulates human movements through barriers and semi-fixed objects. Considering the megalith as a material text, Olsen (1990) rehearses Barthes's idea that in the course of history, being decontextualised from the historical moment of its creation, the literary text 'opens itself to infinite readings as it continuously confronts new readers in altered historical situations', while 'the material signifier remains constant' nevertheless, and thus makes the artefact available to future generations of readers (p. 199). Tilley (1991) argues that it is important to understand the written word as graphic text – as the production of graphic marks on the page, dividing a text into pages or sentences, which take place in the process of 'editing a book', for example (p. 16). Tilley also explains that the title of his (1991) book, 'Material culture *and* text', precisely reflects his attempt to differentiate between the material and the discursive, to lay grounds for the future effort to transcend the position he himself presents, which is based on the semiotic metaphor of 'reading material culture' (borrowed from Barthes).

Second response: the written word in post-essentialism

In the post-essentialist tradition the merits of the metaphor 'technology as text' are discussed as a radical anti-essentialist explanatory device for the social adoption of artefacts (Woolgar, 1991a; Grint and Woolgar, 1997; Woolgar and Cooper, 1999). The textual metaphor is suggested to find a route out of the 'intellectual traffic jam' in the debate on sociality and materiality, which comprises attempts to 'construe one or other's interest in "words" rather than "things," or *vice versa*' (italics in the original). Grint and Woolgar (1997: 93) make the assumption that texts are (inherently?) interpretively flexible, and, by analogy, that technologies can be understood as text to avoid any residual commitment to technological (and any kind of) essentialism: 'the metaphor technology as text is useful because, against essentialism, it stresses the contingency of interpretation.' Textuality is also a key concept to account for the anti-essentialist analysis of political action: 'Research in a wide variety of areas, from literary theory to anthropology, to social studies of technology, tells of the myriad of processes whereby audiences are identified, defined, recruited, configured, enrolled and performed by the textuality of knowledge claims. The rhetoric of truth may feature as a part of these processes, but this rhetoric is emphatically insufficient to guarantee the "appropriate" audience response' (Grint and Woolgar, 1997: 167).

How is textuality understood in post-essentialism?[4] Woolgar and Cooper (1999) discuss the construction of properties of Moses' Bridges, an iconic example in STS. To rule out the above-mentioned 'intellectual traffic jam', the authors suggest 'extend[ing] the notion of "text" to encompass both words and things'. As Grint and Woolgar (1997: 72–73) put it,

> construing the machine as text encourages us to see that the nature of the artefact is its reading. But in trying to escape the dreaded technological determinism, in disassociating the upshot of reading and interpretation from any notion of the inherent quality of the text (what it actually says, what it actually means), we do not mean to suggest that any reading is possible (let alone that any reading is actually possible), although in principle this is the case.

Accounting for delimitations posed by a text, post-essentialists follow Smith (1978), who suggests that the organisation of the text makes one or another reading differentially possible. For Smith, the organisation of the text is isomorphic with the concepts we use to make sense of it.

According to this school of textual analysis, textual organisation provides certain 'instructions' that enable readers to make sense of content in terms of a conclusion stated at the outset. In line with the constitutive approach adopted by post-essentialists, a text is thus seen as constitutive of reality through its rhetorical content. In order to understand how 'a text can be usefully understood as identifying, defining and configuring – in short, as performing – the sets of persons, social relationships and actions/responses which can be legitimately brought to bear in text', techniques of textual analysis are applied. Grint and Woolgar (1997: 73) suggest an amendment to the argument related to the importance of *association* between reader and text in accounting for texts as agents of social ordering:

> A small extension of this analytic stance of texts suggests that the organization of texts hinges not so much on mundane features like the length of sentences, the amount of space devoted to different topics etc., but rather on associations made available within the text and between text and reader. Text, in other words, provides for a certain moral order, in which the reader is invited to join certain groups and dissociate herself from others.

While post-essentialists do not specify the nature of such association, Smith (2001) speaks about texts from the materialist perspective. Smith observes that textual documents, as 'technologies of architecture' of organisations and institutions (p. 173), come in different forms and shapes, yet, when they become incorporated into sociological thinking, they are 'generally viewed as sources of information about something else'[5] (p. 169). Smith suggests that texts themselves need to become objects of inquiry, to be seen at work, in order to reveal the process of objectification: how orders of people, their doings, and time, and locale 'disappear' in a universe of discursive objects (p. 165). The organisation of discursive entities in documents represents these orders as being available, and reproducible, 'out there', separate from the practices of reading and writing texts. It is the particular, local practices of writing and reading that make texts function as coordinators of particular, local and ephemeral people's doings, and objectify social relations, institutions and organisations: 'I need the text's materiality, for it is its material replication that reproduces at least one term, the text's, of meaning in the multiple local settings in which it is read, seen and interpreted' (p. 174).

Some STS authors are also dissatisfied with dichotomising the material and the discursive, and have tried to bring the two together. In Lenoir's opinion, language is always a sign to materiality, and a partial combination of word and object. Lenoir (1999: 271) explores the merits of the semiotic tradition and approves the direction in STS that takes the materiality of language into account:

> Present in the semioticians I find relevant to recent directions of science studies is the notion missing in the work of earlier structuralist semiotics: language itself is not pure sign, it is also a thing. Language is tied to voice, to bitmaps on a screen, to materiality. The word is thus partly object, partly sign . . . We want to call attention to both a materiality of the text and a materiality beyond it. We want, in Rotman's phrase, to put the body 'back in'.

Arguing for the importance of textuality for the stabilisation of artefacts or networks, Latour's notion of immutable mobility suggests that both material and discursive properties of representations may be responsible for the robustness of a textual artefact, which involves the capabilities to travel across social and geographical boundaries. Latour (1990: 42) calls 'immutable mobiles' those visualised, printed and written artefacts created in order to mobilise a network of actants, or to change socio-technical arrangements: 'objects which have the properties of being mobile but also immutable, presentable, readable and combinable with one another'. Combining the material and the discursive is thus offered by these authors as a means to explain how material texts participate in social ordering.

One can of course observe that the terms of debate presented so far reproduce the discursive–material duality that became subject to critique questioning the very idea of duality (e.g. Woolgar, 2002a). Would it be analytically useful to straightforwardly rely on the material/discursive dichotomy to explain how marketing texts work? My further analysis of marketing practices assumes that the language of marketing relies on certain categories that can be unproblematically placed on one or another side of the material–discursive divide that informs the language of academia. However, in order to advance the debate, I am interested in the cultural ways of construing materiality and discursivity as a part of everyday corporate beliefs and rituals concerning material texts. Marketing practice, as I will discuss below, helps us to further problematise, and explore, the merits of both the textual and the material metaphors. In order to take this discussion further, one needs to ask: how is the dichotomy of the material and the discursive sustained in (marketing) practice? The emphasis of the discussion to follow is thus on the material/discursive *ambiguities* associated with marketing texts.

Marcom materials as discursive objects

Tilley usefully points to the possibility of interrogating the *ambiguity* of the parts of the dichotomy: 'to write the material world is the art of ambiguity' (Tilley, 1991: 180). How can the ambiguity of textual artefacts be examined? The post-essentialist critique in STS suggests that ambiguity and dichotomies need to be taken as a topic of study (e.g. Rappert, 2001). Tilley (1990a: 332) in his analysis of Foucault's ideas on discursivity and non-discursivity defines artefacts, as they are constituted in archaeological texts, as *discursive objects*. Drawing also on Smith's (2001) use of the term in her analysis of the objectification through interpretation of discursive entities, I suggest this notion as an heuristic device to examine how discursive and material properties are ascribed to textual artefacts. Namely, this notion helps us to appreciate that textual artefacts can on some occasions be accounted for as written discourse (*discursive* objects) and, on other occasions, can appear as entities, to which certain objective qualities are ascribed (discursive *objects*).

I suggest that marketing is a site that may help us to look closely at the local production of materiality and discursivity. Marcom materials appear to be an instantiation of discursive objects that can be studied empirically. What can a study of this particular *culture* of textual practices add to the debate on the nature of material texts? How can the ambiguity of discursive objects be explored productively through the empirical study of marketing?

As a general observation, marketing vocabulary provides a rich set of terms related to the general category of discursive objects[6] that differentiate between the material and the discursive in various ways. Professional sub-groups in marketing will employ different vocabulary to account for the textual artefacts they work with using their professional jargon. The production of discursive objects in marketing, or writing, is often a collective work. A group of marketers working on a video clip may include a number of professionals with different qualifications across the spectrum of discursive material: marketing managers, copywriters, artists, editors, cameramen, journalists, account managers of creative agencies, printers and post office workers (see also Hennion *et al.*, 1989). Travelling between different professional groups, discursive objects acquire various properties through the situated production of materiality and discursivity. Practical deliberations in the marketing department focus on the 'rhetorical' qualities of texts (or 'content'). Sometimes discursive objects acquire seemingly unusual properties ('look and feel'). And last, but not least, discursive objects are spoken about as mobile entities providing for encounters between reader and text ('content delivery'). Marketers, as producers of inscriptions, sometimes *speak* of discursive objects as if those were merely objects, or merely texts. It can be said that marketers take the metaphorical expression 'to add weight (and also shape, or colour, or brightness, etc.) to one's words' literally: during my ethnography I had to carry or unpack a case containing a heavy banner, or to ask a post-room manager to come with his trolley to collect boxes of brochures.

A post-room manager was surprisingly good at knowing what kinds of discursive objects were in his possession when they arrived at Virtual World from publishers and printers: their quantity, their packaging, their weight. His work involved handling cases and boxes containing discursive objects. Sometimes, when the boxes I needed to ship to another country were too heavy for me to bring to the post-room, I asked him to come with his trolley to pick them up. In order to process the shipment, he usually needed to know the country of production of the discursive objects, their amount, price per unit, a person responsible for the shipment in the marketing department, location in the office and delivery address. The talk about the materials being posted almost never concerned the content of the brochures. The name of a discursive object ('an "airports brochure"') was usually enough to identify what kind of brochure it was and where it should go.

Discursive objects were sometimes accounted for in terms of their mobility. One of the projects I was helping an information management team with was about 'content migration', or the transfer of electronic texts from one document repository into another. In order to delegate the work of 'migration' of texts to an outsourced team, I was asked to do an inventory, or to browse the Web portal and to create a table with information about each document. The properties of the discursive objects included the date of upload, owner and format. This information could be found in the texts or accompanying notes, and I had to skim the texts specifically looking for these data. I was also asked to write a summary of the texts, which was done by copying the first paragraph from the text into the table. In the same project, another group of managers ('content owners') was asked to check the dates of the documents to identify those that required updating. Thus, my task of creating the inventory of discursive objects did not require reading those documents. Reading and understanding were delegated to another group of experts who could (and had the right to) judge the relevance of the content.

An important observation thus is that the material properties of discursive objects were invoked to resolve practical problems in particular circumstances. For example, the marketing managers discussed whether a banner was compact enough to carry around in the airports if a manager went to a trade show in a different location. Or whether a brochure could be shipped in the form of a 'CD' or sent by email in 'PDF format' (some shipping companies, afraid of piracy, did not accept CDs). These instances of ascribing material properties to texts thus always refer to conventions of textual practices invoked to resolve practical concerns in certain situations (carrying it in an airport, going through Customs).

As a site of production of technology discourses, the marketing department is a setting where marcom materials acquire agency. From the ethnographic point of view, agency of textual artefacts occurs as a feature of accounts of (manageable) accountability relations in the marketing department. How are textual artefacts made sense of in marketing? Not every textual document in the 'universe' of discursive objects (Smith, 2001) in the corporation is a marcom material. However, *some* textual artefacts or discourses were identified in the corporation as entities belonging exclusively to the marketing domain of practical action and bore on the way marketing practice was defined. How were marcom materials rendered thinkable in the marketing department in terms of their ability to constitute forms of market relations?

In the marketing department, making sense of properties of marcom materials, their effects and means of production was a part of everyday activities. Marketers' deliberations rely on a variety of framings of textual agency in terms of the ways that textual artefacts may be held accountable for their capacity to produce effects. Sometimes odd-looking, marcom materials at times were meant to demonstrate an apparent difference from conventional communicative forms.[7] It was said that their purpose was to 'draw attention'. Once, upon entering Virtual World, I found that my attention *was* drawn by an enormous balloon hanging under the ceiling saying, in red on blue, '15 years of innovation'. The first thing Alex asked me when we met on that day was: 'Have you seen *it*!?' The marketing managers were excited about this inventive way of announcing the important celebration Virtual World was preparing for, and explained that the balloon provided the best visibility of the slogan in the entrance hall.

There was a sense of thrill about producing those 'artful' objects, about liaising with 'creatives', about choosing colours and images for a brochure or a web page. Visual libraries, font collections, examples of 'creative ideas' that can be purchased or obtained through creative agencies exist to delineate the striking from the usual, the creative from the plain. Virtual World marketers tried to show that they were well on top of creativity. They 'worked with Ogilvy' – Terry emphasised this right away before the very first meeting with gatekeepers. This was an important sign of their access to a source of successful advertising ideas provided by the world-renowned advertising chain that originated on Madison Avenue, which marketers refer to as the cradle of advertising. The library of corporate images that could be used for styling corporate communications was kept on a password-protected Ogilvy website. Virtual World marketing managers were working with some other London-based creative agencies, too, as well as with some in-house designers, mostly Web teams.

It was assumed that not everyone is qualified to write good copy or an article for a website. The ability to produce such texts was a matter of situated assessments. In the beginning of my fieldwork I was not considered capable of speaking or writing on behalf of the corporation, even if I claimed some experience in creative work and in writing promotional materials. However, by the end of my ethnography the demand for my help with diverse tasks, including the production of marcom materials such as videos and brochures, grew significantly. This was explained by my increased familiarity with various local aspects of marketing at Virtual World. I was invited to do copywriting for a highly regarded 'public sector' team. The offer to help the team was considered a 'promotion' in my 'career' and was endorsed by the head of corporate marketing.

Marketers were visibly proud of some inscribed objects they created, and not so happy with others. They blamed the traditionally adopted 'dull' corporate colour palette dating back to the engineering era of the company. Things were changing, but slowly, marketers maintained. Competitors' websites seemed more engaging, more welcoming than Virtual World's own, they thought. Marketing managers were captivated by some images I presented after having done competitive analysis of four other major corporations. Those people at I*** know how to look appealing, to think about customers, I heard. Even if some exciting moments happened, the 'real' creativity always appeared to be somewhere else: on another team, at another agency, in another country. It was said that really creative people were leaving the company. A 'genius' brilliant interviewer and PR man, a star of the corporate TV and a darling of female managers, who had run the corporate marketing department for a few years, was about to leave. He was headhunted by a competitor, which those staying with the company found regrettable.

The fairly chaotic rhythm of the marketing department sometimes demanded quick decisions about the appropriateness of marcom materials for a particular event. The occasioned nature of the creation of marcom materials was acknowledged sometimes when marketers sent to a trade show brochures that in principle were designed for a different event: 'Send whatever we've got.' Sometimes brochures or banners were sent to a trade show without anyone checking their content. Marketers' deliberations on the properties of marcom materials were sometimes complex interactions in which various preconceptions about the nature of interpretive action were invoked and dismissed. The work of marketing managers embodies practical assumptions about social ordering. As such, social orders are thought of as being *manageable* through the creation and dissemination of discursive objects. These assumptions involved folk-theorising of social ordering (including folk and academic marketing management theories), as well as the practical knowledge of producing marcom materials that would pass as good enough.

On some occasions marketers were more willing to provide a rationalisation for their activities. This often occurred in mini-interviews when I asked a marketing manager about his or her rationale for the creation of certain kinds of marcom materials for a particular occasion, such as a promotional video. Often, both the occasional nature of production and its rational properties were presented. The difference between how the production *was* accomplished and how it *should* be done was usually admitted to be inappropriate. If the marketing managers realised that a 'normative' approach did not match the reality of everyday bricolage, they often sought to provide explanations for such incoherence through lack of time ('deadlines'!) and resources. A producer would explain a video's content in terms of corporate style and conventions of technology representation adopted in the corporation. This work would also involve contributing his own experience and materials available to create a plausible (or, in his words, 'objective') image of what a technology can do. The latter may demand additional collection of video and audio materials, such as interviews with users or enthusiastic potential adopters. But he would also admit that he had only limited sources to dig for images, and a minimal budget, and that top executives he wanted to interview were busy, so he had to rely on video fragments already prepared for other products and other occasions instead of shooting new material 'in the field'.

While the details of production of the marcom materials remained confined to the marketing department, the marketers were held accountable for the contribution of these artefacts in the context of corporate performance. One of the examples of assessment of the effects that marcom materials could or should achieve was discussed at the end of the previous chapter. In an attempt at reforming marketing, the new regime assumed that marketers should be made accountable to sales. The reorganisation provoked a dispute about the contribution of marketing (texts) to corporate profit-making. In the debate on marketing metrics, claims were made – by marketers and by the management – about the properties of 'marketing messages' and the ways of assessing those. The role of marcom materials was an issue at stake in the boundary work between marketing and sales.

Boundary work between 'marketing' and 'sales'

Miller and Rose (1996), in their study of the formation of advertising by the Tavistock Institute of Human Relations in London, discuss in what sense advertising was construed as an interpretive act whereby a text actively tempting a reader was received or rejected by an actively interpreting consumer. The authors describe the construction of the modern consumer as an active agent of the interpretation of advertising:

> this was not a matter of the unscrupulous manipulation of passive consumers: technologies of consumption depended upon fabricating delicate affiliations between the active choices of potential consumers and the qualities, pleasures and satisfactions represented in the product, organized in part through the practices of advertising and marketing, and always undertaken in the light of particular beliefs about the nature of human subjectivity.
>
> (Miller and Rose, 1996: 42).

Such beliefs about the nature of human subjectivity – exemplified through deliberations regarding the production and use of marcom materials – were a part of boundary work between marketing and sales. The work of inscribing words onto unusual objects was at times invoked in the conversations about perceptions of marketing by other groups in the corporation, such as sales. Virtual World's marketing managers complained that it was difficult to change their reputation of 'being called T-shirt guys' imposed on them by 'sales'. Those working in sales were responsible for establishing direct relationships with customers. Their ability to make a personal impression and have an impact on a customer through their appearance, designer clothes and speaking skills earned them the nickname 'stars in cars' among marketers. Marketers also said they would prefer to be recognised as contributing to organisational 'strategies'. Those in sales, with their emphasis on achieving real deals in face-to-face engagements, were dangerously dismissing the use of marcom materials, failing to recognise them as an indispensable constitutive element of communication.

At the same time, sales managers received ideas about *what* could be exchanged in communications with customers from marketing in the form of marcom materials. The metaphor of 'armour' used in relation to marcom materials emphasises the purpose of the materials: to win customers. These military expressions (including the term 'sales force') were a part of the corporate language of 'wins' and 'losses', including those of selling as 'winning the battle' and 'fighting the competitors'.[8] Marketing managers complained that there was no consistency in communicating messages to end customers by the sales force because some of the marcom materials were used incorrectly, or neglected. This careless attitude could reduce the effectiveness of marketing campaigns, or could even 'damage the corporate reputation', leading customers to speak negatively about Virtual World. In other words, sales managers were blamed for not providing a good-enough interpretive context for marcom materials.

The latter is an interesting detail since it shows that interpretation was conceived of by technology marketers as a process involving more entities than just a 'text' and a 'reader'. A sales manager was rendered essential to establishing an association between reader and text. In technology marketing, the question of whether efforts to constrain interpretation should relate to assumptions about human subjectivity, as in the fragment above, or whether interpretation should be seen as a collective process, was a matter of deliberation. In technology marketing, assumptions about the nature of organisational decision-making were made and tested. The corporation was exploring possibilities of approaching a different group of decision-makers inside customer organisations, or *accounts*. While traditionally information technologies were sold to technical groups within customer organisations (technology decision-makers, or TDMs), nowadays the importance of approaching business decision-makers (BDMs) is recognised.

The marketers explained that, in their view, a CxO[9] is not an individual buying a piece of technology for his or her own pleasure. Budgets at stake are high, and executives are held accountable for their company's performance. And this, in their view, demanded different skills from those of sales managers. Sales managers needed to be able to identify and approach business decision-makers, and to learn the language of the business benefits of technology, rather than the technical details. Being persuaded of the value of spending on technology, a business executive would then delegate its implementation to his technical colleagues, who usually held less powerful positions in the organisation. These assumptions about the nature of executive interactions in customer accounts led to the creation of different narrative forms of persuasion. The assumptions, according to marketing managers, required new forms of communication.

The head of corporate marketing announced a strict policy with regard to 'demand generation' mailings: messages for BDMs should not be read by TDMs, and vice versa. This kind of marketing thinking, construing the customer as a collective, implied that sales managers were involved in the decision-making process. A sales manager was supposed to establish a relationship with his or her account in order to learn the specifics of an enterprise and to gain access to the main decision-makers. The trouble was that it was sometimes difficult to differentiate the two types in the customer accounts. Is the Chief Information Officer a BDM or a TDM? These questions were often resolved *ad hoc*, when mailing lists were collated for 'organising'.

A widespread view in marketing was that TDMs and BDMs speak completely different languages, and should be approached in terms of their own concerns. OliviaH, a marketing manager, told me the following parable to clarify this strategy (12 January 2005):

> What if I were to sell you a . . . knitting honeymoon? I know it's a stupid example, but anyway. I cannot just say, 'During the honeymoon you'll be knitting all those bootees your baby will need', because if you are the wife, you will like it, but it won't work for your partner. And there are two of you involved in decision-making. You cannot just tell him, 'I'm paying a couple of thousand of pounds tomorrow and we are getting that wonderful knitting honeymoon' because he will say, 'What on earth are you going to do? I won't spend a quid on this.' However, if at the same time he hears that knitting is a modern cool pastime, a fantastic stress-buster, his reaction will be different. He will say, 'Knitting? Oh, fantastic, it's a great stress-buster; I want to be in this club.' That's why we need to target both TDMs and BDMs at the same time when we are running a campaign.

In light of the new approach targeting primarily BDMs, 'too technical' was almost a term of abuse with regard to a selling proposition. A value proposition should now describe the capabilities of a technical solution to facilitate and increase workforce performance, marketing managers insisted. A brochure relying heavily on technical details was defined as poorly written. Corporate brochures and pitches were proofread by marketing managers to prevent the inclusion of too many technicisms. The new style largely used the language of organisational performance, employee mobility and efficiency. The sales force thus needed to understand that business decision-makers, the 'senior people in big customer organisations', could have different motivations for decision-making from those of the 'techies' traditionally approached by sales managers, who were also usually technically trained. Virtual World also implemented this approach in designing two different demonstration halls for technical and business decision-makers. Sales managers had to learn to bring business (not techie!) customers into the luxury Executive Suite, and to invite them to corporate events, conferences and workshops organised specifically for business audiences.

Ensuring that sales managers use marcom materials properly in conversations with customers was identified as one of the urgent tasks for 'vertical' marketers. In one of our first meetings Alex explained that the major goal of the team could be defined as 'sales enablement', or providing the corporate sales force with tools they could use when they entered their customer organisations, or accounts. Marketing managers called sales managers 'the Field'. Configuring the users (Woolgar, 1991a) of Virtual World's technologies implied attempts to configure 'the Field' first. In configuring the sales force, the vertical marketing team was doing 'internal marketing'. This, according to Alex, was probably the most difficult kind of marketing, a task whose difficulty consisted in bringing the (perceived as extremely busy and travelling extensively) sales managers up to date with corporate information, and educating them about new marcom materials (brochures, videos), competitive information and selling techniques.

Marketing managers recognised that educating sales managers required persistence and certain tricks to make sales managers read the marcom materials and utilise them 'correctly'. Alex explained to me what the 'right use' of the materials could mean. A commercial has to be shown at the right moment during a business meeting. A single word can lose or win a deal: sales manuals contained conversational sequences for an 'elevator pitch' in the form of three anticipated questions and answers to exchange with a new customer while going up to the meeting room in a lift. A group of marketing managers gathered to discuss modifications of a Web portal for sales managers. A solution was suggested to provide some interpretive context for the messages that sales managers could recreate in conversations to ensure that a brochure, for instance, produces due persuasive effect. As Alex explained, 'We are now developing a new system of content delivery, where we are implementing a distinction between "knowledge" and "wisdom". "Knowledge" is promotional materials: white papers, success stories, video clips, customer references; "wisdom" is what they [sales] should do with them, instructions on how to use them when they go to a customer. We've had a major problem with this so far – many materials are not used properly.'

How can the 'right use' of marcom materials be ensured? The marketing managers were trying to think of ways to 'deliver' marcom materials to sales managers in the first place. Marketing managers discussed the properties of a Web portal that was thought to become the main source of marcom materials for sales managers. They were trying to understand the informational preferences of sales managers: how much time do they spend reading email? Will they like our new Web portal? What kind of information will they look for? What was more important: the 'look and feel' or the 'content' of the materials? 'Content' was approved as the likely preference for the 'busy' and 'mostly male' sales managers. The colour yellow was good, a friendly colour. The managers were trying to fit as much text as possible onto a single screen page, to avoid forcing users to scroll down in order to read it.

One of the marketing managers observed that the elaborate design, however, was not of much help. The problem rather lay in the general lack of commitment of sales managers to reading the messages from marketing. Another marketing manager agreed: 'They kill our emails before opening them.' This observation puzzled marketing managers: how to solve this? It appeared it was not enough to achieve an appealing design and easily graspable layout for the portal. It was definitely insufficient to try to persuade 'the Field' to read the portal through an email invitation. To win sales managers' attention or, quite forcefully, to 'get them to read', the marketers suggested that the attractive design needed to be weighted down with accountability (cf. Woolgar and Simakova, 2003). Victoriously, it was suggested that the new portal subscription procedure be incorporated as an obligatory element of registration for a corporate seminar compulsory for sales managers to attend.

The creation and use of discursive objects appears to be interpretive action oriented to at least two kinds of audiences. First, sales managers were 'armoured' with marcom materials to approach potential customers whose interpretations were anticipated through the rendering of decision-making in customer organisations a 'collective' process. Addressing BDMs, marketing managers claimed their knowledge of the customer to be superior to the 'technical' knowledge of 'sales'. At the same time, the marcom materials served as a resource for boundary work between 'sales' and 'marketing' as a part of mutual labelling and struggle for the winning versions of communicative arrangements in engagements with customers. To ensure the 'right use' of marcom materials in their way, marketing managers were trying to create complex structures of accountabilities based on their knowledge of the interpretive community of 'sales'. The practical accomplishment of the material and the discursive emerged through the anticipations of possible interpretations of discursive objects by intended audiences.

Third response: Carrie, the marketing manager

Invitation: the local production of action at a distance

A corporation like Virtual World survives and makes profit on a continuous influx of customers attracted to the core product line, as well as on the renewal of offers of technology products and expertise. As in the example of the organising activities that I discussed in the previous chapter, the management of the flow of potential and actual customers is one of the main practical tasks for marketing managers, at least in the 'vertical' marketing department. The tasks of attracting visitors to the events sponsored or organised by the corporation often demand the creation of special kinds of marcom materials, designed to purposefully *invite* the prospective attendees. In some sense, the task of creating the *invitations* can be described in the post-essentialist terms of the creation of *association* between reader and text.

Invitation is a term that has currency in the marketing department just as in common parlance. In the marketing department, however, invitation acquires an instrumental sense as it becomes a feature of market management. An 'invitation' in marketing is a call to be produced, or answered to, or sent to customers, ensuring that it will be read and acted on in a certain way, one prescribed by the invitation. As in Latour (1990), invitation can be seen as the local production of action at a distance. The creation of an invitation is a process whereby various claims regarding its content and anticipated readings are invoked and contested. The organisation of an invitation of a reader (customer) into a text is a matter of practical deliberations in marketing, and takes various performative formats. Marketing managers would work with designers to create an invitation layout and to produce a certain number of brochures. A sales manager would *invite* a customer to read or watch a marcom material, and then make a follow-up phone call to ensure that (travel) action was being taken. But how is an *invitation* accomplished? What kind of practical reasoning is applied by marketing managers who create invitations? We have already seen that deliberations on the nature of discursive objects entail considerations on the nature of interpretive action. Creating or acting on an invitation also relies on the recognition of certain implicit or explicit practical assumptions that become built into an invitation, such as the anticipated readers' food preferences if a banquet option is offered. Invitation is a complex process that involves establishing versions of distribution of accountability, including the attribution of agency to discursive objects. The examples discussed below are taken from my notes and emails collected during a period of intense preparations for various events (customer forums, technology conferences) held or co-organised by Virtual World 'vertical' marketers. Here I invite Carrie, the vertical marketing manager, to share with us her practical thinking. What kind of work do texts do, and what does it take to make them do some kind of work, if seen from a marketer's perspective? An ethnographic analysis of the vertical marketing practical episodes below will stand for Carrie's response.

At Virtual World, discursive objects in the form of 'invitations' were created and disseminated in the course of 'organising' by 'vertical' marketers. I was often asked to help with writing and sending out invitations. There was nothing exceptional about this routine work – a few events (technology seminars, conferences where 'customers' met 'producers') organised or co-sponsored by Virtual World happened every month in EMEA. I became familiar with invitation drafts stored in an electronic collaboratory on the intranet, and was allowed to craft texts of invitations myself, showing them to Carrie only at the last stage before sending them out, for her approval. In principle, an invitation should be approved and signed by a more senior manager, but since those were difficult to catch, Carrie signed invitations for them 'in absence', and taught me how to do it, too.

To collate a database of invitees for an event, sales managers were usually contacted to provide fresh contact information for executives we had to invite. An Excel spreadsheet with data requirements would usually be sent to dozens of sales managers, whose responses had to be accumulated in a single spreadsheet. Some sales managers were sent a list in a Word document or in an old Excel sheet with a different format. I had to put everything into Excel to help Carrie with 'mail merge' afterwards. Making lists meant copying and pasting words and sentences from documents that came in a variety of different electronic formats and meticulously selecting, copying and pasting them into Excel cells. Everyone agreed it was a boring task that just needed to be done. Marketing managers sympathised with my neck pain, arising from long hours spent dragging the mouse, but were happy I was around to help.

It was assumed that business executives were more difficult to approach than technical managers. In terms of their time management, preferences in travel style, and settings, business executives were seen as more demanding and picky. The marketing budget for a business seminar was adapted for more luxurious hotels and venues. In case an executive and/or his or her spouse fancied a cultural visit, the programme should offer such an option. Organising a corporate event in a French town for such an audience that was considered 'difficult', the marketing team had to identify a good restaurant that participants would find attractive. The process included digging deep into the local knowledge of 'good restaurants', learning from marketing counterparts within the country, and ensuring special menu options and flawless service. Marketers tried to elicit the possible taste and style preferences of the invitees, who were perceived as a mostly masculine audience likely to choose more substantial food options: 'It will be interesting for them to experience a traditional restaurant if they are coming to this region' . . . 'I would personally prefer a healthier Italian cuisine with Mozzarella cheese, but men like meat more.'

In the conference programme we created, restaurants were indicated as one of the event's highlights. Pictures of restaurant interiors and exteriors downloaded from the restaurants' websites were included. When the 'meaty' option was finally approved in anticipation of a male audience, the suggestion that the participants would probably drink 'a lot of wine' with this meal was met with approval by Carrie's boss. Drinks in one of the luxury local bars also made a part of the pre-dinner programme. The description of the seminar was more or less standard for events of this format – I copied the 'blurb' from another invitation with minor changes, and added new names of customer representatives attending this time. The title of the event was provided by the organisers and was copied from their brochure (Virtual World, as a co-sponsor, invited its clients personally). The invitation assumed that an invitee would appreciate personalised service, high-standard facilities and the possibilities of benefiting from being in Paris for a few days to explore local cuisine and attractions.

A 'winning' case study?

Peter, a sales manager, asked Carrie to produce a 'case study' of successful technology adoption that could help him to win a prospective client, a hotel manager, 'in a single meeting'. Case studies were a form of success story usually written by an outsourced copywriting agency that specialised in technology, and only with a signed customer's agreement. Companies whose spectacular transformation, as a result of the adoption of technologies, was described had to be real, and preferably well known and reputable. Sales managers were urged to initiate conversations with their customers about writing a case study. While some customers willingly engaged in the process, seeing it as a form of publicity, others were reluctant to do so. Case studies that described examples of a company's dramatic success had the reputation of being powerful marcom materials helping to win *other* customers. In a conversation, Carrie once observed: 'they [sales] leave it with a customer overnight and get a deal next day.' A 'bank' case study would be offered to a bank manager. A hotel manager would read about another hotel. Peter explained that he wanted the prospective client to identify with a situation the case study described: an increase of hospitality business in a declining region due to the implementation of networking technologies.

Peter assumed that during the meeting he would be guiding the customer through the case study, pointing at the obvious difficulty of the customer's situation and at the potential of getting out of it through the purchase of technological solutions. Peter suggested taking another case study and changing the hotel name and some other, minor, as he thought, details, such as geographical location. Carrie promised to help, produced a draft of the case study, and sent it to a creative agency to obtain an estimate to see whether a single copy of the case study, based on the existing file, could be produced quickly. The agency requested a considerable fee. According to the creatives, the work of changing the elements of the text would involve 'shifting the paragraphs', and could only be done in another agency that possessed the necessary software. This work would have cost a couple of thousand pounds. The agency explained this price by 'the necessity to get back to the original pre-frozen PDF file'.

Having no such funds available, Carrie found herself in a difficult situation: she needed to find the two-thousand-pound agency fee or get into a confrontation with Peter. Explaining that Peter 'really needs to win the customer', Carrie asked Jodie to allocate the sum from the shared budget for two 'verticals', 'hospitality' and 'transportation'. Jodie energetically challenged the belief that the outcome of negotiations with the prospective customer might depend on this single text. She wanted to better understand the conditions of the deal. According to Jodie, a win depends on a number of factors, and the required text could not be considered the critical element pushing the deal, a 'show stopper'. She suggested that a case study is a description of a 'won deal' rather than a means of achieving it. There were other means to achieving a deal, without spending budget funds on a mock-up:

> What exactly are the expectations that we are setting with Peter and the customer? If all they want is a case study once it is won then fine I am sure we can find the cash. But we should not spend any money making a mock up for a case study that is not a won deal. Is this customer really going to make a purchase decision based on a mocked up case study? I can't believe this is a show stopper. Could we not put together a pack showing what we have done with the Happy Traveller as an indication of the interest and coverage that can be a result of investment in innovative technology solutions for competitive advantage could bring [*sic*]?
>
> (Jodie to Carrie, 15 April 2004)

Carrie could not obtain the desired sum. Advised by Alex, the team leader, she had to persuade Peter to use the Happy Traveller package during the pitch.

This ethnographic episode is an example of the distribution of accountability with regard to textual artefacts. Inviting the customer into the text by describing 'solutions' for his business 'problems' entailed deliberations on who (or what) would speak to customers in a persuasive way, what would count as a good-enough means of engaging with the customer, and what would *invite* the hotel manager into the universe of Virtual World's discursive objects and technologies. The marketing managers' deliberations show that the content and the effect expected of a 'case study' were not put in a unique correspondence. The same effect – 'a win' – could be achieved by other means, too, thus saving money and preserving the status of 'case study' as a report of an achieved deal rather than a 'mock-up' of an anticipated one.

Materiality as a persuasive resource

An example of a crystal ball invitation illustrates further in what sense, in attempts to produce a desired response in audiences, materiality becomes a resource for marketing managers who attempt to invite readers into marcom texts. For a technology forum of high importance for the corporation, Carrie negotiated the production of a crystal ball invitation box with a creative agency. The example of the material incarnation of a marketing message strikes a chord with Latour's (1991) example of the action of the hotel manager who attached a metal weight to room keys in order to make guests leave the keys at the reception desk. While Latour's account of association insists on the intrinsic capacity of the metal weight to discipline hotel guests, the marketing manager had to engage in the complex work of creating and justifying a material resource. She also had to ensure that the readers of the material text would understand and respond to the message in a certain desired way. This involved recognising and building conventions of interpretation into the material thing.

The crystal ball was created, Carrie explained to me in terms not very flattering to the invitees, 'to help us to move CIOs' fat asses'.[10] A number of explanations of the design were offered. Carrie added that the creative agency simply knew another company specialising in crystal objects, and proposed that they make 'something of it together'. The realisation of the idea was quite expensive because of the need to purchase a few hundred crystal balls. This was not a problem for Virtual World since the marketing team had some funds left before the end of the financial year. This budget had to be spent in order to ensure a similar amount of funding for the next year. The creative brief described the idea of the crystal ball as 'designed to express the idea of seeing the future of hi-tech industries through the crystal ball'. Carrie added that making an invitation in such an unusual and creative fashion, namely as a heavy box,[11] increased the odds that the invitation would not be immediately thrown away. Like Latour, Carrie says the box *is* heavy; however, the achieved heaviness of the discursive objects emerged as the upshot of Carrie's interactions with the creatives and the anticipations of the reactions of those executives who would receive the box.

Carrie apparently liked the crystal ball design. She showed it to her office colleagues, finding it particularly amusing and engaging to see her own name through the transparent mock-up crystal ball the agency gave her in a specially designed paper box. The visible part of an invitation letter placed under the transparent ball read: 'Dear Carrie. We would be delighted to see you . . .' This is what a 'real' customer will see, she explained, and will definitely find engaging, too.

While the invitation box was being produced, Carrie asked the sales managers to send her their executive contacts in potential accounts to create a pool of invitees. One of the questions discussed with regard to the invitation's effectiveness was whether the crystal ball box should be posted or hand-delivered to the invitees. On the one hand, as Carrie explained, it would be better if Virtual World account managers delivered the invitations in person. The sales managers had already established relationships with the customers, so, as Carrie explained, 'they (CIOs) should hear about the conference from someone they know'. On the other hand, posting the boxes all at once would save Carrie time and would ensure that they reached the invitees without relying on 'unreliable' sales managers. Carrie decided to post the boxes, but also to send them with accompanying brochures, in case sales managers were too busy to meet a customer and talk the invitation through. All account managers were also instructed to follow up on the invitations on the phone or in person.

To summarise, allowing a text to speak for itself was a matter of practical judgement. It might involve assessment or anticipation of readership and interpretation, and not necessarily by its intended 'target' readers. A marcom material might be let out of the marketing department on its own, or might be accompanied by other communicative means, such as a letter or a follow-up phone call. Or it might be replaced by another one, assuming that the 'effect' would be the same. I have tried to show that choosing the resources (discursive or material) for the purposes at hand entailed the practical management of accountability relations.

Discussion

The practices in the vertical marketing department offer an opportunity to explore how ambiguities around the material and the discursive properties of discursive objects get resolved. The deliberations about the properties of marcom materials, such as their ability to produce intended action – like inducing someone to travel, or facilitating a deal – notably involved the invocation of folk assumptions about how textual artefacts (or marcom materials, in the marketers' language) work. These assumptions contested textual agency and could variously attribute the effects of a text to the text itself, to a reader, to its content, or to its material qualities. What are the implications of these observations for the scholarly debate about textuality? The heuristically created tension between the textual–technological metaphors opens up new ways of thinking about texts, and technologies, through investigating the cultural conventions of discursivity and materiality empirically. In the marketing department, different cultures of textuality can be formed through, for example, specific tasks delegated to groups or individuals.

As one such example of the production of material texts, I summarised an analysis of everyday work in the marketing department as 'Carrie's response'.

For the material culture studies, the main issue at stake relevant to my analysis is how to capture the materiality of the word. Tilley's (1991) examination of the applicability of post-structuralism to material culture is an exercise in 'pushing it [materiality] to the limits' (p. 180). Tilley writes that 'material culture does not constitute a text, but in order to understand, we need to represent material culture in texts' (ibid.). Thus, in trying to provide a descriptive account of the materialities of grapheme, we will always encounter a problem that he calls a 'doubly textual circuit': understanding material culture as text is equivalent to writing another text (ibid.). In other words, as Yates (1990: 273) puts it, 'The thing itself always escapes.' Archaeology – in the sense of organisational archaeology too – can only come about with(in) the concept of writing, and can be established as contemporary interpretation and writing.

This proposition to explore the limits of the metaphor echoes the post-essentialist treatment of the textual metaphor in science and technology studies in attempts to take the debate further. Woolgar's intent is 'to play against the metaphor' technology as text, to see the limits of the textual analogy (Grint and Woolgar, 1997: 70). These limits arise in the form of textual determinism as a refuge of essentialisms in post-essentialism (Woolgar and Cooper, 1999). In other words, as these authors observe, in attempts to explain how some representations become more persuasive than others, essentialism with regard to the natural properties of real objects gets replaced by the determinism of social and political interests, or textual determinism, such as the 'pragmatic values' and 'rhetorical strategies' of a text. Attention to contingencies of interpretation was discussed in Chapter 2 as a possible way out of textual determinism.

How can the deliberations about properties and agency of textual artefacts in marketing practice inform the debate? The practical management of the material/discursive *ambiguity* in marketing helps us to explore what sustains the dichotomy, and its practical uses. I introduced the notion of *discursive objects* – embracing both discursive entities as linguistic items of a given text, and texts as material objects – to examine the role of textual artefacts in the practical management of accountability relations. Marcom materials were taken to be an instantiation of application of the marketing *analogy* to discursive objects. This particular 'universe' of discursive objects was accomplished in the *marketing* department through deliberations on their ability to intervene in the market discourse.

The properties of marcom materials, their ability to produce certain effects, were shown to be an open interpretive matter in the marketing department, subject to constant assessments and evaluations. Materiality and discursivity were resorted to by marketers for the purposes at hand. Using materiality or discursivity as a resource, participants relied on implicit or explicit assumptions about the nature of interpretive action. The anticipation of the accountability relations in an environment in which marcom materials will be sent to do their work of persuasion was an important part of marketers' deliberations. The ability of marcom materials to 'speak for themselves' – as they go out – was achieved through making marcom materials speak to various audiences, including those in the organisation. One way to summarise Carrie's response to the challenges posed by the textual–technological metaphors is to say that the particular meanings and terms of the text–technology relationship have to be seen as accomplished within the local circumstances of production and use of material texts. The marketing manager, for example, would be interested in the purposes, readership and means of production of marcom materials. As such, her response would mobilise folk theories of the relationship between discourse and materiality, words and things, content of a text and its (material, social organisational) architecture, having currency in the world of marketing. Such folk theories can be contested, or ignored, in the boundary work episodes concerning marketing's role in the corporation. Some of these folk theories were explored in this chapter illustrating the roles of the material–discursive duality in the marketers' practical assumptions about social ordering.

Continuing the theme of the roles of materiality in the marketing discourse, the next two chapters follow my transition to the 'advanced technologies' marketing group at Virtual World. As such, I became involved as a project manager in the production of a corporate discourse about a new technological product related to radio frequency identification (RFID) technologies. I will offer a discussion of the corporate practices of product launch, and of the role of technical demonstration in the launch. In particular, the chapters to follow discuss in what sense a new technology was accomplished as a *tellable story* in the marketing department.

6 'Softly, softly' tagging the world[1]

Introduction/transition

The corporate practice known as a product 'launch'[2] occurs in a variety of settings, including in the information technology (IT) industries. Launching involves the announcement of a new technological product or expert service, and may or may not be accompanied by selling or monetary transactions. It can be seen as an organisational ritual through which a company offers a 'novel' product to 'the market'.[3] Ideally, a launch brings together corporate representatives, a version of a product, and some external audiences (such as journalists or potential consumers), and may be accompanied by a media release. My transition to a new team at Virtual World presented me with an opportunity to examine ongoing practices and beliefs around attempts to launch a technological product and, in particular, around the role of technological demonstration in a launch.

As such, this discussion joins the body of research on the role of mediators, such as corporations, in forging relations between technological artefacts and their publics that has been addressed previously in science and technology studies (for example, Oudshoorn and Pinch, 2003). I will examine the co-construction of technological constituencies and material technologies through the practices of a launch, and through technology demonstration in particular. Technology demonstrations are often a highlight of launch activities: they attract both public and media attention. Some demonstrations, such as Steve Jobs's public presentations of new Apple technologies, became prominent media events and news items.[4] Although his performances still exemplify newsworthy demonstrations,[5] in this chapter I focus on more mundane, and less public, practices of launching and demonstrating technologies. The cases of interest here were either performed on a smaller scale (with less public exposure), or confined to technological exchanges between business organisations. Apart from the use of star demonstrators (often top corporate executives or professional demonstrators), some corporate employees (marketers, marketing managers) routinely prepare and organise product launch and technology demonstrations.[6] I describe demonstrations as they are achieved through social interactions by the parties who perceive – and dispute – them as a critical part of the launch.

The particular technology examined in this chapter is radio frequency identification (RFID) – a system using small electrical tags that can transmit limited amounts of information on radio frequencies over fixed distances to a receiving device called a 'reader'. RFID tags can be attached to objects and people in order to monitor their presence and trace their movements. In some renditions, RFID is seen as a successor to bar codes for the purposes of information storage and manipulation, and data analysis. Currently established RFID applications include public transport passes (such as the Oyster card in London, or Navigo in Paris) and goods scanned in some supermarkets.[7]

During my time with Virtual World in 2003–2005, trade publications promoted the potential of RFID for tagging and tracing virtually 'everything'. Applications for the retail industry were promoted early on (along with potential military applications for tracking soldiers and objects). One of the more notable promotions occurred in May 2003, when Metro AG supermarket opened its Future Store in Rheinberg near Düsseldorf in Germany, with Claudia Schiffer, the supermodel, on display. The doors opened to over forty companies, including Virtual World, that were invited to view the store 'as a life-sized technology Petri dish' (*Deutsche Welle Online,* 2003).[8] Despite such fanfare, Virtual World approached the potential of RFID with caution (Simakova and Neyland, 2008). Rather than buying into claims about the instant success of RFID, the corporation favoured approaching specific industries with carefully crafted proposals, technology assessment offers and pilot projects, before articulating plans for product launch. RFID was evaluated as a potentially profitable technology, and a launch was proposed as the necessary step towards making an official public announcement of Virtual World's interest and expertise in RFID. The accomplishment of the launch – as an instantiation of corporate practical deliberations on the roles of technology demonstration – is the main focus of this chapter.

In the style of STS writings that explore the 'decentered' worlds of technoscientific objects (Law, 2002; Latour, 1996), this and the next chapters continue offering a personalised ethnographic account that includes a set of reflections on uses of the launch metaphor in a corporate setting. My account follows the actors, through my encounters with them, as they express various opinions at different locations and for different audiences, moving back and forth across corporate boundaries. Without intending to overly generalise the findings based on one particular case of RFID launch and demonstration by Virtual World, this study introduces a sensibility towards the nature of deliberations in IT industries, at least. As ethnographic observations with other IT corporations suggest, the situated participants' inquiry into the status of a technical product as being 'ready' to leave a corporation is an observable feature of organisational life (Licoppe and Simakova, 2007). The search for acceptable framings of occasions of a new technology crossing corporate boundaries includes formulating and defending certain bottom lines, such as the technical conditions of the device, or, as in another case, the existence of a market for it. Perceived as the necessary condition for technology to cross corporate boundaries in an orchestrated way (for which 'launch' is shorthand), these bottom lines become a matter of deliberations, provings and organisational politics.

Can marketing help?

In August 2004 Alex left the 'vertical' marketing team to become responsible for a new project with another marketing group called 'advanced technologies'. His concern was that the forthcoming marketing reorganisation would mean cutting the marketing budget, and that apparently everyone was looking for a safer position since some redundancies had already occurred. The 'advanced technologies' team had just started to explore the commercial potential of RFID. The executive deliberations about this new technology had been going on for about a year, and the corporate intranet archives contained records of the first steering committee meetings devoted to RFID from 2003. The position of RFID Marketing Manager for EMEA was offered to Alex. The appointment did not mean that RFID was occupying Alex exclusively, as he and I were soon thrown into another 'advanced technologies' project running in parallel to RFID. The team was also managing other projects in various stages of preparedness for launch. These were designated by acronyms, and largely related to offering new network applications associated with emerging technological developments in IT, such as middleware, or wireless, and seen by the management as potentially profitable.

RFID is an interesting case of the application of the marketing analogy in the organisation, as discussed in Chapter 1 (Wensley, 1990). It presents an opportunity to discuss another instantiation of attribution of agency in the marketing discourse. In the case of RFID, marketing was called upon in attempts to understand the potential for and to eventually achieve profitable performance based on an RFID product. Attempts to implement marketing thinking in relation to the technological product aligned with a perceived need for a change in relations between the corporation and its audiences. The support for RFID came from top corporate management in both Europe and the United States, including the CEO and the newly appointed VP of Marketing in EMEA, who were mentioned in conversations as the executive 'sponsors' of the RFID project. The VP held the view that successful corporate performance had not always been attributable to 'clever marketing': the decade of Virtual World's phenomenal success and its growth into a global corporation was generally attributed to the 'Internet firestorm'. It meant that customers were seeking to buy products from Virtual World without much effort on the marketing side. Nowadays, however, the corporation felt the need for a serious marketing effort in order to survive in what was recognised as a much harsher competitive environment. RFID was seen as one of the promising products for the growing market of advanced technologies, where Virtual World wanted to expand its presence. Claiming Virtual World's expertise in this new market was perceived as a difficult task given its public image as a more traditional technology business oriented to basic network solutions. It was anticipated that business media and analysts would doubt that the corporation had sufficient knowledge and resources to offer sound expertise in RFID to the market, as had happened before in relation to other advanced technologies. Could 'clever marketing' help to redress the situation?

Alex offered me a chance to follow him as an opportunity for me to learn some other kind of marketing in exchange for help with the RFID launch. While staying with the 'vertical' marketing team did not require any special approval, changing teams had to be justified with senior management, as it potentially meant a different access configuration for me. The appropriate reason for me to leave the vertical marketing team was formulated in terms of this being a useful move to explore a different perspective on marketing at Virtual World. It was also recognised that I had already spent a considerable amount of time with the vertical marketing team. One year with 'vertical' marketing was seen as a good achievement for marketing managers. Moving to a new team was interpreted as a sign of good career planning. At the same time, there were rumours that the vertical marketing team was in danger of being reorganised, and that some key people were leaving, or had been fired. Everyone thought it would be wise for the employees to look for a different position. A preliminary agreement with Alex stated that my fieldwork end date was envisaged to be in October 2004, according to my fieldwork extension plan. However, in following the new project, I added eight months to my fieldwork term with RFID marketing, including the virtual mode[9] period, from March to June 2005. The continual extensions of my fieldwork plans were closely intertwined with practical decisions about the timing of the RFID launch.

The everyday uses of the launch metaphor in marketing implied a nuanced crafting of launch as an event that takes, will take, or took place. Although the normative launch talk (e.g. solidified in the marketing plans) requires certainty, the participants' informal statements about the project's current situation allow for a considerable degree of flexibility. This notably includes deliberations about the launch deadlines. My new placing with the 'advanced technologies' group allowed me to collect some materials about the marketing practices in this group. The transition captured the first moments of preparing the RFID product launch, the deadline for which was planned for January 2005. A launch plan had been written earlier, and now required action. One of the first steps for me was to liaise with another 'advanced technologies' marketing manager in order to learn 'what it means to launch a product'. Contrary to the fixed dates one could see in the plans, the conversations at that time revealed less certainty about the deadlines and the content (or the 'value proposition') of the launch. The reservations expressed about the launch date, usually explained in terms of 'delays' with getting the value proposition right, led to speculations that the launch would be ('endlessly') 'postponed'. Some managers who became involved with the RFID expressed doubt that the launch would ever happen. Any further extension of my non-disclosure agreement did not seem worth the effort for them: there would be nothing to disclose. Indeed, I did not witness the full-blown RFID launch planned for the EMEA theatre, having left the field in the summer of 2005. The delays in getting the technology demonstration kit ready were employed as a good reason to postpone the launch. However, I took part in the preparation for and participated in a series of tentative local launches. These observations contributed to my reflections about the construction of the role of marketing as an adequate measure to ensure that the corporation would come up with a credible RFID value proposition.

One can say that RFID was introduced at Virtual World as a *category* (Bowker and Star, 2000: 4) around which formal and informal discourses began to form. Both practically and ethnographically speaking, making sense of what was going on in the organisation in relation to RFID was not a straightforward task for a beginner. In one of the first RFID corporate trainings arranged through an EMEA conference call, participants referred to RFID as a 'virtual organisation',[10] signalling the lack of centralised management. The use of the RFID acronym to denote the technology's *organisation* presented RFID as a set of disparate activities, members of which wanted to know what was going on in the other groups identifying themselves with RFID. The conversations at that time implied that RFID was high on the corporate agenda. When I joined the RFID team, Alex subscribed me to two internal mailing lists devoted to the technology so that I could receive daily updates, media reports and corporate news. The messages posted on the lists further contributed to the impression of the RFID 'buzz'. Claims of the upsurge of interest in RFID in various industries, companies and governments could also be heard in conversation with Virtual World managers. Alex received requests for information from some corporate managers, some of whom expressed interest in the project and wished to participate in the monthly updates.

The RFID acronym performed some kind of organisational ordering. Participants were busy defining members' identities in the 'RFID space', and at the same time RFID became a means by which to identify oneself in the organisation. My role at Virtual World later became recognised through RFID as well. Some individuals were mentioned as having managerial or advisory responsibility for the new technology. The members of the RFID 'core team' were listed on the special RFID portal of the corporate intranet and gathered weekly for a conference call. The documents of the RFID steering committee, which involved top executives, marketing managers, engineers, business solution managers, legal reps, strategic alliances managers, and marketing managers responsible for specific markets, also indicated these individuals' previous and current RFID-related activities.

It was also admitted that not everyone in the organisation possessed equal knowledge of RFID or authority to speak about the technology on behalf of the corporation. The practical management of RFID boundaries implied deliberations on who could speak on behalf of RFID, to whom, and under what circumstances. External consultants from the United States were invited to provide an overview of the technology for Virtual World's employees in the EMEA. Sales managers received basic training in RFID, but were not yet exposed to a definitive value proposition that they could use in their conversations with customers. The executive board thought it was too early to speak forth about RFID, to articulate Virtual World's interest in the technology. During the initial stages analysts were briefed about Virtual World's interest in RFID under a non-disclosure agreement: the analysts could 'know', but not 'write' about, the association between RFID and

Virtual World. In other words, attempts were made to identify and limit the RFID knowledge to some groups within and outside of the organisation, as well as to restrict Virtual World's association with RFID in the public's eyes to certain conversational situations. At the very first stages, rather than acting as public spokespeople for the new technology on behalf of the corporation, marketing was assigned certain responsibilities in *situating* the RFID discourses. This is not to say that the ways the technology was talked into the corporate discourse were perfectly controlled by some authoritative power, but just to indicate an attempt at congealing the effort in terms of the managerial agency. As opposed to, for example, letting everyone mention RFID as a potentially profitable technology freely, the title of 'RFID Marketing Manager' assumed attribution of individual agency to someone who was presumably capable of establishing acceptable corporate discourse vis-à-vis the technological product. The success or failure of launching RFID would be attributed to the marketing manager, for whom carrying such responsibility demands the work of maintaining the boundaries of marketing knowledge contested in the corporation.

In other words, it can be said that marketing managers were responsible for deciding what kinds of RFID descriptions could be available and to whom. The distribution of marketing knowledge about RFID was accomplished through establishing and managing mailing lists, as well as Internet and intranet resources. These resources delineated information available to various reader groups at Virtual World. As above, Alex was the owner of several RFID mailing lists performing the politics of inclusion and exclusion. A 'General' RFID mailing list was in principle accessible by all members of the organisation showing interest in RFID. They could join the list upon Alex's written approval. A smaller 'Retail' RFID mailing list existed to stimulate special interest in RFID in the marketing team working with retail industries. An employee of Virtual World needed to prove his or her affiliation with retail industries in order to be added to the list. The RFID 'Core' mailing list was restricted to the twelve members of the RFID steering committee. As an ethnographer, however, I requested and received a subscription, too.

Alex was also responsible for a special RFID portal on the corporate intranet, which displayed RFID materials created specifically for sales managers in the EMEA regions. A dedicated RFID home page on the corporate Internet site was also available. The two performed a distinction between 'competitive' information that had to be kept hidden from competitors' eyes and 'public' information that could be 'accessible to everyone on the planet'. For instance, a document for sales managers called 'Q&A about RFID' contained sections on partnerships and strategic alliances, while the one 'for the rest of the planet' did not include this information. Marketing beliefs assume that disclosing technological discourses under various circumstances serves certain ends, and requires careful judgement regarding who can be made aware of (or speak on behalf of) technology and who cannot.

In brief, the new technology did not bring clear sets of identities, responsibilities and expertise available in the corporation at the outset. Those were a matter of practical concern. At Virtual World, the participants were engaged in elaborating their status and roles in relation to the new technology. This work involved learning who did what in relation to RFID, identifying top executives supporting the new technology, as well as assessing status and perspectives for the project in the corporation in conversations with peers. The application of the marketing analogy in the case of RFID assumed that the attribution of agency to marketing managers as active promoters of RFID would hinge on the promise of a transformation of RFID into a profitable corporate product through the creation of a credible value proposition. This opened up a space for deliberations about who could speak on behalf of RFID, to whom, and under what kind of circumstances. In other words, as I would like to argue, RFID was accomplished as a *tellable story*.

RFID as a tellable story

The articulation work in relation to the technology entailed accumulation, discussion and rejection of certain descriptions of possible RFID discourses and of the circumstances of narration of RFID stories. I will discuss how the formation of an RFID discourse created by the advanced marketing team was closely intertwined with recognising the existing discourses and their convenors, and discerning potential audiences; as well as anticipating (and attempting to control) interpretations by them. The section will explore the articulation work, or the creation of discursive formations (which I term *tellable stories*), connecting technological artefact and various constituencies by marketing managers who prepare to intervene, to speak forth on behalf of Virtual World and of RFID to certain audiences.

Defining the product

During the period September–October 2004, one could rarely hear definitive replies to questions about what RFID meant for Virtual World EMEA regions, or about visions of the directions for future efforts to bring the technology to market. There was not much to say about the content of the RFID product (or its value proposition) at that moment either. Although RFID was positioned within the category of 'advanced technologies', the definitions of the technology remained somewhat basic. The educational seminar for sales ('RFID 101') – delivered by the US counterparts through a conference call – did not connect the RFID descriptions to Virtual World's existing expertise. In conversations with customers, a sales manager would only mention that the company was taking an interest in RFID but had no product yet. The marketing managers' talk defined RFID in terms of a combination of tags carrying digital information and scanning devices called readers. Discussing the design of a technical demonstration for RFID, marketing managers assumed that there might be a need to connect cables and switches, but that would be a task for the 'techie' guys with whom the managers were trying to liaise, and who were showing some useful enthusiasm about this new 'funky stuff'.

Assimilating into the RFID Marketing Manager role for Alex (and for me into the role of assistant) entailed the need to become familiar with as much available and accessible RFID knowledge as possible. A body of knowledge had to be acquired from the outside. A number of voluminous market reports from the world's leading analytical firms were bought in order to make sense of the 'current situation', to look at how the technology is spoken about by other companies, and to assess the potential markets and their future. I spent my time studying market reports and organisational documents related to RFID, while also working on a market analysis for the producers of RFID technology components. Making sense of the new knowledge also required a delineation between knowledge useful for the marketing task and the technical aspects of RFID. Alex confessed that he found it difficult to speak to engineers. He was trained in branding and marketing communications, and had never studied the sciences. Although he had worked as a marketing manager in IT industries for more than ten years, the RFID talk was yet something to be learned.

Figuring out how the marketing talk could accommodate the technical language was a matter of further deliberations and practical work. The reports alone did not seem to provide enough information, and neither did Internet searches. Learning the current talk adopted by the industries assumed going out to 'liaise' and 'partner' with various organisations both inside and outside of the corporation. This is known in hi-tech corporations (and in business academic literature) as 'establishing an ecosystem' around the product. Alex had to recruit Virtual World's technical and marketing specialists, as well as establish contacts with outside companies.

The RFID project also had to demonstrate that it was worth the investment – in the sense of marketing salaries, office space and equipment – to senior executives in the corporation, including the new VP of Marketing. The latter was a believer in the ultimate revenue potential of RFID, and so the project, from its early stage, was established as a legitimate corporate unit. During the initial exploratory stages, the profitability of RFID was not a part of everyday concerns. The financial goals and outcomes of the RFID effort remained undetermined until at least the end of my fieldwork. Attempts to incorporate a so-called ROI[11] calculator into the early value proposition that would show potential revenue for a company deploying Virtual World's expertise were dismissed as premature. Rather, other kinds of assessment were applied. At the moment of my leaving the field, Alex received an email signed by the members of the executive board congratulating him on his five years as a Virtual World employee. His work was appreciated, and the board members urged Alex to 'keep it up'. Bemused, Alex interpreted the commending statement in terms of perhaps 'them' wanting him to establish 'more relationships with partners'. This interpretation was not mere speculation – achieving the validation of Virtual World's effort in RFID by other members of industry was considered a crucial element of the building of a credible statement of corporate expertise that could not be easily dismissed by business analysts and other potential critics who would be brought into the statement through the building of such relationships.

From the inside of the marketing department, the nascent RFID discourse performed the distinction between the technical work and the work of marketing and sales to potentially communicate the new product to customers. What seemed to take much of Virtual World's marketing managers' time and attention was what can be called the folk sociology and folk ethnography of RFID. The participants were interested in what was going on in the 'RFID space' in terms of worldwide legislation, announcements introducing new players entering the RFID markets, accounts of successes and failures of RFID adoption and trials, and opportunities to establish connections between Virtual World and a number of market players, corporate partners, standards bodies, governments and potential customers. The IT world was carefully watching the RFID trials mandated by one of the largest retailers, Wal-Mart, and the US Department of Defense. In the summer of 2003, Wal-Mart decreed that its top hundred suppliers would put RFID tags on certain shipments by 1 January 2005. There was no agreement on the outcomes of the trials in terms of the value of RFID to the businesses agreeing to participate in pilot projects and technology assessment exercises. A *Business Week* article forwarded to the corporate RFID mailing list emphasised the uncertainty associated with RFID implementation in retail despite the industry's push and impatience: 'RFID: Plenty of Mixed Signals. Despite Wal-Mart's push for radio-frequency identification, skeptical suppliers are still foolishly slow to embrace the new technology' (*Business Week*, 31 January 2005). Another article, from *eWeek*, presented the disputes around standardisation, property rights, interoperability of the functional units and the reluctance of Wal-Mart suppliers to invest in RFID in full scale, which made it difficult to give a comprehensive conclusion of the value of the trials ('RFID Struggles Mount as End of Year Approaches', *eWeek*; this article from 22 December 2004 was sent to 'RFID mailer list' on 5 February 2005 by a business development manager).

For my own part, explaining RFID to colleagues wishing to learn about my research unexpectedly turned out to be enormously difficult. Delving into RFID meant being exposed to various RFID descriptions, which often seemed to share only the RFID acronym. I read technical documents containing specialist XML[12] talk used by engineers. Marketing managers told RFID anecdotes. RFID producers promoted various versions of RFID functionalities. Market reports established different visions of RFID futures. Whose talk to adopt?[13] Not just my individual sense of confusion, a similar question became a matter for discussion, and consequently of boundary work, for RFID marketing managers. The issues the managers had to deal with concerned exactly the task of spelling out technological functionalities and the business value of the company's RFID product. One of the immediate features of the RFID discourse that was spotted and taken cautiously by the marketing managers was the atmosphere of the extreme hype of RFID that seemingly proliferated from the press into the corporate talk. As such, the potential of tracing 'everything' was a common feature of RFID hype statements. Virtual World's marketing managers claimed they were careful not to embrace the RFID hype for the production of their own RFID statements. They were also reluctant to adopt any existing RFID definitions for their own product. Rather, the

EMEA managers were considering adopting a 'cautious attitude' towards RFID as opposed to repeating claims about its quick success. Discussions were held about the appropriate field for RFID pilots in EMEA. One of the first potential applications of RFID (also widely discussed in the media because of the visibility of the Wal-Mart trials) was considered for retail industries.

The various possible ways of partitioning the world for the purposes of articulation of a corporate statement was a source of tensions between the 'global' (the US) and the local teams. In a discussion about how to ensure a statement that would be robust across the transatlantic audiences, some statements, such as the US 'global' marketing communication proposals, were accepted as master discourse, and their applicability for other audiences such as the EMEA had to be 'tested' and 'adapted'. These descriptions of the technology would be used in various communicative engagements with customers, press and other interested constituencies. What was conceived of as a universally applicable message became a matter of interpretation and contestation in the local 'RFID space'. Corporate claims can be challenged and contested, while corporations notice the critique and attempt to incorporate it into their own accounts, or to ignore such criticisms. The corporation may feel the need to mobilise a response if public concerns arise.[14] The examples of such contested territories for RFID that may or may not become parts of corporate statements include local governments and standards bodies contesting the implementation of certain radio frequencies; privacy activists contesting the application of RFID to persons; and suppliers refusing to employ RFID tags in order to keep their prices low. In other words, within a global corporation that tries to define its own role in the cultural technological discourses, participants construct competing versions of partial views of the world. Trying to understand the ways in which Virtual World could join the RFID with propositions 'influencing things in the direction that are favourable to its needs', a discursive boundary work to prepare intervention was about identifying potential 'favourable' interpretations (and interpreters) of Virtual World's statements. Preparations for product launch, as it will be discussed in the next section, serve as such an effort.

Product launch as organisational practice[15]

On its face, the term 'product launch' refers to a single, momentary action, through which a company introduces a specific product (in this case, a new technology) to constituencies beyond the corporation. Empirical observations rarely confirm such a simple, straightforward conception. In line with other STS studies of innovation that critique a linear model of technological development, I believe that it is more productive to define innovation, and product launch in particular, in terms of partial and practical heterogeneous encounters, and temporary, unstable (market) relations between socio-technical constituencies (see, for example, Callon and Muniesa, 2005). An ethnomethodological perspective also emphasises the importance of moving away from a view of invention as a singular event, to taking 'an interest in ongoing practices of assembly, demonstration, and performance' (Suchman *et al.*, 2002: 163). Such encounters between technologi-cal artefacts and their social constituencies can be understood as occasions that are produced through socio-technical assembling and affiliative practices that constitute encounters and frame their accountability (Suchman, 2005).

I will begin with the proposition that a product launch can be seen as the prac-tical work of organising encounters between a technological product and various constituencies inside and outside of an organisation, or as an ongoing work of encounter-ing.[16] The chapter will look closely into the accountability relations accomplished around and through product launch. Namely, I will analyse attempts at organising and at accounting for encounters between a new technol-ogy and its constituencies. Such accountability relations are of practical concern and are subject to management by participants in organisations. The organisation of access to launch activities illustrates what I mean by management of the accountability relations around new technology. The practice of launching a product assumes that little must be revealed beforehand to anticipated audiences, so that the preparations must be hidden from outsiders. Participants can even show hostility towards others who attempt to gain information. Sometimes care-fully selected audiences, such as business analysts or researchers, are briefed by corporate representatives 'under NDA' in order to transmit carefully crafted messages about the new technology. Such briefings also serve as means to explore reactions from business analysts, or to gain information from analysts to incorporate into public corporate communications such as white papers. In other words, when viewed as the practical management of accountability relations surrounding a new technology, a launch involves the creation of boundaries around technology talk.

A product launch is one of various discursive resources that companies employ to portray innovation activities as developing in a predictable, controllable way, in contrast to the messy interactions that often occur between a corporation and the outside world. Launching a product involves practical knowledge, and may entail performing a form of expertise. Corporations may use different resources to account for the release of a product (such as 'distribution', or 'communica-tion', or simply specifying a series of events as a part of a 'marketing plan'). When the term 'launch' is used, it most definitely belongs to the marketing domain. At the same time, preparations for a launch involve interactions with other corporate specialties and units, such as R&D, sales, or business develop-ment (cf. Workman, 1993). Various claims are made regarding what counts as the right timing and circumstances for a launch. Marketers have a particular basis for privileging their expertise over the opinions of other 'lay' members in a corpora-tion.[17] As an element of textbook marketing knowledge, product launch is taught in marketing and branding courses to executives and future marketing managers. Gurus are keen to offer their advice, and consultancies thrive.

A launch also is used internally to a corporation to display marketing activities as coherent, linear or parallel sets of actions that offer solutions to organisational and industrial problems such as meeting the demand to innovate or gain profit. In normative organisational talk, product launch is portrayed largely as an event for which preparations should begin long in advance, proceeding through a series of meetings, conference calls and approvals by senior executives. In a corporation, launch-related documents (plans, Excel sheets, PowerPoint slides) are construed as accountable resources that can be transferred from one product to another. Managers pass such documents around as a way to share knowledge of what it means to do a launch. Ideally, these documents need to be filled in with content related to a new product or commercial offer, and to be regularly updated as the action plan changes or new 'best practices' emerge.

For instance, in the corporate projects dealing with certain 'advanced' products, such as RFID, a document called the 'launch master plan' was used.[18] The document suggested that actions were assigned to individuals working on a set of parallel tasks. These tasks included preparing marketing materials, technical demonstrations and pricing strategies, as well as furnishing answers to anticipated questions from journalists, and analysing competitors' activities. According to the plan, relevant groups such as sales managers or distributors should be briefed (in conversations, through sales manuals and meetings) in anticipation of encounters with customers inquiring about the new product. During a launch, other external audiences (including the media) receive renditions crafted by marketing and PR managers of what the corporation has to say about its new product. If accepted as newsworthy, these renditions then go to wider audiences (for example, as press releases). The launch events are publicised to establish the facticity of the product/service and to provide a means of access to the new corporate product. As sometimes happens during after-launch assessments, actors verify the exact dates, locations and audiences for the planned launch events.

Another important detail of the master plan document was how it represented various organisational practices (e.g. R&D, marketing, PR, business development) that were formally assembled for the purposes of the project. It did so in such a way that a launch appears to be a singular action, or a particular event announcing the product. The actors were portrayed by this document as aiming to achieve a coherent outcome by a certain deadline culminating in a public event. In practice, however, a launch allows for a considerable degree of spontaneity, emergence and opportunism when managers use resources at hand to communicate a new technological product to audiences. Some marketing managers specialise in emergency product launch, and are able to bring together a set of connections (in media, in creative agencies) to produce necessary materials and publications within a short time.

Dates and deadlines are an important part of the launch discourse, as they define the circumstances of when and how a corporate story will go public. The deadline initially planned for the RFID launch discussed in this chapter was continually postponed as the circumstances for the 'right' time for going public were deliberated upon. What sorts of deliberations lead to decisions about what can be communicated to publics, when, and how? In general terms, decision-making around a launch involves the routine work of producing versions of what is going on at the corporate inside/outside boundary through categorising and ordering. A crucial element of the boundary work achieved through launch is the ongoing movements back and forth across the organisational boundary. This involves the assessment and anticipation of interpretations of 'internal' corporate statements, for example, about a product or expertise, by 'external' (consumers, press) constituencies (Woolgar and Simakova, 2003). Participants preparing a launch in organisations engage in constructing these 'internal' and 'external' contexts. A version of 'internal' contexts may involve statements of corporate expertise available and relevant to a new commercial offer. These statements are elaborated in deliberations upon how to present a corporation in association with a product. Versions of the 'external' contexts may consist of possible images of the 'competitive environment', the state of the market ('market analysis'), or of consumer or user profiles. Preparations for a launch thus comprise achieving and displaying a version of a product ('the offer'), profiling contexts for the launch ('consumers', 'partners', 'competitors', 'distributors', etc.), as well as re-articulating what the very corporation is like.[19] Corporations characterise the intertwining of these entities as having certain properties favourable or unfavourable to a launch.

Having started with the proposition that a launch in practice is best seen as a series of encounters, the analysis of such practices of launch at Virtual World suggests the idea central to this chapter that these communicative occasions constitute how a new technology may be spoken about. This approach can be summarised as the creation of *tellable stories* about emerging technologies. As argued elsewhere (Simakova, 2007; Simakova and Neyland, 2008), corporate participants try to create and defend *tellable* versions of possible relationships between the corporation, market/users and product involved in a particular launch. A tellable story can be described in terms of a narrative connecting particular attributes of technology constituencies inside and outside of an organisation; as such, a tellable story 'narrates boundaries, relations, agency and identities for entities' (Simakova and Neyland, 2008: 96). From this point of view, and returning to the initial proposition made in the chapter, framing accountability relations around socio-technical encounters becomes a matter of practical concern for participants who aim to create 'narratives which turn out to be sufficiently compelling to draw together and hold together constituencies of people and things focused around a new technology' (Simakova and Neyland, 2008: 97). How was Virtual World's tellable RFID story accomplished? And what was the role of technical demonstration in the creation of RFID tellable stories?

Preparing a product launch

As discussed earlier in this chapter, the task for marketing managers in preparing a product launch can be described in terms of the organisation of encounters between the product and various constituents inside and outside of the company. The discursive framings of such encounters may be achieved through product description and slogans; demonstrations; coached speakers and sales force; and the results of technology trials solidified into 'case studies'. The launch plan specified marketing events and 'marcom materials' that needed to be 'launched' to the preselected audiences at certain dates in the financial year. Such events and materials included a guided tour or a demonstration for certain pre-booked customers; verified and tested messages used in press releases and pitches; a prepared sales force who could sound knowledgeable and confident about the RFID proposition; and a selection of specialist journals whose editors engaged expert writers and whose readers could appreciate the hi-tech and business issues involved.

One of the central concerns associated with the launch, which was articulated in the interviews and in the working conversations, was the practical steps to achieving the credibility of Virtual World's expertise in RFID. Creating the RFID story linking the company's name and the RFID technology in a 'unique' way[20] meant for the marketers achieving a credible statement, as opposed to a 'wild . . . statement, with nothing, nothing behind it'. The credibility of a possible statement was tantamount to matching knowledge about potential recipients of the company's statement with claims about the properties of the RFID product. Such claims would need to anticipate and take into account possible criticisms. Shaping up statements about RFID, marketers got involved in the gradual work of recognising and categorising audiences. The need to create statements appropriate for Virtual World entailed an addition to the team. Abigail, a PR[21] manager, was invited to join in. One of the public relations manager's tasks was to define the ways of talking about the new product to the press.

The broad group of journalists ('journos') was considered a special, and a difficult, category of the public to engage with. The 'riskiness' of this group resided in the anticipation of a possible negative statement about the company. Journalists were viewed as a group who follow the motto 'bad news sells'. Technology and business analysts, in turn, were placed in a similarly 'difficult' but 'more mature' and 'easier to deal with' category. Analysts were believed to be more interested in 'knowledge itself' than in generating news. Marketers said they were trying 'to be careful in what exactly we are trying to say'. This meant that marketers were trying to achieve knowledge of the audiences to ensure the desired interpretations. Target audiences' interests were captured and operationalised for occasions of briefings and pitches in the forms of questions and answers (Q&As).

Analytical firms were the audience of considerable concern for the RFID marketing managers. Gartner, Yankee Group, Forrester and others publish authoritative reports assessing companies' strengths and weaknesses and establish hierarchies of the IT market players. It is considered prestigious, for example, to be among the top ten in the rankings, or to get into the 'leaders' corner' of what is known as the 'magic quadrant' of Gartner's rating.

Virtual World had received coverage interpreted by managers as negative with regard to some of its products in the 'advanced technologies' category. According to the managers, avoiding a similar failure was important in the case of RFID. Marketers maintain that the position of a firm in the rankings is not a straightforward reflection of its performance or its product quality. They believe that rankings can and should be influenced. The task of an 'analyst relations' manager is to manage Virtual World's position in the analytical publications. An analyst relations manager, such as TonyS, had to be constantly available to analysts. The analysts could have Tony's mobile number and could ring him up whenever they needed more or new information. He also scheduled some update calls once in a while with the analysts on his list, for thirty minutes or so, and these were in addition to the regular corporate analyst briefings and press conferences associated with new product launches, updates and emergencies. Tony needed to be constantly updated about the company's business and its new products. He had to have a clear view, coordinated with his peers and seniors in the company, of what could be made public and what could not. He admitted some possible influence on the rankings through the corporation's own efforts to establish a relationship with the analytical firms.[22] Virtual World, according to the manager, was one of the major subscribers to such analytical materials, 'spending millions' on the reports. This, according to the manager, worked well as an incentive for the analytical firms 'to speak good about us'.

One of the main questions the marketing managers expected from analysts concerned demonstration of 'proof points', or the display of Virtual World's connections to key players in the industry. It was important to show that Virtual World was well connected to key industries, universities, standards bodies and governments in 'the RFID space'. Those other players had to be represented as supporting and appreciating Virtual World's effort and expertise. Some companies were approached with requests to provide a reference for Virtual World. Virtual World had committed to a number of trials with a few enthusiastic 'early technology adopters' who volunteered, or were persuaded, to explore the business benefits of RFID. The results of such trials would provide for the possibility of writing RFID success stories (including Virtual World's own) and thus contributing to the RFID market 'take off'. According to the marketing managers, the trials did not signal successful outcomes, being not 'in favour of our current value proposition'. Seeking 'validation' from other powerful companies was considered crucial for a successful statement to be presented to analysts. In other words, a network of supporters of the RFID project was created in order to be demonstrated to those who could make an authoritative decision about the potential of Virtual World's RFID product.

An important part of the corporate talk concerned conversations that could be held once an account manager[23] entered a prospective customer organisation with an RFID story. To define the outcome of future interactions, the marketing managers, through consultations with sales, were trying to articulate answers to questions such as 'What do you expect to see in customer engagements?' and 'What should I plan on hearing or what will I soon be hearing from my customers?' The RFID talk anticipated the 'concerns', 'thoughts', 'motivations', 'religions', 'fears' and 'responsibilities' of existing or putative customers, as well as potential scenarios of possible engagements. Knowledge of 'what's on the customer's mind', their 'careabouts' and 'pain points' was defined as a prerequisite for a sales manager before an engagement would happen. Through the lens of the marketing tasks, the way of referring to a customer organisation as an *account* usefully reflects the marketers' effort to equip sales managers with stories (such as, for example, elevator pitches) that would help to win a customer in communicative events.

As in the previous chapter, encounters with customers are thought of as occasions on which some pre-designed narratives can influence the outcome of such an encounter. So, according to such thinking, it is certain ways of talking about the corporation, and the technology, that make the customer accounts responsive to the pitches. Such folk belief in the power of communication entails competing ideas about the ways to produce and perform accounts: sales managers' secrets of how to achieve a deal, marketing teams' different ways of advertising technologies. For marketing managers, one detail of their task to create the winning accounts (both narratives, and customers) was about the difficulty of finding out what exactly happens in the conversations between a sales manager and his or her customers. Sales managers were known for their unwillingness to disclose the content of a deal apart from its financial outcome; attempts to gain such information through an intranet forum where managers were invited to share their experience did not succeed; and there was no mechanism to make such disclosure compulsory. The knowledge of what's going on in the accounts, however, was rendered an essential element for achieving successful marketing strategies for RFID.

The 'novelty' of RFID for Virtual World was described in terms of the need to start talking to different professional groups inside the customer companies. This aligned with the fashionable-at-that-moment corporate sales strategy built on the idea of different ways of talking about the product by a company-buyer's management and its technical staff. These audiences were categorised in terms of 'business decision-makers' (or BDMs) versus 'technical decision-makers' (or TDMs) in customer organisations.

As one of the first steps to bring potential customers into the RFID story, Virtual World commissioned a study and a white paper from one of the analytical firms. Writing the white paper thus involved interviewing a number of key technology adopters whose testimonies would contribute to 'validation' of Virtual World's RFID proposition. The paper was to be made available to various audiences through the corporate website, at conferences and expos, in exchanges with account managers, and so forth. Writing the paper also entailed a number of iterations between the analysts and Virtual World's managers, who advised the analysts to accomplish a certain number of interviews and to change the wording. The analysts' contributions, however, were not reflected in the paper's authorship; it was presented as an independent study. Writing the white paper was seen as a way to gain greater credibility earned through the involvement of the current and potential RFID technology adopters, who, as members of the 'very industry', speaking of their RFID experience and expectations, would help to persuade other prospective customers: 'If it [the research] is compelling, so maybe it gives us an opportunity to say something to the industry. Because again it's a validation . . . *not by us,* but by the very industry that we are talking to' (a PR manager).

Writing and publishing the paper entailed certain difficulties, which the managers framed in terms of a timing question. It seemed to be too early to seek support or professional advice from business analysts, who were themselves in learning mode. The results of the 'messaging testing' to solicit the opinions of hi-tech analysts and customers were interpreted as showing that neither potential customers nor business analysts yet showed due understanding of the relationship between RFID and Virtual World's expertise. According to the focus group results, the business leaders just did not see IT as a potential solution for their business problems when RFID was deployed. In this situation, going public with an 'aggressive' statement, according to the marketing managers, would make the company look 'pretty stupid' in the eyes of those 'not in the know'. This did not, however, mean passively waiting for the moment when analysts' knowledge would become mature enough to produce an expert writing of Virtual World's RFID statements and readers would be able to apply informed judgement to these statements. The corporation actively engaged in educating the RFID partners and analysts. The moments of 'enlightenment' sometimes happened 'coincidentally' when Virtual World commissioned research from an analytical firm: 'We need to get them, you know, think [*sic*] about that . . . And that started to happen, for example, I think, interestingly it happened to people that we talked to when we were putting the brief together for the research, which is quite fun' (a PR manager).

Preparing for an engagement with audiences, the marketers' reasoning was about constructing knowledge of, and influencing, the accountability relations they were going to enter while presenting their proposition to various groups: who will say what in reaction to their statement; how they can achieve certain reactions and avoid others; what kind of allies they need to have inscribed into their technology in order to achieve recognition and credibility. In order to find its own 'unique' voice in RFID, the work inside the corporation concerned identifying, recruiting, or avoiding relevant members of the industry and 'external' groups, partners and competitors, or, in other words, drawing the boundary between 'us' and 'not us'. Speaking forth, articulating connections between the entities of a discursive formation (Virtual World, RFID, analysts, audiences), was achieved through anticipating and actively providing for possible 'positive' and 'favourable' interpretations.

Tentative launch

Narrating a PR strategy

Earlier in this chapter I introduced the notion of the *tellable story* in order to conceptualise a bounded attempt in articulation, in speaking forth to certain audiences in marketing. I contended that the tellability of narratives needed to be understood as an ongoing accomplishment. This section examines the nature of practical judgement related to the production of tellable stories in technology marketing. I will discuss in what sense the performance of a marketing community, the boundaries of marketing knowledge, is a part of articulation. I take a particular example of what was termed by the participants a 'soft launch' in the course of preparations for a 'real' product launch. In February 2005 the RFID marketing managers acknowledged that they were under pressure to go public with a corporate statement, but at the same time they recognised the lack of any appreciative audiences. What can participants' deliberations tell us about how RFID was made a tellable story?

The marketing managers envisaged the growing interest in RFID in various industries due to the 'buzz' around it created by media and various RFID interest groups, not without contributions from Virtual World itself. Encounters with press, business analysts and customers were perceived as becoming increasingly more likely, but without a clear vision about who exactly the story should be told to. 'RFID is a moving target at the moment,' Abigail, the PR manager, said on starting an interview. The interview was a means for me to enter the side of the preparations for the launch that were not visible to me. Although I was involved in the RFID activities as the demo project manager (see next chapter), the PR activities were not accessible to me, if not to say that they were concealed, as if nothing else apart from the RFID demo was going on. When we finally discussed the possibility of an interview about PR, Alex and Abigail said they had been working on a PR strategy and presented it to me as a product of their thinking, a carefully designed set of documents and ideas they had nurtured together before making them known to the other (marketing) managers and the researcher. The interview was set up as our special meeting with Abigail, who was in principle accessible for more casual conversations, but who preferred to talk about the PR strategy under these particular arrangements, unusually welcoming a voice recorder. This was one of the most clearly recorded interviews[24] during my field-work, designed to *reveal* the PR strategy to the ethnographer. Thinking of tech-nology in terms of *audiences* ('RFID is a moving *target*') was presented to me as a special prerogative and skill of marketing/PR managers, a kind of precious expertise, which, as I will show below, was recognised by marketing managers as receiving little appreciation in the corporation. The materials analysed below are based on the interview with Abigail, on more informal interactions with Alex, and on RFID team meetings I became increasingly involved with after the first three months with RFID.[25]

As above, six months before the agreed launch deadline the marketing team found itself in an uncomfortable situation in which it needed to tell a public story about RFID, but at the same time could formulate a number of reasons why it was somehow not exactly the right time to go public. As the managers acknowledged, the corporation needed to tell a story first of all because of the fear of being left behind its competitors and losing the element of novelty in the eyes of its potential customers: 'If you take into account what our competitors are doing around RFID, before they are going public, we can't be quiet.' The marketers were also aware of the sales force's concerns about being left without answers when their customers approached them with questions about RFID: 'They want to know *what do I sell?*, so it would be great to create noise and awareness about it' (a PR manager). And finally, the managers acknowledged the pressure from other corporate groups: 'Everyone got quite excited at the beginning of the fiscal [year]: *"RFID is gonna happen", "Next best thing", "We gonna get something out there", rush, rush, rush, turn to PR,* you know, *"let's PR this immediately"'* (a PR manager).

At the same time, the marketing managers were insisting on the impossibility of 'doing something credible' unless certain criteria had been fulfilled. One of the major worries of marketers was achieving at least some kind of presence of the RFID product (the RFID demonstration discussed in the next chapter was meant to become the product). Showing a kind of material bounded entity was considered integral to achieving 'credibility', and the lack of it was seen as a major impediment to the launch. The creation of the RFID demonstration was Alex's responsibility, and meant liaising with and persuading his colleagues inside the company as well as Virtual World's strategic partners to work towards assembling a working demonstration of and specifications for the RFID product. The dialogue with the customers also seemed to be premature because of the lack of a firmly formulated value proposition and the 'actual' availability of the RFID product through the reseller channels.

As opposed to the 'let's PR first' approach, marketing managers claimed they had *methods* for capturing the right moment, the right publics, and the right content for a public announcement. Abigail, the PR manager, said that 'a sanity check' in the form of a 'SWOT'[26] analysis would help them to locate the pressing demands and interests coming from various groups, including those in the company, and to anticipate possible customer, press and analyst reactions. The marketing managers also emphasised the important role of a document called a 'go-to-market checklist', which enumerated criteria for the possibility of product launch. The document was created in order to promote marketing knowledge to other members of the corporation. The PR manager called it a 'killer slide', meaning that it incorporates all possible criteria of readiness for product launch that should be accepted by all other participants involved in RFID. Each red or green cylinder box on the slide represented a marketing task being accomplished in cooperation with other groups in the organisation. By the time I spoke to Abigail and Alex in February 2005, only one out of fifteen boxes was ready: the green one containing the 'top 20 most difficult questions' expected from journalists and analysts. Only after all boxes had been marked green could the 'GTM' (or 'go-to-market') plan be finalised.

Abigail explained that they used the checklist to seek and promote internal understanding of the challenges marketers faced in preparing a public announcement and to persuade the other relevant groups inside the company to take responsibility for cleaning up the 'bottom-line' corporate RFID realities before a statement could be issued: 'to educate non-marketing experienced people inside the company on what they had to get right before they were ready for PR' (a PR manager). Indeed, getting an internal 'executive commitment' from and an understanding of the 'marketing realities' by Virtual World's top managers was considered crucial for the launch success. In one meeting Alex showed the GTM slide, explaining that the majority of the elements of the process – selected in red – were still in need of approval from the currently disagreeing top managers, with a minor proportion of those elements where a commitment was secured marked green: 'until reds become greens,' he explained, 'there is nothing to talk about.' The documents I discuss contain claims made by marketing managers about a discursive formation that would potentially provide for a 'positive' interpretation: 'So, the purpose of this . . . checklist, and in a way it applies to all of our RFID story, is really because there are a couple of things you kinda need to . . . at least you need to have fairly baked before you go and turn to the outside world' (a PR manager, 8 February 2005).

The role of these documents as presented to me by the marketing managers is interesting from the ethnographic point of view. Alex and Abigail presented the sheets to me as 'the most important take-aways' from the field. The documents were their best achievements, they said, in educating other people in the marketing thinking. They hoped the sheets would provide a good representation of how marketing is done at Virtual World (forgetting, perhaps, that the company would have to be anonymised). Having acknowledged how the documents got into the ethnographer's hands, I have included some descriptions of the documents here as an example of marketing knowledge. A note to the reader: this is done not in order to illustrate the 'factual' account of the 'necessary conditions' for articulation of a tellable story. Indeed, the 'let's PR first' and the more cautious approach advocated by the marketing managers somewhat blurred later as the encounters with customers and other audiences where RFID was mentioned became more frequent. Rather, presenting the marketing strategy in the description of an *ethnographic* episode opens up questions about the performance of organisational relations and boundaries of marketing knowledge. The function of the documents in attempts to persuade the 'non-marketing' people (including me as ethnographer) shows that boundary work around marketing knowledge was an integral part of articulation. The alternative claims available in the organisation contesting marketing knowledge of possible interpretations of Virtual World's RFID discourses ('Let's PR it immediately!') contended that positive interpretation might be achieved by means of attracting immediate attention. From this perspective, speaking forth about RFID was not an outcome of careful judgements regarding the readiness of technology 'bottom lines'. How was the contest between these various claims about tellability practically resolved?

A first RFID story

Deliberating about the content of RFID-related statements, and of the timing and circumstances of narration, the marketers were trying to manage the uncertainties associated with the lack of a definitive RFID discourse that Virtual World could project to the outside world, the perceived lack of the firm's knowledge about the audiences, as well as of what these audiences would know about RFID and how they would judge Virtual World's potential to show expertise in RFID. They referred to the way they were juggling the simultaneous impossibility and necessity of launching the product as 'gaining a marketing momentum', 'filling the vacuum', trying to 'connect what will be in August, when we launch, and what will be in April, with this first announcement [of the Partner programme]'. Matching the statements and the audiences, expanding their presence in the RFID space, and defining it while at the same time addressing new readers, the marketers were trying to avoid any kind of 'aggressive' definitions and propositions, saying that it's rather 'education, really, it's not an announcement, it's not a launch': 'We will try to attract Retail and Logistic media, you know, *what's new in Retail at Virtual World,* and have some murky "new thing"' (a PR manager).

In February 2005 the RFID marketing manager observed that the pressure to launch the product was escalating. Sales managers wanted to be able to answer customers' questions about RFID or to initiate conversations about the increasingly fashionable technology. A decision was made to attempt a product launch, even if the bottom-line requirements had not been fulfilled – not a 'real' launch, it was said, rather a 'soft' launch. The managers invented oxymoronic expressions in order to account for what was happening, such as 'quiet announcement', or 'quiet launch'. These are examples of discursive constructs portraying tensions between meeting the requirements from different groups inside and outside of the corporation, in accommodating various anticipations of positive and negative interpretations: 'Quiet launch . . . is no launch . . . bizarre . . . hmm . . . internal launch [laughs]' (a PR manager).

One of the first press releases was devised for the occasion of Virtual World's joining an RFID Expo (see the next chapter for a more detailed discussion). The Expo opening was considered one of the RFID 'soft launches', to which only partners and sponsors were invited. The PR manager writing the press release[27] had to take into consideration a number of circumstances and anticipated audiences' reactions. Abigail mentioned that she was 'using the original scope of words' found in the Expo's self-description on the website. She also mentioned the difficulties she faced while trying to provide a description of the purpose of Virtual World's engagement with the Expo. She needed to take into account a possible negative reaction of the standards bodies who might become suspicious of the word 'testing' [of RFID devices] taking place at the Expo. The word 'testing' *(against what?)* would allegedly indicate a lack of loyalty to the standards currently being endorsed by the standards body. She needed to 'steer away from this concept'. She was also working on the first Virtual World byline on RFID. But taken together, all these activities, she said, were 'not an announcement, not a launch':

> So, that's the kind of stage we're in at the moment in terms of . . . softly, softly, we put small announcements out . . . a lot of these are specialised publications, they don't have skills and resource within their editorial capacity to be able to write something specialised about IT and RFID. So, I'm working with a writer, who's actually a freelance journalist, and he's producing our first byline actually, which will be placed in a UK magazine called 'Logistics . . . Manager' or something very . . . hm . . . interesting. So, this is just general visibility, really, nothing too aggressive.
>
> (A PR manager)

The first 'bylined' article (authored by a media company and not by Virtual World) in *Logistics Manager*[28] tried to discursively resolve the tensions between widely reported discouraging results of the first retail industry pilots involving RFID implementation in 2004 and the desire to move forward with RFID. Members of Virtual World suggested that resolution would emerge from the company's expertise in network applications since implementations of the technology were deemed to produce large volumes of data related to tracing and tracking products and goods, in need of management. This was an area where Virtual World could claim some expertise.

The internal constituency of marketers was quick to acknowledge (and celebrate) the success of the article that was published. The article had proved to be compelling: 'As the magazine is now published we are offering the article to be repackaged by other EMEA press titles.' Subsequently, small sets of audiences could be identified and offered the story. The next story was on its way. It would narrate another bottom line: Virtual World's participation in the board of EPC Global, an important standards-governing body: 'Next byline due will focus on standards featuring Moses Mansfield.' The public relations manager sent an email to an internal constituency termed 'All' – a list of those interested and engaged in RFID at Virtual World. The email leaves room for concerns that the other participants might have about the content and dissemination of the article ('Any questions please let me know').

> Dear All
> Please find a copy of a bylined article created by EMEA which the UK PR team placed in Lgistics [*sic*] Manager magazine. As the magazine is now published we are offering the article to be repackaged by other EMEA press titles. Next byline due will focus on standards featuring Moses Mnsfield [*sic*]. Any questions please let me know.
> Best regards
> Abigail
> Abigail Smith
> Corporate Relations Manager, Vertical Markets, EMEA
> dl: +44 XXX XX XXX
> mobile: +44 XXX XX XXX
> email: asmith@virtual_world.com

Preparing and disseminating such stories is an everyday task of marketing and public relations managers in corporations. This means staying up to date with current ways of talking about technologies, defining what are perceived as fashionable trends, being in tune with the corporate discourse, or developing means to resist all those. At the same time, as the next chapter will discuss, this work is contingent on the everyday opportunities and practical options that are constantly recognised, adopted and defended as the marketing way of getting things done.

Discussion

During the early stages of the development of the RFID discourse, the participants were especially concerned about the construction of credible corporate
statements about RFID in the situation of uncertainty about the properties and
potential of the technology. Product launch was thought to be the culmination of
their attempts to evaluate potential benefits of the new technology and to create
understandings of how to market the product. Preparations for RFID product
launch exemplified a number of folk assumptions about the nature of socio-
technical change, and construed a particular version of marketing knowledge that
comprises a set of practices of, beliefs about, and organisational commitments to
socio-technical ordering. RFID technology was made amenable to corporate
management processes and practices that purport to prepare the moment of going
public with a proprietary technological offer and expertise attached. Such work
entailed struggling with the indeterminacy of the content of the new technology
and the constituents performing the cultural discourse of RFID both inside and
outside of the corporation as an important feature of everyday deliberations.

Some corporate narratives were accepted as ready to go public, while others
were not. I discussed the tentative, careful ways in which such stories were
created by Virtual World's managers. The deliberations on the appropriateness of
a corporate story for a particular moment in time entailed an organisational
dispute. Some claims concerning timeliness, content and audiences were attributed specifically to marketers, delineating their professional knowledge. What is
RFID? What kind of discourse should Virtual World adopt? And when? Virtual
World marketers answered these questions through accomplishing folk sociology
and folk ethnography, as well as through proposing a methodology that had to
find supporters in the corporation. This work was accomplished through contesting knowledge claims regarding possible interpretations and boundary work
defining marketing knowledge. Making sense of alternative interpretations in the
effort to make certain interpretations stick is not a straightforward process.
Alternative interpretations and unexpected audiences always remain a possibility.
The practical ways of getting the corporate statements and their audiences to
'hang together' were achieved through performing the corporate ritual of product
launch.

The marketing managers' ways of creating credible corporate statements notably included the work of categorising and ordering, or of 'configuring' (Woolgar,
1991a), the audiences for technologies marketed by the corporation. Some of the
general audiences were already preconfigured (known, described), to some
extent, in the folk theorising of launch that relied on certain audience categories
(such as analyst firms, peer industries, journalists). Their voices were to be
brought into (or avoided in) the Virtual World tellable RFID story through the
articulation of corporate narratives, such as the white paper. Other audiences
recognised as specific for the RFID technology (such as logistics managers, or the
standards body) had to be identified and addressed with specially crafted wording, such as in the first byline, or in the press release.

Achieving a tellable story was equivalent to achieving recognition of audiences, constructing social categorisations and knowledge claims regarding possible interpretations of artefacts by various interpretive communities (Fish, 1980). The next chapter is now moving into a discussion of further deliberations on the RFID product launch inside Virtual World that concerned creating and displaying a technical demonstration.

7   RFID 'theatre of the proof'

The organisational politics of technology demonstration

As deliberations on the content of Virtual World's RFID talk went on, the idea of having a working demo as prerequisite for launch emerged as an element of the corporate tellable story. Technology demonstration – an element of the launch 'master plan' document – became a notable matter of concern for the marketing managers. Demonstration (or 'demo') occupied a special section of the master plan as a set of actions leading towards the final version of the demo. The actions listed included the creation of the demo concept and design; approval of the concept; identifying and engaging with a demo contractor; demo production 'to first draft', and consequently to its 'final version'; as well as installation of the demo in a showroom. Responsibility for the demo production was assigned to two managers: Alex, the RFID manager, and his senior. Other managers and engineers involved were listed in brackets.

The inclusion of the demonstration as a necessary element of RFID launch was the outcome of an organisational dispute. Possessing a working technology that could be shown in operation was discussed in terms of the kinds of interpretations it might receive. The organisational politics of demonstration notably involved deliberations on the persuasive powers of demonstration, and judgements about what counts as good corporate conduct. The two polar viewpoints that I shall discuss differed in an important way: while the first opinion attached little importance to the existence of a working technology for initiating corporate conversations with the outside world, the second position defended the need to display a working demo before any public communication could happen.[1]

Some managers suggested that the corporation should 'PR RFID immediately'[2] rather than wait until the time-consuming work of building a demo was completed. This step was perceived by some as a useful means to ensure that the company did not appear laggard in joining the newly fashionable RFID movement in the telecom industries, as well as a means to gain leadership in potential markets by capturing the attention of the technology's 'early adopters'. Other managers perceived a different possible interpretation, and defended the need to produce a demonstration kit first. The latter viewpoint was supported by a number of arguments that construed a particular world of the telecom industry of which Virtual World was presented as being a part.

First, the idea of having the demo ready aligned well with the 'demo-ing' tradition in telecom industries.[3] Demonstrating was considered an important element of corporate life. Virtual World's CEO was a great believer in well-prepared and performed demonstrations, often providing demonstrations himself for the corporation's own sales force. His performances were available on the corporate intranet as video files. Managers coming back from corporate meetings in California spoke about the CEO's new performances with inspiration. Sales managers were advised to encourage their customers to attend demonstrations provided by the company under the auspices of the corporate 'demonstration programme'.[4] Technology showrooms dedicated to demonstration tours and seminars were arranged as luxury executive halls also offering fine cuisine, and were staffed by engineers who guided customers through. The effect of exclusivity of access to technological demonstrations was reinforced by separation of the halls from the rest of the premises by a transparent wall displaying lush furniture inside. A special swipe card was required to access the demonstration facility[5] and, formally, one needed to sign up for a demonstration tour in advance. The US counterparts were also reported to have a working RFID demonstration. Virtual World's CEO performed an RFID pitch in a sales meeting, and his performance featured the material design, thus setting up good practice.

Second, the particular marketing managers with whom I worked opposed going public without a working demo and were ready to defend their rationale. The marketers were especially concerned with an anticipated public reaction to what could be perceived as 'empty' statements unsupported by any kind of proven expertise. In their view, this would be an example of poor industrial conduct that could affect the corporate reputation negatively. Having a demo on display thus had two main advantages for aligning with common ideas of what it means to achieve good corporate conduct.[6] First, Virtual World could report on the existing product to media, analysts and customers, who would portray the corporation as a good industry citizen. Building the demo would require liaising with various partners in order to display the partnerships in public statements, showing implementation of technical solutions in Virtual World's versions of RFID. This measure had to be taken in anticipation of analysts' questions about corporate expertise with RFID, and had to be supported with testimonies from other members of the industry. Second, the demo had to demonstrate that certain 'customer issues' could be solved by using Virtual World's expertise. The precise content of RFID commercial propositions associated with the demo had yet to be developed. The first RFID demo rationale relied on very general terms, such as saying that the demonstrations would show how technological architecture can 'leverage the company's core expertise' or 'align with' some other currently popular technological propositions made by Virtual World, for example open standards, or wireless solutions. As the rationale document specified, RFID demonstrations consisting of two prototypes with different functionalities would serve the purpose of 'demonstrating Virtual World's proof points'. Customer representatives would not only hear about the advantages of the technical solution but would also be given an opportunity to witness the technology at work, and to 'tinker' with a demo in order to have first-hand experience of the working technology.

The RFID launch by Virtual World was thus construed as a case for putting a demo on display before going public. Displaying and reporting on a demo that was ready to be shown in operation was presented as the 'bottom line' for any public statement. It reflected a wider societal assumption that material demonstration would make corporate statements more durable. Being a 'good industry citizen' thus appeared, according to the winning ideology, to hinge on the company's ability to demonstrate the material practices of building technology as a proof of corporate expertise. The contrary, 'Let's PR first' argument assumed that the developing technology discourse could rely on a different set of conventions that circumvent the materialist assumption, and could help the corporation to assemble a constituency of potential adopters curious about the new technology. As it turned out, this was not perceived as good corporate practice. The communities enrolled to substantiate the demo-ing strategy clearly outweighed the 'early adopters'. As I will discuss below, the two practical strategies for going public, though separated at the beginning of the launch activities, became somewhat blurred later when building the demo intermingled with communicating to external audiences.

The organisational politics of demonstration at Virtual World prompts certain critical questions about the existing analytic treatment of demonstration in the corporate discourse. Both historical[7] and contemporary analyses of technical demonstration often rely on the observable presence of a demonstrable technology, and the activities of scripting and de-scripting a technical object. Material presence and the ability of a technical object to influence the way innovation becomes spoken about is seen as a necessary condition for a successful demonstration that educates and constrains witnesses' readings of new technology. Thus, much emphasis is placed on the central role of a technical object in operation for the dissemination of a technical artefact. Bloomfield and Vurdubakis (2002: 120) stress the centrality of demonstration for corporate conversations among actors engaged in trade show exchanges: 'cometh the moment, cometh the artefact.' Hence, success or failure is often explained in terms of the performative content of a demonstration.

Much is attributed in these works to the creation of a persuasive moment when 'influencing the psychology and atmosphere surrounding the emergence of new technologies' (Lampel, 2001: 304) takes place to manage the uncertainty associated with innovations and to produce durable interpretations. These researchers try to dissect demonstration 'scripts' (Akrich, 1992), in order to identify their narrative content, such as 'heroic content of time and space, revolutionary breakthroughs, magic acts, or the triumphal celebrations of a new technology' (Lampel, 2001: 305). Similarly, Bloomfield and Vurdubakis view demonstration in terms of the 'construction of expert knowledge and client ignorance' (2002: 116). Their analysis scrutinises demonstrations in terms of representing technology in a persuasive and favourable way for a company, or 'the symbolic rendering of the world into a form amenable to prediction and control' (ibid.: 118). Smith (2009) stresses that a demonstration is a manifestation of multiply framed experience and ways of knowing, which is 'intended to afford controlled freedoms' (Smith, 2009: 475). In brief, this perspective seeks to explain the construction of credibility and public acceptance of technologies by ascribing what can be called certain *persuasive affordances* to material objects: 'one advantage of material artefacts over the written or spoken word is that they enable the physical construction of, and immersion in, such imagined worlds' (Bloomfield and Vurdubakis, 2002: 121).

The perspective taken in this chapter suspends for analytical purposes the assumption that material artefacts have an inherent persuasive capacity to motivate desired action.[8] This is done in order to problematise that assumption as a managerial belief and focus of deliberations, rather than treating it as an accepted fact of life. One way to do so is to show the contestable nature and cultural and organisational boundaries around demonstration and its persuasiveness: does everyone agree on what counts as a persuasive performance, or on whose strategy is better? From this perspective, one can also ask: what kind of work (design, assessments) goes into deciding what counts as the adequate persuasive powers of a demonstration as material artefact?

To start answering these questions, I can note that Bloomfield and Vurdubakis and others have paid attention to *discursive* negotiations over whether a technology is good enough for participants' purposes at hand, in reference to objects existing somewhere else (such as, for example, a future-shaping Self-Stocking Refrigerator existing in a lab far away but not at the location in question) as an element of demonstrating cutting-edge innovations. Quattrone and Hopper (2006) also observe of the SAP system that the acronym (which stands for Systems, Applications and Products, an integrated software system for resource planning) was important for the work of social ordering in conversations with potential users (also see Woolgar, 1997). The acronym was a part of technology talk, of referring to the system as a material entity, and was used to account for what it means to act with it. The acronym provided for emerging definitions of its users and uses, and other constituencies, but without the presence of any material object. The remainder of this chapter further questions the role of demonstration in a technology launch by asking to what extent it mattered, and how it was made to matter, for the RFID demo that the material object was shown in operation.[9] What was the role of the material technology in the organisation of RFID witnessing and the construction of RFID corporate discourse? In what sense was the technology rendered demonstrable and accountable?

Holding marketing and engineering together

Corporate documents emphasised that Virtual World's goal was not to become a manufacturer of the RFID product itself. Instead, it was to use technical components purchased from other manufacturers. The corporation sought to demonstrate its expertise in network data management with RFID systems that had already been adopted by customers. Due to the strategic absence of a proprietary

RFID product, creating the demo required selecting components in relation to which the company would display its expertise. This task could not be delegated to engineers alone, who mostly liaised with their technical colleagues in potential partner companies. Rather, it was assumed to be a marketing job. In order to assemble and make sense of the relevant elements of the RFID demo, Alex, the RFID marketing manager, initiated conversations with other groups in the company, including engineers. Alex, who had an MA in marketing focused on branding, confessed that he had little technical knowledge. He hoped that the engineers would carry out the technical work (in terms of negotiating the demo functionalities), but he was unable to fully avoid technical details.

Preparing the demo thus depended on identifying and recruiting relevant expertise within and outside of the corporation. It involved maintaining interest and support for the idea of RFID within the company by 'building up a community around the project'. The required task included collecting relevant expertise, learning a number of technical details and getting in touch with partner organisations who marketed RFID technology in order to explore interoperability. The marketing manager also tried to identify and establish good working relationships with 'independent third parties' such as an educational centre or a governmental agency that administered radio frequency standards. In line with the earlier suggestion that a launch is not a linear process but instead involves a set of encounters, negotiations, opportunistic actions and assessments, the process can be described as development-through-launch rather than develop-then-launch.[10]

Building the demo required that roles and responsibilities for implementing the project be introduced, and I was invited to become project manager. The demonstration was established as a potential outcome of a collective effort, including my own efforts, to the extent that the ethnographic 'output' depended on the ethnographer-as-project-manager's ability to keep the project alive. The development of the demonstration kit exhibited accountability at work as the intertwining of multiple, intersecting constituencies and audiences in decision-making.

One of the main tasks was to move a demo that had been developed in the United States to London showrooms. John, a US-based engineer, was recruited to provide technical background for the EMEA version of the demo to Paul, a London-based engineer responsible for showroom installations. The communications between the two engineers flowed as email exchanges on our laptop screens. John developed a version of Virtual World's RFID demonstration that had already been successfully shown on a couple of occasions in the United States. But, according to him, the demo design required constant revision and improvements. It was not clear which of several versions of the US demo had to be replicated. The selected version also turned out to be highly contextualised, in terms of negotiating radio wavelength standards and technical devices, and thus was not easily mobile. The engineer's continuing reports on the demo modifications did not fascinate Alex, whose marketing concern was ensuring the availability of a working version of the demo by the launch deadline.[11] He tirelessly insisted that the 'final version' of the technical documentation be forwarded from John to Paul. Alex acknowledged that the demo architecture was never static: 'the technology changes constantly, and we will need to revise the demo every two or three months.' How then was it possible to make judgements about the acceptable demo design for the moment? To achieve a final version that could be replicated and displayed, Alex figured that elements of the demo configuration that had already been used in a US show, or had already been communicated to sales managers, could be accepted as a good enough configuration for the EMEA demo kit. He was particularly interested in the technical features that John had already presented with some success to an authoritative solutions development group in the United States. In other words, the stabilisation of results achieved in other situations, for other purposes, and for other audiences, was deemed acceptable for inclusion in the demo in progress.

The RFID marketing manager reported on the demo preparation in a monthly conference call open to other members of the corporation. Conference calls of this kind can be seen as corporate rituals for signalling interest or commitment to a new initiative. The assembly of attendees changed from call to call. Marketing managers, business development managers, strategic alliance managers, technology development managers and engineers episodically joined particular calls by invitation, and some stayed on with the project. Alex was disappointed when only a few people turned up for the first monthly call in response to his widely circulated invitation. Although RFID was a hot topic in corporate shop talk, the interest in the project, Alex regretted, was not substantiated by the 'real' action of joining in the call.

Alex was trying to develop a sense of the kinds of communicative engagements in which RFID could be talked about, and of what sorts of other elements of current corporate talk could, or should, be employed. These very first attempts at 'talking RFID' in EMEA were mostly internal to the corporation, with the exception of independent business analysts who were briefed under non-disclosure agreements (and as a means to get information from the analysts). The conversing managers displayed unease with me observing their deliberations, so almost no recording was allowed. Through these partial, bounded attempts at 'talking RFID' the new technology began cropping up in corporate talk under various guises. It should not be assumed, though, that the marketing manager and his close group were the only sources of the RFID talk in the corporation. As I discussed in the previous chapter in more detail, the technology featured in the news, disseminated through a conference call from the United States in the form of a corporate educational seminar on RFID that managers were invited to join, and also featured in shop-floor conversations. Consequently, the marketing manager's task was to produce and sustain an officially authorised corporate discourse of RFID that would later become part of Virtual World's EMEA presentation of a new technical solution. Questions from those who joined the monthly updates helped Alex to identify currently popular technological propositions. In these conversations, such as the one below, different characteristics of RFID were suggested for communication to different audiences. In a meeting with David and Alain, two solutions development managers, Alex discussed different attributes of RFID in light of the different communicative events they planned to fit into the thematic talk. Consider the following fragment of the conversation in which these managers discussed 'differentiation' of Virtual World's solutions and where RFID could fit as a part of value propositions:

Alex: Is it a [data] volume discussion?

DAVID: YOU CAN APPLY THE VOLUME ARGUMENT. BUT EMPLOYEES ARE SOME-
        TIMES NOT TRAINED TO DEPLOY . . .
ALAIN: SO WE CAN SPEAK ABOUT QUALITY MANAGEMENT?
ALEX: THIS IS GREAT. WHAT ROUTINE TRAINING DO YOU HAVE WITH THE FIELD?
        CAN WE GET RFID AS AN APPLICATION INTO THIS TRAINING?
DAVID: WE CAN DO THAT. THE TRAINING IS ONCE IN TEN WEEKS. WE CAN INTRO-
        DUCE RFID INTO THAT.
ALEX: WOULD YOU LIKE SLIDES SUPPORT?
DAVID: YES, ONE TO TWO SLIDES.
ALEX: OKAY, TWO SLIDES.
DAVID: WE ALSO UPDATE ANALYSTS. ON MONDAY WE BRIEF ANALYSTS ON NEW
        SOLUTIONS.
ALEX: GOOD. MENTION RFID AS SECURITY.

As the fragment shows, sales managers anticipate subsequent conversations with their customers, and imagine presenting RFID as a 'quality management tool' (and not as a means of handling large volumes of data). Alex anticipates that analysts would be receptive to an account of RFID 'as security'. Were the logics of inclusion of certain features driven by concerns about technical design (the 'technical perspective') or rather by concerns with addressing certain audiences in communications ('the marketing perspective')?

When asked about this distinction, Alex dismissed it as rather artificial ('Both!' was his reply, as he said he was busily trying to tie 'the two' together). On the one hand, the features had to be compatible with the demo design agreed on with the engineers. On the other hand, the features should mesh well with the corporate image, technology value propositions and other products. After collecting opinions from business development and sales managers who claimed knowledge of current customer interests, Alex had to consult engineers about possibilities for including such features, such as the popular wireless capacity, into the demo design. And correspondingly, technical features were discussed in terms of their potential to sell well and look good in press releases. As an example below will illustrate, a demo had to please marketing colleagues or answer technical concerns, as well as meet anticipated customer concerns reported by sales managers.

One of the concerns was finding a producer of reader devices that could meet Virtual World's demo requirements, as well as look good as a corporate partner in the go-to-market campaign. In December 2004, BestReaders (a pseudonym), a manufacturer of RFID reader devices, announced in a press release a new version that was developed against Virtual World's interoperability standards, and that was now compatible with European radio frequency standards. Although, it was said, Virtual World's demo could operate well with a reader device based on US frequency standards, an EU-standards-based reader promised easier adoption and deployment in the EMEA regions. BestReaders was recommended to Alex by John as one such producer. Marketing managers in both companies contacted each other. The partnership, as an RFID marketing manager in BestReaders explained, appeared promising because of its potential to win against Solar, a common competitor of both BestReaders and Virtual World, due to its ensuring a strong technical solution and merging the customer base of the two companies. Thus, partnering with BestReaders seemed to satisfy the requirements of achieving working demo functionality and helping marketers to take advantage of presenting BestReaders and Virtual World in public statements as partners. Alex's task was now twofold: to acquire a reader prototype from the BestReaders supply division and to persuade BestReaders to become an official partner under certain conditions. The technical content of the demo now needed to be made visible through textual and visual elements. The managers began discussing that BestReaders could, for instance, put their posters together with Virtual World's in trade shows: 'overlapping design will demonstrate a joint working solution.'

Locations, audiences and selling cycles

In parallel with the tasks of developing the demo and achieving partnership agreements, Alex tried to find and validate locations, or venues, to install the showcases. The task implied justifying their selection and persuading colleagues that the chosen locations would be a 'great showcasing environment'. Alex engaged in exploring possibilities through visiting various technology expos, as well as technology business seminars and conferences. Some organisers of such activities were invited in with sponsorship propositions, which were evaluated by Alex and his boss. Locations not only had to be chosen in view of their access or capacity to provide technical support to host the demos, but also were discussed and defended as elements of Virtual World's tellable story about how RFID could be differentially included in the selling pitches.

In January 2005 the media provided a diverse range of estimates and predictions regarding the functionality or business values of RFID. The RFID marketing manager's concern was how to speak about the technology given the apparent contestation among players in the industry about RFID capacities. Inside the corporation the managers maintained that no single opinion was considered credible enough to form the basis for a corporate public statement. Therefore, Virtual World's press campaign began with some cautious statements about the potential of RFID – on which industries could base their goals – to establish its long-term presence in the market. As a way of achieving credibility for their own commercial propositions, the RFID marketing team considered participating in an 'independent' RFID project.

Alex examined a brochure of an establishment called RFID Expo that had announced a call for sponsorship for companies wishing to install their technological demonstrations 'in a neutral environment'. Eric, the Expo Director and originator, had already spent one year persuading industries, governments and scientific labs to become sponsors of his project. Eric's proposal to the companies, which included some global players such as Virtual World, was based on the idea that a physical demonstration was a unique selling point. Exploiting the dictum 'seeing is believing', the Expo Director successfully sold sponsorship packages to IT industries. At the same time, the Expo administration was conscious about persuading potential publics that attending the demonstrations installed by the sponsors was what Michel Callon (1986) would call 'an obligatory passage point' for building up their knowledge about RFID.

Becoming an Expo sponsor, according to Alex, meant trying 'to achieve some momentum in RFID space'. In other words, engaging in RFID involved 'the continual reflexive management of social organisational boundaries and boundary relations' (Woolgar, 2004: 253). To justify a considerable sponsorship budget, Alex had to pitch participation in the RFID Expo to his seniors and other interested colleagues. His PowerPoint presentation called 'RFID Expo Leverage' emphasised that other major corporations had already joined, or were considering joining, the Expo as sponsors. Alex reported that in the previous months Expo managers had attracted a good mix of customers and vendors to their events, thus providing the basis for communication and for building up new relationships. Virtual World's marketing managers also appreciated Expo's connections with representatives from government and science, which, presumably, added credibility to Expo's positioning of itself as an 'independent RFID environment'. Visitors to RFID Expo would have needed to be convinced that RFID was a part of science-driven rather than commercial pursuit, through rhetoric about an 'independent environment' and the scientific origins of RFID.[12] Explaining that RFID Expo was under-resourced and seeking to improve its financial status, Alex reported that he had already benefited from 'some expertise on RFID' that Eric had given him, along with intelligence on the other joining sponsors from Eric as he tried to convince Virtual World to join in. Two other major corporations had already bought available 'gold' sponsorships, so, eventually, Virtual World signed a 'silver' sponsorship agreement with the Expo. This assumed a different set of showcasing opportunities in a less expensive package. In a brainstorming meeting held by the marketers to discuss the potential benefits and problems associated with the purchase of a showcase space, Alex described the sponsorship as a 'good marketing buy'.

The agreement document established a moral relation with RFID among identified actants ('the Expo', 'the Sponsor', 'the competitors') and also provided for the distribution of obligations and responsibilities regarding the technological demonstration. According to the agreement, Virtual World was entitled to a number of 'sponsor's benefits'. The important advantages of the package were described in terms of what kinds of other constituencies could be reached through becoming a sponsor. Alex stressed that participation would give Virtual World an annual showcasing opportunity, the details of which were specified in the sponsorship agreement. The Expo provided the company with a 'permanent' showcase for the calendar year 2005. That 'year of showing' included not only the presence of Virtual World's stand and the demonstrations, but also an agreed upon number of 'Virtual World's days', in which visitors would be invited specifically to explore Virtual World's RFID demos. Virtual World would also receive opportunities to nominate its speakers for events held at the Expo. Commitment to the sponsorship meant engaging in the work of persuading other members of the organisation to take part in the Expo as speakers, representatives, demonstrators and technical engineers. The 'category exclusivity' sentence in the sponsorship contract meant that 'no competitor could showcase their technology'. Juggling the elements of the sponsorship packages was a part of the politics conducted by the Expo management. Alex realised later that the principal competitor Virtual World had been careful to avoid neighbouring with on show-casing occasions during the RFID campaign had sneaked in as a business partner of a non-threatening sponsor. The last, but not least, benefit of becoming a sponsor was the opportunity to partner. Alex and his colleagues discussed the possibility of 'leveraging the venue' by persuading other Expo members to use Virtual World's expertise for their own RFID products.

While the first demo location at the Expo was assumed to be open to the general public, Alex also kept in mind the goal of convincing his counterparts at Virtual World to work more specifically with retail industries to include the RFID demonstration in their sales activities while executive customers were visiting corporate showrooms. Alex initiated the effort to install the demo at another location inside the EMEA headquarters. Although the demo designs for the show-room and for the Expo were assumed to be identical, the two venues were not considered equal. In terms of a procedure called the 'sales cycle', the 'independent environment' of the Expo suggested an earlier opportunity to bring the customer in to provide some 'general experience' with RFID, without necessarily accompanying the customer or doing a 'hard sell' as in the headquarters show-rooms. The locations were thus an important part of accounting for the value of demonstrating RFID to various groups and individuals.

Cometh the moment, cometh the artefact?

As the engineering work got under way, Alex began installing a show booth at the RFID Expo. I joined him during one of his visits to the venue to assess the configuration of Virtual World's stand. The Expo had rented a hall from a telecom company that was willing to host the innovative activity. Showing us around, Eric explained that he was not entirely happy with the location. He explained that the telecom corporation from which he was renting the hall was an 'outdated monster' that could not keep pace with the modern world, and that an association with it could negatively impact the innovative image he wanted to maintain of the RFID Expo. One of the signs of this old-fashioned attitude, according to Eric, was the company's reluctance to adopt a marketing way of thinking in terms of audiences. He also complained that, being constrained financially in the first stages of Expo development, he could not refuse the host corporation's offer of a carpet for the Expo floor. The carpet turned out to be brown, a colour Eric found depressing and not a reflection of the Expo's modern spirit.

He said the old-fashioned corporation did not recognise the requirements for creating a dynamic business environment that would possibly be better met by a blue carpet.

Upon our arrival, we found Expo managers and engineers busy arranging stands according to a document called the 'Expo floor plan'. Some were gluing posters onto show panels. The Expo hall was already full of plastic panels, some of which had been assembled into booths (Eric apologised for their having not been prompt enough with the layout for 'our' stand). We observed a messy assembly of plastic shelves, tables and panels designating demonstration spaces, sometimes unnamed, sometimes with company name written in large letters. This led us to realise that there were other companies who had prepared to demonstrate their RFID to the world while 'we', at Virtual World, were struggling to get 'our' demo done. Before, we could only guess at the competitive activities: figuring out what the competitors were doing was a significant part of our conversations. Suddenly we were walking between panels, while recognising that other companies had their RFID stands and posters up and running. What had they brought as branding? Were there any working demos?

After a quick tour around the hall, Alex said he was not happy with the suggested location of Virtual World's stand. To prove his point, he pretended he was a customer entering the Expo through the front door. Describing his visual impressions, he said that while the two 'golden' sponsors' logos (whose stands had been assembled earlier) immediately attracted his eyes, Virtual World's logo was hidden from his immediate view. He insisted on rotating the stand so that the logo was clearly visible to the visitor. Alex also asked that the panels (called 'pods') be placed closer to each other in order to convey the impression of the elements of his stand 'all being together'. The Expo managers protested. They argued that the new configuration would ruin the spacing and unity of elements at the Expo. In addition, they said, the stand's walls were not designed to fit when placed together, and the stand's central placement would 'clutter a nice window view', which they claimed created an attractive 'green' atmosphere in the room. These reasons, however, did not prove persuasive: the stand was assembled according to the 'silver' sponsor's requirements. BestReaders' marketing manager, who accompanied us on the tour, also wanted to install a demonstration kit on a separate pod. To highlight the relation between the two companies, the managers persuaded the Expo director to allow the two stands to be close together to achieve the desired proximity in the eyes of potential customers. Instructing technicians to change the arrangements, the Expo director said that it was his job to be flexible. He complained again that the two 'golden' sponsors 'basically did what they want', to the extent that they installed their own stands, made of metal, not plastic, which not only severely damaged the intended uniformity of the Expo design, but also could interfere with the radio frequency devices' performance.

At the moment the Expo began to invite in some visitor delegations, Alex still could not report on the completion of the demo. The manufacturer of the reader devices justified the delay with another delay in the shipment of a detail from another manufacturer. Virtual World was not the only sponsor whose demonstration was not physically present. Some Expo sponsors provided makeshift demos. As a representative of another global corporation explained, for the big launch, they would have something else. Some other sponsors realised that their demonstrations did not quite work after being transported to the new location. In the absence of the demo, Alex stressed the importance of putting some 'branding' (in this case visual and textual materials, such as posters) onto the stand walls. As he explained, 'because we don't have any demo in there, branding plays the central role. It helps recognition by visitors to the Expo that Virtual World is associated with both Expo and RFID in general.' The RFID branding had been produced and displayed specifically for the Expo. Alex received a branding poster design and a 'typical demo unit design' from his US counterpart in corporate marketing. The design scheme suggested a branding 'set-up' in the picture, portraying the poster size and its position on the wall in relation to the standing figure of an anticipated viewer – recognisably an ideal-type executive man.

Alex was also working on a script for demonstrations, hoping that John, the US engineer, would be able to provide a draft. The script, he said, followed a formula that was transferable from one technology to another, and he (or rather John, the engineer) was trying to fill in the RFID content: 'These are the problems, this is the technology, I'll show you how it works and what the benefits for the customers are.'

Concerns about empty shelves were heard, as sponsors and administrators gathered to discuss the situation. As Eric was pushing for letting some selected visitors in, the sponsors were struggling to get the demos ready and working. Agreement was reached: the Expo director and the sponsors accepted that 'visitors' must be categorised in terms of their 'riskiness', anticipating possible negative interpretations of empty shelves. For instance, the managers agreed that it was 'too early' to let journalists into the Expo area since they were 'too risky' as a category of visitors who could negatively report on the lack of working demos. The 'branding' thus was doing its work of creating 'virtual witnessing' for limited groups of visitors, prominently including scientists and governmental representatives, who were carefully selected by the sponsors and the Expo managers. Once the demo was in operation, it would be shown to other visitors. Different groups were to be exposed to different versions of the Expo configurations, which were being progressively improved. The technology thus was rendered variously demonstrable and accountable in reference to anticipated interpretations by assumed audiences.

RFID Expo: tentative opening

Thus far in this chapter, I have discussed the backstage activities of preparing and displaying the RFID demo, but at the anticipated Expo launch deadline, the question remained: What are the criteria for success, and what kinds of concerns have been articulated and addressed at this point? At the start of this chapter, I suggested that launching a technology implies ongoing assessments and evaluations, through which accountability of the activity is managed. Collins (1988) observes that participants in public experiments (scientists in his case) made a distinction between 'an experiment' (finding out something about the world) and 'a demonstration' (revealing that something to an audience). He shows that certain kinds of scientific activity may receive the label 'demonstration' (and not, for example, of 'experiment') as an outcome of interpretive activity defining the purpose of communicating the event.

A similar observation can be made regarding a product launch. As I shall illustrate below, deliberations on the status of a public event as a 'launch' or 'opening' are closely intertwined with assessments of the readiness of the entity (e.g. the product) to be shown publicly. The deliberations equally include assessments of the kinds of publics to whom the demonstration in its current status can be shown. These deliberations take place to ensure that the launch is interpreted as a (potential) success. One of the framings employed by participants to account for launch in pre- or post-launch deliberations is to characterise it as a tentative effort. This is a pre-emptive strategy that allows participants to direct its interpretations in case things go wrong.[13]

As I indicated earlier, much work went into reaching agreement on what would count as the demonstrable condition of the Expo, and for whom. The Expo management's 'trick of the trade' (Moeran, 2005) can be characterised as maintaining the 'gap' between the backstage and frontstage actions, as well as creating subtler distinctions between the groups of actors in each region. Sponsorship packages and other forms of involvement with the Expo were offered to companies, but at different values that were concealed from other Expo participants. The details of the offers constituted 'commercial secrets', though they sometimes could be disclosed. The Expo website addressed visitors as well as sponsors, establishing two distinct roles and codes of conduct. Sponsors had permanent showcases, while visitors had to sign in using a special form and had to follow a predefined schedule. The work of construing the visitors' experience remained concealed from them in order to achieve the Expo's 'genuine', 'independent' character. It was crucial to show that the industrial field of RFID was now able to demonstrate rather than merely experiment with RFID. This meant that accidental divulgence of technologies malfunctions must be avoided. Eric shared his concerns about letting the crowd in. He wanted to be 'in control of end-user experience'. As he said, everyone was aware that RFID is a delicate technology, and one sensitive to interference. Therefore, he did not think it sensible to go for a big launch from the very start; doing so would be 'high risk'. The sponsors and the Expo director preferred a so-called soft opening, which would assemble the parties, such as the sponsors themselves, who were already involved in the Expo activities. Eric explained his decision to avoid doing a 'real' opening with a metaphor: 'They never do it with ships; I mean, launching it immediately after it's built. They give it at least three months of a sea trial while it still leaks.'

The date for the 'soft' opening was chosen, and representatives of commercial sponsors were gathered. The event ran according to a programme, indicating time slots for business presentations and for a tour around the demos that had been installed by that date. Alex invited me to attend, but did not show up himself.

Another Virtual World manager who confessed to me that 'he was not really in RFID and was just asked to read the slides' gave a PowerPoint presentation. He disappeared shortly after his talk, and I was left alone as Virtual World's sole representative until the end of the day. During the event, I was approached by a marketing manager from another sponsor company, who asked me to discuss a partnership proposal. I explained that I could not make decisions, since I was a researcher, an ethnographer observing what was going on.[14] My humble explanations did not impede the manager's pursuit. For her, the fact that I was placed as a Virtual World representative was enough to treat me as the right person to approach. I took her business card and promised to pass it along.

The opening tour revealed that Expo participants held their own views on what RFID should look like and which presentation of their product would sell better. Best ways to direct visitors to read the technology were a matter of discussion and debate. Each stand differed in size and configuration, and contained imagery and texts with variously elaborated designs. Some of the presenters installed PCs, and sometimes TV monitors, to show video clips in addition to (or instead of) providing guided demonstrations. The Expo director commented that he found some stands looking rather dull, not providing enough entertainment for visitors, and suggested that success could be achieved through 'bringing in more elements of drama', through adding 'some theatre'. According to Eric, the RFID witnessing experience needed to go beyond the conventions of industrial technical demonstration.[15] The Expo administrators felt they needed to perform impression management to make it an attractive business pursuit for future visitors. Establishing other criteria helped the Director of the RFID 'theatre of the proof' manage his own enterprise according to desirable visitors' reactions. The appropriate elements of dramatisation were subject to discussion. Eric's talk provided good examples: he praised the UK Post Office for having 'literally, literally bought some elements from Disney!' for their RFID showcase. One of the sponsoring companies used a toy train with RFID tags attached to it, offering visitors a chance to play with the technology. Those 'interesting' examples, according to some managers, would be remembered by visitors, who would tell other people, creating a 'snowball effect'. The marketing managers shared the idea that the Expo would succeed 'if every visitor will tell about his positive experience of the Expo to no less than seven people'.

During the opening day of the Expo, the invited founding sponsors and partners were demonstrating RFID demos for other sponsors. A noticeable feature was that an active group of photographers attended the event. Their task, as Eric explained, was not to take vanity pictures but to produce some content for the Expo website. He added that the aim was to give the impression of a 'vigorously running Expo: it's open, it's got content and interesting players'. While the participants were standing around a demonstration kit observing a demonstrator attempting to reboot a failed operational system, a photographer approached and asked the viewers to stand closer to each other, and suggested that the demonstrator engage in a lively dialogue, while he asked the others to show more attention. After a short moment of embarrassment, the participants found it easy to adopt those ideal roles of witnesses and demonstrator.[16]

Later, while browsing the Expo website, I discovered to my great surprise that I was in a photo on the Expo website representing an 'RFID demonstration' among a group of some other opening day participants. The pictures established visual conventions of the RFID demonstration now appearing in Expo promotional materials and on its website. In the photos scattered throughout the website, people gather around objects portrayed as RFID technologies, as prompted by the website text. Some people show objects to others standing around. Groups sit and listen to a presenter showing PowerPoint slides. In the photo that captured my attention the evidence of my presence in the field had been furnished by someone else. I appear in the natives' visual artefact as an element of their persuasive discourse. For the invisible others (Expo managers, photographers), I looked like a participant in the RFID demonstration, like a 'typical witness' whose reaction could be presented to Internet audiences. The photo appears to be an artefact from a 'tribe' of boundary workers whose activities I was trying to understand, and who enrolled me in their boundary work via displaying the photo.[17] The reflexive management of the frontstage/backstage boundary in technology marketing, as it is presented in this chapter, appears to be an upshot of the ethnography. The ethnographer's presence in the setting provided access to the 'backstage' of the event: we know that in the pictures the 'demonstrators' who gathered for the tentative opening were transformed into 'visitors'. This impression was achieved through the visual intensification of activities taking place during the 'opening' day, making the images depict an idealised, glossy performance. The accompanying text ('we welcome visitors across a wide set of industries'), like a caption, reinforces the impression that a 'real' moment of demonstration, to 'real' visitors, has been captured by a photographer. As I tried to show throughout the chapter, the ethnography served as the instrument for both achieving and deconstructing this impression.

Discussion

The marketing of RFID has been discussed in this and previous chapters as the process of managing accountability relations around a new technology, or as the creation of tellable stories. I showed that the process of introducing a new technology in and by the corporation implied not only the creation of RFID stories that were then sent out into the world. It also involved organising the story so as to let the organisation itself be inscribed into the story by means of organising conversations within the corporation. As discussed elsewhere (Simakova and Neyland, 2008), Virtual World's 'soft' launch of RFID at the Expo operated on the basis not of sending stories out into the world, but of attempting to bring (an allegedly controllable version of) the world into the organisation. RFID Expo was defended as a suitable forum for launching Virtual World's compelling RFID story to what was assembled as a pre-educated and preselected audience. The marketers selected RFID Expo on the basis of the Expo management account that access to the (still under construction) RFID story could be closely controlled. It has been noted, at the same time, that the construction of the story, of the audience and of the circumstances of narrating such a story is a contingent process implying the performance of organisational boundaries.

From the standpoint of an outsider, the process of launching a technology may appear to be momentary and linear as one looks at ready-made artefacts and statements that congeal the corporate deliberations taking place before a corporation goes public with a new technology. Opposing this received view, the chapter revealed much tentativeness in the process of product launch. Although operating with managerial 'tools' such as the launch plan, corporate routines and understandings of 'what it means to do a launch', much of the process deals with the everyday work of trying to hold together the new technology and its audiences, conversations and communicative engagements. In the folk theories of marketing much room is also left for handling the uncertainties associated with anticipations of success and failure of a launch, and to the active ongoing construction of criteria for launching a product and of means of achieving the launch, such as in the folk notions of a tentative opening.

The RFID technology demo provided for positions of insiders and outsiders in the hi-tech corporate culture of demonstration. Members of such a culture share (and occasionally contest) the assumption about having a working technology being a prerequisite for a definitive statement of interest in a technology by the company. The boundary appears to be a practical resource. Suffice it to say that for the Expo managers the boundary around such a culture of demonstration was a means to reach out without relying on showing the actual technology in operation. The Expo began inviting scientific and governmental delegations whose expectations of the initial workability of technologies were perceived as low. In such conversations working technology could be plausibly deferred (Rappert, 2005) to the future, and support could be obtained on the basis of technological promise rather than demonstrated achievement. Thus, assumptions about demonstration as a 'bottom line' provoked the work of categorisation of witnesses to the demonstrations ('risky' and 'non-risky' audiences) and managing such audiences (away).

Displaying the demo in operation, or managing its absence, was equivalent to achieving distinctions between technology constituencies and furnishing different RFID stories. By analogy with previous observations in science studies (Lynch and Woolgar, 1990), the search for appropriate storytelling circumstances and audiences is best seen as the *bricolage* of resources and materials at hand as well as of managerial practices, as debating and agreeing on the 'right' circumstances of the launch. The participants also propose and dismiss folk theories of product launch entertaining various assumptions about interpretive work. All these appear to be open interpretive matters in corporations. Providing an insight into the corporate practices of launching, this and the previous chapters also raise questions about the nature of ethnographic work as an interpretive practice. What does it mean, and what does it take, to take technology descriptions 'out' to the world in order to render a technology to wider (academic, student, practitioners) audiences? A discussion of this follows in the concluding chapter.

8　Concluding remarks

Revision of the post-essentialist approach to the market

Marketing Technologies has offered ethnographic reflections on technology marketing as a strategic research site for science and technology studies. As an exploration that aimed to examine the constitution of technical capacities in market relations, the book has offered a set of arguments to enrich our understanding of markets, marketing and technology. The empirical study of technology marketing in practice, in turn, brought up questions about the nature of ethnographic inquiry with corporations. Technology marketing was approached ethnographically as a kind of practical reasoning on the nature of socio-technical relations in attempts to intervene in cultural technological discourses. This was achieved through deliberating upon the 'appropriateness of particular narrative forms' (Rappert, 2001: 562) as a basis for construing winning technological claims, which I termed 'tellable stories'. The conclusion will discuss some of the contributions of the analysis to the contemporary debate on the nature of socio-technical change, in terms of the stabilisation and dissemination of technological artefacts, in the context of market relations.

The book has offered an approach to the market that brings together the French and the British traditions in the anthropology of the market. The purpose of this move was to find analytic ways of accounting for the construction of agency in market relations without prioritising either material or social explanations. While the actor-network theory approach usefully draws attention to the role of material artefacts (such as 'marcom' materials, or demonstration kits) in social ordering, the discursive approach in the anthropology of the market emphasises the importance of language as constitutive of the properties of material artefacts. The discursive approaches in science and technology studies and anthropology contributed to the elaboration of the approach to the market as text. This approach urges us to stay alert to the possibility of multiple interpretations of relations between the entities composing 'the market'. From the discursive perspective, the attribution of agency to entities participating in market relations is seen as a textual phenomenon. 'The market' was treated in the book as sets of conventions and attributions of agency (Dilley, 1992a; Miller, 2002a; Carrier, 1997), whose currency was examined. Holding responsible specific forms of agency in market relations (Dilley, 1992a) was discussed as interplays of contesting claims. These claims can be seen as certain narratives providing for agency distribution, including the positions of insiders/outsiders of marketing.

Markets, technology and accountability

The discursive approach to the market offered in the book employed an understanding of relations between the market constituencies in terms of the distribution of accountability relations. As in the title, *Marketing Technologies* is thus about marketing, technologies, and markets as performing and being performed in certain accountability relations. As a summary term, accountability has been used in the book to draw attention to various ways of talking marketing, and technologies, that emerged in and through deliberations in the marketing department. In particular, I explored two possible directions of thinking about accountability.

First, accountability as understood by Garfinkel as an omnipresent feature of social condition: 'Any setting organizes its activities to make its properties as an organized environment of practical activities detectable, countable, recordable, reportable, tell-a-story-aboutable, analyzable – in short, accountable' (Garfinkel, 1967: 33). As such, the accountability of the marketing setting – in the sense of everyday conversations, professional jargon, remarks exchanged, documents produced and read, and meetings talk – was made available to me as ethnographer through interactions with the setting. And, second, as *managed* accountability.

This second meaning emerged through questioning the nature and boundaries of marketing knowledge that renders accountability, as the work of production of accounts of and by marketing, a matter of practical reasoning. A specific kind of accounts is solicited, for example, through organisational audit and reporting. This form of accountability was discussed in Chapter 4, which looked at the vertical marketing reporting. Accounting for 'vertical' marketing was tantamount to learning the language of adequate contribution in interactions with the line manager. As argued in Neyland and Woolgar (2002) and Power (2003), a commitment to accountability (audit, measurement, evaluation) needs to be sustained. Chapter 4 in particular discussed the ethnographic encounters with centres of accountability, accountability rituals, and accountability trials in the corporation. These activities for measuring and evaluating marketing have provided versions of marketing that were assembled in the context of these very efforts to evaluate, as well as to establish the authority of evaluators. Marketing was assembled as subject to measurement and performance evaluation through invocations of different communities – such as sales, or customers – whose relevance was contested. Under this rubric, marketing as a research site was also made accountable to the ethnographer in interactions as I followed marketing managers around and discussed the terms of access.

One can also think of marketing attempts to intervene in cultural technological discourses in terms of *managing* accountability. I discussed these attempts in terms of the reconfiguration of accountability relations vis-à-vis technological artefacts. Particular examples included the production of marcom materials with intended readings, and the creation of the first RFID statements. Achieving accounts was an ambiguous and uncertain task. Accomplishing the accountability of and by marketing was shown to be the continuous work of identifying the relevant audiences, and of constructing the content of statements as well as the circumstances of narration that would take these relevant audiences into account. Through this lens, Garfinkel's 'natural' accountability of a setting was shown to be not fixed and given, but rather an achievement such as accounting and audit, or claims of ability to intervene in societal discourse – through, for example, the invoking of normative marketing knowledge, the proposing of marketing strategies, or the articulating of situated practical claims.

The actual, potential, and imagined audiences – readers of marcom materials, visitors to the Expo, business analysts, journalists, corporate sales force and other members of the corporation – were notably a matter of deliberations in the course of the managed production of accounts in marketing. As such, one can think of managing accountability relations as the work of 'configuring' (Woolgar, 1991a) relevant audiences. However, as this ethnography suggested, joining other authors, it is not always clear, on any particular occasion, which audience(s) of a performed action are relevant (Woolgar and Coopmans, 2006). The attention to managed accountability in the book indicates the variability of relevant audiences that marketing managers had to identify and address. In this respect, other scholars even stressed the need to speak about the multiple accountabilities since accounts of practical action are oriented to different audiences. For example, Power (2003) defines the audit explosion in terms of 'institutional' and 'behavioural' (or the level of interactions between individuals) 'effects'; Garfinkel (2002: 173) talks about different 'layers' of accountability: 'accountability to the populational cohort and the scene in which one does something; accountability to the populational cohort to which one reports a description of what has been done'; Suchman (1993) observes that the immediately present interactants are only a part of all the relevant potential participants to whom the work in the airport operating room is oriented; while Woolgar and Coopmans (2006: 18) speak in terms of 'interlocking' accountabilities, referring to the multiple relevant audiences to which the practical actions to sustain technology development are oriented. If scientists are 'savvy strategists' managing multiple accountabilities in Woolgar and Coopmans (2006), marketers are no less so. These strategies were understood in the book as local, partial, if not idiosyncratic, claims about the appropriateness of practical action through at times contesting relevant various audiences. At the same time, the book offered an exploration of the tensions in regard to content and context of social science research on, and with, marketing and its audiences.[1] Not intending to make generalisations about the presence, roles and utility of such thinking in other – social science and everyday – discourses, my aim was to explore in ethnographic detail the (marketing) culture of thinking in terms of the audiences and, importantly, the *boundaries* of such thinking.

As one example, the most straightforward distinction between audiences to which marketing claims and actions were oriented was one achieved in the contestation of the strategies of going public with the first RFID statements

(Chapters 6 and 7). In this organisational dispute, audiences both inside and outside the organisation were rendered differentially significant. In the dispute, enthusiastic 'early adopters' in the 'Let's PR immediately' strategy, and critical 'industry insiders' in the rhetoric of responsible corporate conduct, were nominated as the relevant audiences. The creation and interpretation of the go-to-market checklist – which served as a categorisation device for different constituencies inside and outside Virtual World – was a part of construing the 'right' circumstances of going public. As such, the ethnography of technology marketing in practice proved to be a rich source of observations about deliberations on the nature of audiences and the 'right' circumstances of accounting for technologies in and by the corporation.

Marketing knowledge: an ethnographic perspective

Studying marketing knowledge was equivalent to exploring the particular commitments to and assumptions about social ordering exercised in the marketing department. I suggested that 'marketing' is best approached as a label for a practical activity employed in various discourses of socio-technical relations seen through the lens of production–consumption dynamics. Wensley's (1990) suggestion was helpful to understanding marketing as an analogy that can be accepted or rejected in the accounts of corporate practices performing social or business identity, distribution of expectations, responsibilities and power relations. As such, marketing was called upon as a means to transform RFID technology into a successful technological solution aligning with the corporate image. Developing an anthropological stance towards marketing, I proposed that marketing is best seen as both a culture and a cultural artefact (Hine, 2000). This approach helps us to appreciate marketing in its contingent, plural and differentiated context (McFall, 2004), or to understand marketing as a locus of practical activities of marketing professionals, as well as a part of broader social, managerial or organisational discourses.

As discussed in Chapter 2, marketing as an actant in various societal and organisational discourses is portrayed in various ways. In the marketing normative literature, marketing is widely construed as a set of techniques and instruments of intervention. However, while some accounts present marketing as a powerful agent of societal change, others ascribe to marketing knowledge only a moderate ability to exercise influence. This is what Willmott (1999) described as 'the paradox of marketing', which, as I proposed, needs to be approached sceptically through a careful examination of who makes what claims about marketing and in what circumstances. At Virtual World, the invocation of the 'paradox' played a role in the boundary around technology marketers. On the one hand, marketers lamented the unrealised potential of 'marketing thinking'. On the other hand, difficulties with establishing marketing as a mature and resourceful discipline and function within the organisation were acknowledged, and some techniques of intervention offered by marketers, such as the use of 'marcom' materials, were a matter of boundary work between marketing and sales.

From the ethnographic perspective, marketing knowledge was not a single set of techniques, practices or descriptions. Rather, as diverse accounts achieved for various occasions, marketing knowledge was a matter of continual elaboration. As a situated practice, marketing knowledge depended on the local ways of getting things done, establishing contacts within the organisation, and knowledge of how to account for one's work in appropriate ways. Made amenable to audit and performance assessment, marketing knowledge was construed as subject to evaluation and change. In everyday practical discussions, marketing managers articulated competing views about the properties of marcom materials. Marketing knowledge was also assembled as accessible and describable in the ethnographic engagements in different ways. The choice of the field site itself entailed the co-construction and alignment of assumptions about both marketing and ethnography as being useful, or at least not threatening, to marketing, whereby the rhetoric of access was playing with the assumption of the lack of knowledge about how marketing is done in practice. The ethnographic experience of climbing 'the corporate ladder' construed a particular version of a progression from 'basic' marketing skills, such as 'organising', to 'project management' and 'copywriting'. Accessing the PR strategy through an interview prepared to reveal the existence of such a strategy is another example.

This is not to say that the moves and transitions from sites where different kinds of marketing knowledges were performed were smooth. Rather, on joining the corporation, the ethnographer behaves like an 'awkward student'[2] incapable of grasping the marketing organisation immediately, and then learning the signs of competent membership with varying degrees of success. Ethnographic stories not told here (and there is an archive of emails and documents related to projects and encounters that never took off as longer-term engagements) would present a much more diverse picture of marketing in the organisation. As a 'student' of marketing, I was accepted, and progressed, at some sites within the corporation, but not at others. Eventually, this book offered a particular, if not idiosyncratic, version of marketing knowledge informed by the ethnographic experience. Technology marketing, as the object of research, thus features in this book as tellable stories created by many actors. These actors include marketing managers (who may have imagined the study would appear in marketing textbooks), marketing scholars, STS colleagues and the ethnographer herself. As a participant observer making sense of marketing, I attempted to conceptualise marketing by introducing a set of terms such as articulation, tellable stories, and discursive objects, pulled together under a summary term of the practical management of accountability relations. As such, these terms serve as textual devices to help me, as analyst, introduce a distance between myself and marketing discourse. They also accomplish displacement, or make the 'marketing analogy' – as the abstraction of the organisational world that I describe – to connect the empirical study with the science and technology studies and anthropology scholarship. The book shows marketing knowledge as contingent sets of practices and assessments of (accounts of) marketing practices, as an elusive object of study that constantly needed to be made available to the ethnographic gaze.

Marketing technologies and intervention

Marketing has been characterised in this book in terms of attempts to change cultural technological discourses. This approach aimed to critically explore the ways technological artefacts achieve market success. Such exploration, I argued earlier, had to take into account the boundaries of marketing knowledge. Together with this book, other studies of marketing *in situ* have shown neither that marketers' expectations always come true, nor that marketers have the indisputable authority in the construction of a marketing campaign through the anticipation of audiences' reactions (Moeran, 2005; Lien, 2003; Woolgar and Simakova, 2003). The analysis of the deliberations inside the marketing department revealed a rich set of folk theories concerning the explanations of product success, depending, or not, on the effort of marketing. The folk sociology of marketers also involved competing practical means to achieve market success. As in Chapter 6, the explanation of a success of an artefact (such as the Internet) can be told in the passive voice, too. This book speaks yet another time in favour of research on 'unfolding institutions and practices' (Woolgar and Coopmans, 2006: 19) associated with new technologies, such as RFID, in terms of the practical management of accountability relations. What can this study, as an anthropological effort to make marketing knowledge strange as an element of practical knowledge in the organisation, add to our understanding of technology?

The book has highlighted at least two points that enrich the STS premise that the nature (value, utility) of scientific and technical artefacts derives from the performance of relationships across organisational boundaries. As such, I analysed how marketers constitute an understanding of which claims about the distribution of agency and technical capacities have the best chance to win out. The book advances a post-essentialist argument that supposedly intrinsic features of a product are contingent and thus not the reliable basis for explaining market success. The construction of durable claims about such 'intrinsic' features is a matter of practical concern inside corporations. In marketing practice claims about such intrinsic properties are continually made and contested. As a positive suggestion, the book argues that deliberations around success and the stabilisation, currency and mobility of 'intrinsic features' can be seen as the creation of tellable stories. Anthropologically speaking, the organisational beliefs and rituals around the creation of tellable stories involve sustaining marketing expertise. In the situation where multiple and radically different versions of the 'right' circumstances to go public were heard, presenting and validating marketing knowledge was achieved through the organisation of particular arrangements. One such example is the construction of the special communicative moment in which the PR strategy was presented to the ethnographer as a single worthwhile take-away from the field. The presentation indeed won out, now appearing in the book as an instantiation of the creation of tellable stories. As above, constructing tellable stories is what a novice *learns* to do in joining a corporation.

Another area of analytic concern that elaborates on the creation of tellable stories as organisational rituals is the deliberations around the role and properties of discursive objects. The discussion offered in Chapter 5 raised questions about the role of materiality in the production and assessment of the 'marcom' materials that were approached ethnographically as a specific 'universe of discursive objects'. I discussed in what sense marcom materials were construed as agents of intervention. The practical resolution of ambiguity between the material and the discursive properties of discursive objects in the marketing department entailed the construction of 'speaking for itself' as a form of agency that was deliberated upon as participants tried, evaluated and adopted complex versions of accountability relations, or attempted to solve practical problems for the purposes at hand. The materiality of discursive objects appeared to be a discursive resource employed by participants to create the persuasive power of discursive objects. However, the conventions of accounting for the material properties of texts that were sent out to the world in order to produce action at a distance (such as the invitations) featured competing versions about the potential effects that such discursive objects would produce. It can be said that the debates in the marketing department related to the role of materiality in establishing interpretive constraints. The question that emerged from a more detailed examination of these organisational disputes revealed tensions and the occasional nature of accounting for the association between reader and text (Woolgar, 1988a). The practical questions about who/what bears the burden of interpreting and fixating the moral order of a text remained an open interpretive matter in the marketing department.

What deserves further discussion is the nature of situated claims about the (potential of) technologies to achieve successful adoption. Changing societal discourses was shown in the book to be a local, situated practice informed by managerial beliefs and sustained through organisational rituals. Suggested as a corollary of marketing attempts at assembling a compelling corporate narrative, tellable stories should not be understood in an instrumental sense. Nor is the introduction of the term another attempt to offer a textual determinist (see Chapter 2 for more detail) explanation of technology. Below I discuss in what sense the notion was proposed to account for the complexity, messiness and ambiguity of organisational life, and for the continuous work of identifying and addressing relevant audiences.

In particular, I discussed product launch, and the role of technical demonstration in it, in order to develop an understanding of contemporary organisational practices in IT industries. In line with the general thrust of the argument, the book looked at technology demonstration in terms of the practical management of accountability relations. This move was made in order to depart from the perception of technology launch as a singular event and a linear process leading to such an event. Emphasising messiness, ambiguity and the actors' everyday need to engage in the practical management of accountability relations around new technology encountering its publics is perhaps not enough to develop a thorough understanding of launch practices. As above, I suggested that the marketing practice of launching could be characterised in terms of the production of tellable stories about RFID. The notion was proposed to sensitise us to the ways in which marketers construct claims about the distribution of agency and technical capacities, or to the ways in which new technologies are talked into existence. *Tellable stories* refer, for example, to the discussed throughout the book instantiations of (the construction of) communicative occasions whereby the new RFID technology was talked into existence by, and within, the corporation. In the case I presented, this work was scrutinised via offering an analysis of Virtual World's construction of the circumstances of the presentation of the technology in relation to Virtual World, and the management of audiences for these occasions. The development of the demo, the selection of the locations, the RFID Expo, and the partnering episode can all be seen as the construction of tellable RFID stories that feature the deliberations on the 'bottom line' status of the demonstration, the entities involved in narrating the RFID corporate story, and the circumstances of narration. Thus, these communicative occasions are treated in this chapter as bounded attempts at narrating RFID that offer for (anticipated favourable) interpretation versions of the technology to particular audiences.

My analysis of uses of the launch metaphor for the organisation of sociotechnical relations by corporate actors in an attempt to intervene has revealed much deliberation around the process. To arrive at a version of an event that would count as launch, numerous actors and audiences – anticipated, imagined – were invoked. These invocations were intertwined routinely with evaluations of the status of the nominated 'bottom line' realities, such as demonstration. I drew attention to the observation that the event's status as either a tentative or a definitive launch was established differentially for participants and for outsiders. While publications (the website, press releases) ascribe a definitive status to the launch ('opening'), participants were more careful and nuanced about defining the status of the event among themselves. Being conceived of as a definitive corporate effort in the planning stage via the use of a master plan, the event quickly became subject to (anticipatory, simultaneous, or *post hoc*) questioning and investigations, undermining its definitive status, changing its scope and moving it into the area of the tentative. Equally, it can be said that being a 'participant' in launch practice was equivalent to recognising the tentativeness of launch, to being immersed in the plethora of deliberations and uncertainties associated with launch, as opposed to taking for granted the event 'as it happens', as presented to outsiders.[3]

Reflexively, the distinction between the tentative and the definitive status of launch was also accomplished by the ethnography. Deconstruction of the definitive statement appearing on the Expo website was achieved (assuming the plausibility of the ethnographic presence there[4]) through revealing and describing backstage activities via becoming an insider. Transitions between the tentative and the definitive (such as the Expo 'opening' event and its website portrayal) can thus be seen as interleaved with achieving distinctions between the communities of insiders and outsiders of such events in ethnographic writing. Perhaps oversimplifying the insider/outsider distinction, the ethnography somehow assumes that everyone present at the opening shared the knowledge of the event as tentative; hence the need for impression management in order to present an idealised image of the event. The analysis, following the events unfolding, culminated in the deconstruction of a visual/textual 'definitive' version of the event on the Expo website; but that was preceded by ethnographic moves across the boundary constitutive of the shifts between the tentative and the definitive.

Chapter 7 suggested that demonstration provided for the emergence of categorisation and ordering performed by launch. The demos as a material 'bottom line' were an element of the discursive management of the tentative/definitive dichotomy and, at the same time, of attempts to manage the inside/outside boundary through categorising and exclusion. Corporate cultures perform (and occasionally contest) the assumption about a working technology being prerequisite for a definitive statement of interest in a technology by a company. The boundary appears to be a practical resource. Suffice it to say that for the Expo managers the boundary around such a culture of demonstration was a means to reach out without relying on showing the actual technology in operation. The Expo began inviting scientific and governmental delegations whose expectations of the initial workability of technologies were perceived as low. In such conversations workable technology could be deferred (Rappert, 2005) to the future, and support could be obtained on the basis of technological promise rather than demonstrated achievement. Thus, assumptions about demonstration as a 'bottom line' provoked the work of categorising witnesses to the demonstrations ('risky' and 'non-risky' audiences) and managing such audiences. Displaying the demo in operation, or managing its absence, was equivalent to achieving distinctions between technology constituencies and furnishing different RFID stories.

In summary, the book offered an ethnographic discussion of corporate beliefs about, and of implicit and explicit commitments to, social ordering. As an instantiation of accounting for messy flows and connections, technology marketing is a particular setting where technology is deliberated upon in terms of changing the cultural discourses around it. Sustaining the situated practices of ordering and managing interpretation entailed the organisational politics in which human and non-human agency was deliberated upon. The production of claims about the winning technology and about the means to achieve it was shown to be a contingent accomplishment. To follow is a discussion of how becoming a participant in the corporate deliberations and rituals had implications for research practices and for the ways that the account of the corporate life was created and delivered to the readers of this book.

Living with unrest: research strategies and tellability

One final question that requires special attention in view of the above discussion of the construction of technology accounts in the marketing department is this: how did the 'Marketing Life' project fulfil the common expectations in science and technology studies to attend to the *content* of technological artefacts?

Some answers have already been offered in the previous chapters as I discussed the ethnographic attempts at holding the setting accountable. The very possibility of gaining access to the setting was an outcome of negotiating the terms of engagement in the form of a non-disclosure agreement. The document, as in

Chapter 3, embodied a particular configuration of relationships between the field and the researcher through mutual elaboration of the ethnographic and marketing knowledges. I highlighted the ways in which my role within the corporation was construed in terms of being a marketing apprentice while doing participant observation. In the course of participant observation, being able to *receive* accounts of marketing action was often equivalent to learning to maintain communicative engagements with the field in the form of input to the corporate activities, or small talk. The main examples of participation discussed in the book included participation in the vertical marketing 'live projects', and RFID project management. The intermingling of the accounts of marketing and ethnography in the course of access negotiations, and further in the course of research, finally contributed to a particular mode of *giving* ethnographic accounts of marketing in practice, which I will discuss below.

The emphasis of the book's argument on the organisational politics around the creation of tellable stories provokes questions about implications for studying these practices from STS perspectives. If marketing can be seen as the creation of tellable stories, what might follow for STS's own writing practices attempting to render technology to readers? The account of the organisation of relations of accountability around and through RFID demonstration was intertwined in this book with questioning and elaborating the role of ethnography for rendering the field to academic audiences. Would the account remain the same if the ethnographer relied on, for example, ready-made representations of RFID demonstration (the demo technical layout; the website portraying 'vigorously running' activities)? Would the analysis arrive at an understanding of the tentativeness of launch as social ordering and the differential importance of demo as material object had it been confined to an event from an outsider point of view? And were such 'outsiders' invited?

For the purpose of this discussion, social science research – like marketing (Chapter 7) – can be usefully seen as the 'continual, reflexive management of social organisation of boundaries and boundary relations' (Woolgar, 2004: 453). As such, the production of social science texts can also be seen as being guided by multiple accountabilities and oriented to various audiences. In other words, achieving a tellable marketing story for STS audiences meant engaging with participants' ways of construing such stories and the circumstances of narration. What is at stake in such accounts is the *content* of technologies and of practices sustaining these technologies. As it follows, an author bounded by a non-disclosure agreement becomes engaged in figuring out what can and cannot be said about Virtual World's versions of the technologies in question, such as RFID, sometimes with help from readers sensing possible breaches of anonymity. Anonymity is one of the instances of negotiated technology descriptions to render technology to academic audiences as the ethnographer tried to fulfil her obligations. As such this condition informed, but certainly did not dictate, the ways in which the ethnographer gained access to and accounted for the technology and the activities in the field to STS. Presenting some parts of the book earlier at a number of conferences provoked questions from the audience asking for more detailed descriptions of the RFID technology.

Is it not that, in some sense, the realist element in the 'culture of content' is similar to the 'cultures of demonstration' as in the analysis above? This certainly reflects the widespread assumption in STS about the *content* of science and technology as prerequisite for an analytic statement. But this expectation of analysis of the technology in question does not seem to show enough sensitivity to the distribution of such knowledge in socio-technical relations. Nor does it exhibit appreciation of the conditions of ethnographic inquiry in settings where anonymity and non-disclosure are routinely negotiated, and where the very possibility of letting certain accounts of technology in/out are a matter of negotiation of terms. The examples include sponsorship providing for a possibility to participate in developing technology discourses, and to gain an audience; or negotiations of terms of access to a corporation that include non-disclosure. In other words, the traditional approach leaves underanalysed the practical (participants', analyst's) ways of achieving technology content, or, in other words, of going about leaving a technology unpacked for some while opening up its content for others. This analysis is strongly suggestive of the idea that answers to the question of 'what is the technology like?' are highly contingent and are a matter of contestation. What we do deal with are achieved (sufficient, acceptable, conventional, adopted for the purposes at hand) technology descriptions.

Negotiating conventions of disclosure of (technical) content in attempts at intervention and ordering such as launch appears to be a practice neglected in STS. The book has sought to gain insight into the accountability work sustaining the demo in focus of social relations, which assumed distribution of technical knowledge. The approach taken in this book, and especially in Chapters 6 and 7, promotes sensitivity to the instances when the very portrayal of what technology is like in relation to its various (anticipated) readings becomes subject to practical questioning and negotiating.[5] A working suggestion might be that the current moment, when scholars' attention is increasingly drawn to activities behind corporate walls,[6] might be better characterised as 'the age of non-disclosure'. This assumes different possibilities, practices and conventions of accounting for socio-technical ordering in science and technology studies. How does the ethnographic attempt at holding the field accountable, as in this book, change our expectations of what counts as acceptable analyses of a given technology? How successful can STS writings be '*without*' rather than *as a result of* attending to technical content?

One useful way of continuing this discussion is to resort to the earlier post-essentialist rationale developed in this book concerning an alternative research approach for studying marketing. As with McFall's (2004) proposition to move from the analysis of the content of advertising to the practices of creating advertisements, the same research strategy, of shifting the research focus towards practical circumstances of interpretation, was proposed for social research seeking to redefine the terms of debate in STS (Rappert, 2001). The condition of anonymity as in this study has offered an apt case to explore this approach by focussing on the practical resolutions of contingencies of interpretation. The proposed 'shift away' from the rhetorics to the circumstances of interpretation arguably helps us to appreciate what kinds of deliberations constitute the practical management of accountability relations. This book has explored, through attending to the detail of practical action and of writing the experience up, the ethnographic ways of living with the unrest within as one engages in the *production* of narratives. This analytic strategy also offered a basis for a move helping the ethnographer to adopt anonymity not as an exasperating constraint, but as an analytic device raising questions about the interactive achievement of accounts of technologies and of marketing practices that one can play with. As a report of participant observation in the marketing department, and as a version of marketing practice that is constitutive of the technologies in question, this book can be seen as a set of tellable stories attending to practical deliberations and to ethnographic experiences in acceptable detail. As such, the book conveys the lasting and haunting sense of the indeterminacy of interpretation – of technology, of the outcome of marketing effort and of the content of social science research – experienced and shared with participants for whom this was a matter of productive ongoing concern.

Notes

Preface

1 In particular, marketing emerged as a worthwhile topic of research for me in the course of workshops and conference sessions that began looking at various aspects of market-making from STS perspectives, such as those that took place in Sweden (Workshop on Market[-ing] Practices in Shaping Markets, Stockholm School of Economics, June 2003), in Paris (Society for the Social Studies of Science [4S] / European Association for Studies of Science and Technology [EASST] Joint Meeting, Ecole des Mines, Paris, August 2004), and at the European Group for Organizational Studies (EGOS) Colloquium (2006 and 2007).

Chapter 1

1 Apart from Michel Callon's group at the Centre for Sociology of Innovation at the Ecole des Mines, Paris, a recent centre for market studies formed in Sweden, with two notable international workshops in Skebo (2003) and in Stockholm (2010) exploring the merits of STS for the studies of markets and marketing. See also Araujo *et al.* (2010).
2 An overview of literatures shows that agency narratives in actor-network theory differ as they search to account for the actants' capacity to influence (or resist) sets of networked relations. The examples comprise the 'fluid' technology and the engineer who attempts to accommodate network requirements in De Laet and Mol (2000); a pro-active Machiavellian hero Pasteur in Latour (1999a); and non-human actants such as scallops in Callon (1986) and the door-closer in Latour (1992). In Latour (1999a) powerful actors employ non-humans (such as 'metal weights'; 'microbes') to 'persuade' associations, or socio-material orders, held together by virtue of the newly gained formations that the non-human entities bring in.
3 Attempts have been made to theorise agency as a shifting, contestable category. Pickering (1993: 567) discusses the possibility of a 'post-humanist decentering of agency' through the metaphor of the mangle: 'the contours of material agency are mangled in practice, meaning emergently transformed and delineated in the dialectic of resistance and accommodation.' Middleton and Brown (2002) suggest that agency is a shifting category emerging in interactions of unstable configurations of actants. Agency is 'invoked', 'deployed', such as in their example of the neonatal care unit: 'A particular form of agency embedded/enmeshed in the baby as a hybrid of intentionality and technical practice (equipmentality) is invoked' (p. 17).
4 'Sociologie des dispositifs d'achalandage' in the original; the translation is mine.
5 Shifting away from the heterogeneous 'hybrid' model of market relations, Cova (1999) argues for the replacement of 'marketing' with a new concept, 'societing'. Social relations are thus seen as providing for market performance, where the linking practices are central: 'the link is more important than the thing' (p. 75).

6 As it follows from the discussion above, the same assumption about the instability and different meanings can be applied to ANT and STS. Cf. Woolgar *et al.* (2009a) for a discussion about the performance of the STS acronym.

7 The problem of reinterpretation of what the actors do in order to produce descriptions of context has also been raised in anthropology. With regard to the problem of context in general, Dilley (1999a) writes: 'Context has been shown to be an emergent as well as generative property of knowledge. Indeed, contexts are sets of relations and not self-evident things in themselves. We must therefore be alive to the possibility that there are two parallel processes of construing contexts: for us from within our own bodies of knowledge; and for them within theirs' (p. 38).

8 Or, in Strathern's (1996) own words, 'Who cuts the network?' (p. 520).

9 The spirit of this study accommodates some ethnographic sensibilities in relation to technology formulated by Woolgar (2000a) under the summary term 'technography'. By analogy with ethnography, 'technography denotes a form of study of "technology" that engages a similar form of tension between the exoticism of the technical . . . , and the dispassionate distance of the observer wishing to address questions formulated in terms more familiar to outsiders' (p. 172).

Chapter 2

1 This is of course a rather straightforward realist rendition of the constructivist approach to marketing as practice, adopted at this point in order to circumvent the normative literature. In the next chapters I will discuss the importance of paying attention to the textual representational practices in the construction of accounts about marketing practice.

2 Building an approach to marketing as an organisational practice, I adopt Barbara Herrnstein Smith's (1997) understanding of beliefs not as fixed statements of faith in reality, but as contesting claims. As she puts it: 'The historical process of testing and verifying beliefs, scientific and others, may be seen, then, not as the gradual shaping up of our more or less errant but malleable beliefs by the autonomously resistant features of a fixed reality, but, rather, as the continuous mutually shaping interactions, between our more or less changing beliefs and the more or less changing worlds in which we operate with them' (p. 43).

3 McFall approaches advertising as a cultural economy in Foucault's sense of 'genealogy'. She contends that, for instance, advertising is best seen as 'a diverse, haphazard and uneven array of institutions, practices and products' (2004: introduction).

4 Rabinow (2005) specifies markets as a problem for anthropology in the sense of the power of corporations to change the ways we think about ourselves. As Rabinow puts it: 'following in the wake of the venture capitalists, biotech startups, and multinational pharmaceutical companies, more and more people around the world are growing accustomed to thinking about themselves (and their pets and plants and food) as having genomes. These genomes, it is believed, contain precious information that tells the truth about who they (and their pets and plants and food) really are, as well as providing clues to what their future holds' (p. 45). For Rabinow, powerful 'companies' succeeded in imposing genomic thinking on people around the world.

5 This echoes the proposition to maintain the symmetry between producer and consumer based on the principle of generalised symmetry of the actor-network approach, as discussed in Chapter 1.

6 See, for example, Dubuisson-Quellier and Lamine (2008) for a discussion of Fair Trade network building that involves deliberations about the individual choice and the collective action; as well as negotiations of boundaries between producer and consumer identities that emerge in these new forms of engagement *ad hoc* as forms of solidarity, organisation of lobbying, and involvement in legal disputes (see also a discussion of Fair Trade as hybrid forums in Neyland and Simakova, 2010).

7 In the sense that such an attitude helps one to appreciate the wider social and political contexts in which marketing, as a kind of interactive social science, is sustained as a set of knowledge and utility claims (cf. Woolgar, 2000b: 175).

8 The notion of boundary work was used by Gieryn (1999) to analyse the nascent relations between science, religion and mechanics in Victorian England.

9 I understand discursive objects both in the sense of texts as sets of discursive entities (language items) whose properties become objectified through the textual practices, as well as in the sense of texts as material artefacts themselves (see Chapter 5 for discussion).

10 The creation of representations by marketers can thus be approached by analogy with the analyses of representation in scientific practice (Lynch and Woolgar, 1990).

11 Cf. also Smith's (2001) discussion of the actualisation of the texts through reading: while texts (e.g. documents, files) can be seen as (containing) discursive objects *in potentia,* it is through the conversation between reader and text that the properties of and relations between the elements of the text actualise.

12 Woolgar and Coopmans use the following references: Shapin, Stephen. 1984. 'Pump and Circumstance: Robert Boyle's Literary Technology.' *Social Studies of Science* 14 (4): 481–520; Shapin, Stephen and Simon Schaffer. 1985. *Leviathan and the Air-Pump: Hobbes, Boyle, and the Experimental Life.* Princeton: Princeton University Press.

13 RFID seemed to have gained greater currency in the United States than in Europe at the time I finished my dissertation.

14 Dilley mentions that the notion of articulation has been developed by writers such as Stuart Hall, Ernesto Laclau and Jennifer Daryl Slack to confront the problem of context, to attempt to map context – 'not in the sense of situating a phenomenon in a context, but in mapping a context, mapping the very identity that brings the context into focus' (Daryl Slack, 1996: 125, in Dilley, 1999a: 37).

15 The term 'articulation' also features in STS literatures. Examining the merits of actor-network theory, Fujimura (1992; also in Lenoir, 1999) applies the term to describe the ways standardised packages are used in 'attempts in articulation', or to link up different social worlds.

Chapter 3

1 I believe that the theme deserves a longer ethnographic discussion due to the 'difficulty' being a persistent feature of accounting for a variety of practices and disciplines. A discussion in Woolgar *et al.* (2009a: 18) about what counts as 'the hardest possible case' in STS emphasises the need to consider the difficulty as a part of the rhetoric of the radical character of STS. The authors examine the tendency to shift the focus from science to politics (Barry, 2001), or even marketing, as an element of the construction of new research questions, and new audiences, for STS.

2 This kind of designation is used for names of top managers at Virtual World.

3 Virtual World agreed to pay my travel expenses, as I was commuting from Oxford to West London through Heathrow airport by bus.

4 Cf. Chapman (2001: 32) on the possibility for anthropologists of business to switch careers through acquiring the subjects' professional skills.

5 This remained Terry's attitude towards the ethnographers. In a friendly way, he recalled the episode in our further conversations, and was helpful in explaining practical matters to me while settling me into the corporation.

6 EMEA stands for Europe, Middle East and Africa. This is one of the global 'theatres' where Virtual World claimed its presence. The abbreviation is adopted by other corporate giants, too. It can be pronounced differently. The US way is to say [i:-mi:-]. When I learned this variant first, UK managers thought I was 'pro-American', and made it clear to me that their variant – [i:-em-i-ei] – sounded 'right'.

7 For comparison, while this rhetoric worked in the context of this study, a different way of framing ethnography as conducting a more document-oriented 'archaeology' of a business project – instead of emphasising direct observation of and involvement in projects – was successfully adopted for my access to a national corporation in France in 2006–2008.

8 'Crossing the chasm' between 'early adopters' and 'laggards' is the key to success in technology marketing, according to Moore. The set of normative recommendations provided by Moore contains tips on how to identify and where to find those groups and what kind of rhetoric needs to be employed to address the putative users.

9 But see Rappert (2009) on the practices of non-disclosure and anonymity in diplomatic and security settings, in particular the discussion of the 'Chatham House Rules' in Part 1.

10 See Ashmore (1989: 107) for a discussion of the tensions between, and the mutual construction of, the inside–outside categories as a part of participant observation. Anonymity can be seen as one example of how the complexities associated with balancing on the boundary – e.g. achieving insider knowledge about a technology and attempting to render that knowledge to the academic audiences – are managed through the textual practices of describing the ethnographic experiences.

11 I refer in particular to Trevor Pinch's talk at the S&TS Graduate Conference on research methods, Cornell University, December 2006, and also to personal communication with Professor Pinch at that time.

12 See Neyland (2008: 11) for a discussion of ethnography as being a fluid and unpredictable kind of inquiry that has to deal with contingencies of the situations in the field. Law (2004) discusses fieldwork in terms of the unfolding of fluid research strategies.

13 Louise Woodward, a nineteen-year-old English au pair, was accused of murdering eight-month-old Matthew Eappen while fulfilling her duties in 1997. Hine describes her ethnographic journey as she was following the news and online supporter groups.

14 The M25 is a peripheral road around London.

15 Abolafia (1998) observes that conducting ethnography of markets and marketing means passing several levels of gatekeepers. As Abolafia mentions, the natives can be highly protective of information and somewhat suspicious of the ethnographer's motives (ibid.: 81).

Chapter 4

1 A Natuzzi success story explains this as follows: 'The company distributes its product "vertically" in the leather furniture market: It sells to only one company in each price and quality category. For example, Natuzzi will sell one type of couch to Siemens, a lower-end retailer, without selling to any of Siemens' competitors. It will also sell a different couch to Bloomingdale's, a higher-end department store, but no other company in that category' (Lucas and Conlon, 1996: 91).

2 For example, critique was put forward against the static and singular understandings of 'the market' as a phenomenon out there, disconnected from the practices of market-making, or marketing (Araujo *et al.*, 2010).

3 Marcom stands for 'marketing communications'. See Chapter 5 for a discussion of the ascription of agency to marcom materials in the marketing department.

4 Cf. Abolafia's (1998: 78) reiteration of this perception that 'market-making is the province of the corporate elites'. Although marketing gatekeepers may appear to be members of the corporate elites, marketing on the ground, or 'middle marketing', is less so.

5 My identity as a 'researcher from the Said Business School' was rarely invoked in the vertical marketing department. Malefyt (2003: 159) observes that advertising has created its own language and rhetorical style, and that ethnography needs to fit the advertising accountability conditions to be accepted: 'Indeed, abstract models and rhetorical styles

of language about consumers and brands have become the true "goods of advertising," increasingly valued over the actual people and products those signs intend to represent ... Ethnography will continue to be of value to the agencies. Yet, it will be esteemed not for its "true" representation of consumers, but for the way in which it allows an agency to add value in the presentation of itself to others.'

6   Articulation of customer careabouts was a part of the configuration of the customer. In Chapter 5 I discuss the construction of a collective customer and the anticipation of the collective process of decision making in the customer organisations accomplished by marketers. In this sense, it is important to note that customer careabouts were often categorised in sales manuals in terms of the executive positions of the targeted individuals in the accounts. For instance, the careabouts of a Chief Information Officer (CIO) would be different from the careabouts of a Chief Executive Officer (CEO).

7   I did not go. My Schengen visa expired shortly before the proposed trip (I am a Russian citizen so I needed one), and the 'bonus' was offered on very short notice. Also, I was not sure how serious was the intention to send me to Germany. For instance, a trip to South Africa with the goal to study how marketing managers in the country worked never materialised. The trip was discussed during my introduction to the company with the gatekeepers, who seemed interested in sending the ethnographer to the remote place. However, it was never mentioned again afterwards.

8   Personal assistant.

9   In Chapter 5 I discuss the importance of the group of senior business decision makers ('hi-touch') for the participants. A new business approach urged marketing and sales managers to be able to identify and engage in a conversation with business decision makers (BDMs) rather than with technical decision makers (TDMs) in customer accounts.

10   Purchase order.

11   Cf. 'centers of calculation' in Latour (1987).

12   This builds on Grint and Woolgar's suggestion that 'the completion of an artefact is itself achieved and displayed through "stabilization rituals" which implicate and define prospective user communities' (1997: 24). See also Woolgar's (1989) unpublished paper on stabilisation rituals.

13   See Chapter 7 for further discussion.

14   See the next chapter for a discussion of boundary work between sales and marketing based on the use of textual artefacts as an attribute of 'tribal' differences.

15   A lead can be defined as a relationship established between a sales manager and his or her account, potentially leading to a deal.

16   Return on investment.

17   The number of people who visited a show.

Chapter 5

1   'Marcom' stands for *mar*keting *com*munications.

2   A special issue edited by Pels *et al.* (2002) offers a useful insight into the status of the debate on sociality and materiality in STS. In this chapter, however, I limit the discussion to some specific perspectives in the material culture studies and in STS concerned with exploring the nature of the relationship between technology and text.

3   The post-structuralist approach is represented in the material culture studies through such authors as Barthes, Derrida, Foucault, Geertz, Ricoeur and Levi-Strauss (Tilley, 1990b).

4   Through this brief summary of the argument, this chapter continues the discussion about the interpretive constraints initiated in Chapter 2 (page 00).

5   See also Riles (2006) for a discussion about making documents an object of anthropological inquiry through attention to the bureaucratic cultures sustaining certain documentary practices.

6 Marketers, of course, do not use the term 'discursive object'. However, I employ this term heuristically in order to connect the empirical materials with the academic debate.

7 That is of course only one of the folk strategies related to marketing messages, which in other contexts may be crafted as inconspicuous items in the universe of discursive objects. The work with business analysts and proliferation of Virtual World's statements into the media as independent publications and bylines was also hosted under corporate marketing. More on this in the next chapter.

8 Strathern (2005) points to the military metaphor as a part of textual practices in her analysis of the university mission statements designed to be 'bullet-proof' against the attacks of critics.

9 A CxO stands for Chief 'x' Officer, a general acronym for Chief Officers. In particular cases 'X' can be replaced by 'E' (Executive), 'I' (Information), 'F' (Finance), etc.

10 The difference between the registers of the invitation text itself and of the hectic work of its production is a part of accounting for textual agency in the marketing department.

11 'Inscribed in solid medium', as material culture studies scholars would say.

Chapter 6

1 The fragments of this (and to some extent of the next) chapter were presented and discussed in a co-authored paper (Simakova and Neyland, 2008) that explores the role of marketing in changing the cultural discourses of mobility. I would like to acknowledge a continuing fruitful collaboration with Dan Neyland on the topic of markets and marketing.

2 'Launch' is a participants' term, and the quotation marks are intended to alert the reader that it should not be taken literally, but metaphorically. For readability, however, the quotation marks are dropped hereafter.

3 How corporate actors ritualise the emergence of new technological entities is also noted by Woolgar (1989) on stabilisation rituals.

4 See, for example, BBC coverage in June 2008 of Apple's announcement of a new, cheaper version of the iPhone, as well as preceding speculations and post-launch criticisms: http://news.bbc.co.uk/2/hi/technology/7443543.stm.

5 As Rosental (2002) observes, a demonstration can be viewed as an element of the culture of technology developers, broadly understood. Although Steve Jobs, a co-founder of the Apple Corporation, passed away in October 2011, his demonstration clips are still available online on YouTube, and are being watched and commented upon by viewers. 'It's always a joy to see Steve Jobs performing,' as one IT professional declared during a conversation. The developers' jargon also features widespread use of a short form of the term 'demonstration', or 'demo'. Historical studies of demonstrations of scientific apparatus and techniques, which also focus on notable historical figures, include Latour (1988); Shapin (1984); and Shapin and Schaffer (1985).

6 Marketing practices, including product demonstrations, have been studied ethnographically, and some helpful suggestions can be found in the literature. For instance, some ethnographers use Goffman's (1959) dramaturgical metaphor to account for marketing in terms of staging performances. Moeran (2005) and Prus (1989) speak about marketing's 'tricks of the trade' as arrangements for impression management. Examining Steve Jobs's public presentation of the NeXT computer, Lampel (2001) questions the role of 'spectacles' and 'technological dramas' (also see Pfaffenberger, 1992). In his study of the presentation of self in everyday life based on the dramaturgical metaphor, Goffman concludes that the metaphor was, after all, 'in part a rhetoric and a manoeuvre' (Goffman, 1959: 254). An action staged in a theatre is relatively contrived and explicit, prepared and implemented by professionals whose everyday job is to put on theatrical performances. Further connections with Goffman's work can be developed. See, for

example, Smith (2009) for an interesting attempt to apply Goffman's frame analysis to the present-day IT demonstration. Although this is a useful approach, I give a somewhat different treatment to demonstration. I will try to shift the analytic focus away from the content of demonstrations and interactions with the artefact during the actual demonstration, in order to look into the circumstances under which demonstrations are developed and sustained by actors in organisations.

7   To what extent and in what sense RFID allowed or improved the functional capacities of traceability was a contested matter during large- and small-scale pilot projects. For instance, Wal-Mart's mandating that its suppliers implement RFID tags for tracing goods delivery to supermarkets in 2004–2005 was considered questionable at the moment Virtual World and other corporations began to develop RFID technologies.

8   One of the folk theories of technological change reproduced a microeconomic assumption of economies of scale, which was invoked in order to justify Virtual World's becoming a player in RFID at an early stage of the technology when uncertainties were perceived as high. According to the assumption, the greater the number of industrial players that engage in RFID development and piloting, the more rapidly technical improvements can be achieved. Presumably, a buzzing field would also promote a faster price reduction for RFID tags, whereas a high price would be perceived as an impediment to mass adoption.

9   Being in 'virtual' mode meant being able to access my email remotely through a secure login and to join conference calls. See Chapter 3 for more discussion.

10 Such use of the names of technologies – referencing a technology in terms of its *organisation* – is not uncommon in the speculative deliberations about emerging technologies. Elsewhere (Simakova, 2012) I discuss similar uses of the word 'nano' as it may occasionally indicate either or both the social and institutional aspects of the technological initiative and its technical content.

11 Return on investment.

12 Extensible Markup Language.

13 Cf. (Woolgar, 2000a: 177): 'Our uncertainty about the correct characterization of technical capacity is a reflection of the availability of the many different ways of making that characterization.'

14 For reasons of anonymity, I cannot refer to a recent attack in the press on Virtual World's 'misuse' of RFID by a privacy rights group.

15 The discussion of launch as organisational practice was first developed for a co-authored conference paper (Licoppe and Simakova, 2007).

16 The idea of developing an ethnomethodological perspective on product launch in terms of encounter-*ing,* and of approaching the launch as a basis for criticising the linear model, was fruitfully discussed with Christian Licoppe (personal communication in 2007). The approach also builds on an earlier study of communication technologies (Licoppe, 2004). Elsewhere (Simakova, 2007; Simakova and Neyland, 2008), the framing of accountability relations around technologies by marketers was conceptualised in terms of the creation of tellable and compelling stories.

17 For further discussion of practices for establishing marketing knowledge as the main source of expertise on an RFID launch in Virtual World, see Simakova and Neyland (2008).

18 This particular master plan did not specify the financial side of the launch. The corporate attitude towards promising products such as RFID was that 'if the idea is good, you need to do it in style.' It was, of course, a tongue-in-cheek observation, since marketing managers eventually had to conduct *ad hoc* pitches for budget for each item in the action plan.

19 In Simakova and Neyland (2008) we argued that marketing need not simply be conceptualised as launching a product into the world. Instead, marketing can be understood as launching a world into the product.

20 In hi-tech marketing, getting the 'unique value proposition' right was considered to be crucial for product success.

21 Public relations manager.

22 These interactions are usually kept concealed from the audiences outside the corporation. The analyst reports are construed in such a way as to present independent evaluations of corporate products and performance.

23 Account managers are responsible for establishing and maintaining the relationships with the *accounts,* or customer organisations.

24 See Chapter 2, the section on data gathering and organising, for a more extensive discussion of interviewing in the corporate setting.

25 I started to receive invitations to more general meetings after I extended my fieldwork deadline, showing my commitment to the RFID project.

26 Although 'SWOT' analysis usually stands for 'Strengths, Weaknesses, Opportunities, Threats', the version of 'SWOT' used as a generic name for the document by Abigail contains 'Requirements' instead of 'Threats'.

27 Because of anonymity, I cannot insert the full text or fragments of the press release. This is another example where the research strategy of shifting away from analysis of rhetoric to the conditions under which interpretations are made productively highlights the tensions arising when writing up under the non-disclosure agreement. The absence, in this book, of the content of the press release performs different communities, of practitioners and of academics; what exactly has to be anonymised and how – the terms of the press release and/or the audiences these terms speak to – are open interpretive matters.

28 The journal's title is fictitious and does not refer to any existing journals.

Chapter 7

1 Readers may be reminded at this point of earlier research by Collins (1998) on the evidential cultures in scientific labs that searched for gravitational waves in Italy and in the United States. The contentious matter of whether the data were ready to go public was debated in anticipation of interpretations of publications by peers and funding bodies. Just as in this case study, the resolution of the dispute depended on reconciling different notions of a 'bottom line', or of what counted as sufficient evidence for the simultaneity of an energy burst in two separate metal pieces. This study highlights the similarities between the scientific and corporate communicative strategies for going public. However, while Collins emphasises what he calls the institutional context of research, which would make the two cultures rather distinct, this study looks at corporate communicative strategies in terms of decisions about going public made for the purposes at hand.

2 To 'PR immediately' meant to begin mentioning (to customers, to press) that Virtual World had an interest in RFID. The tentative and careful process of going public with RFID statements by Virtual World is discussed in greater detail in the previous chapter.

3 See Rosental (2002) for a discussion of the currency of 'demo-cratic' practices in Silicon Valley cultures, in which Virtual World's main headquarters also were located. Livingston's (1999) study of mathematical proving also suggests the possibility of investigating the demonstration anthropologically, as an activity sustained in a certain culture of demonstrating.

4 A showroom brochure read: 'The overall objective of the Demonstration Programme is to support Virtual World's sales and marketing functions by providing our customers with demonstrations that emphasise Virtual World's product solutions, major product features and related customer benefits.' The brochure also explained that 'the mission of the showroom is to enhance Virtual World's sales growth by creating a highly personalised customer experience which optimises company's expertise and expands business opportunities and relationships.'

5 For example, I could not walk in and out freely, although I had a badge that allowed me to have access to the premises.

6 I acknowledge that the achieved standards of corporate conduct may certainly differ across various industrial fields. Launching a drug would require a biotech company to treat clinical trial results and intellectual property as 'bottom lines', whereas neither was prominent in my case study. Instead, the corporate talk concerned negotiated licences and commercial offers with external vendors. Such differences open up broader research issues associated with the function of the launch metaphor in various industries, as well as the translation of (marketing) practices from one industry, or product category, to another.

7 Latour (1988: 86) describes how Pasteur's achievement of 'the evident clarity of his experimental demonstration', performed in his 'theatre of the proof', helped him to expand his laboratory across France.

8 See, for instance, an earlier debate on the notion of affordances between Hutchby (2001, 2003) and Rappert (2003).

9 Analytical attempts in STS to theorise the object and its absence can be found in some 'after-ANT' forms of theorising (e.g. Law and Mol, 2001; Law and Singleton, 2005). The object is theorised in terms of unstable sets of relations between absence and presence, as in Law and Mol (2001). Law and Singleton (2005) usefully suggest that analysts need to ask: 'What *counts* as an object?' (p. 334). They propose that analysts need 'to work on different models of imagining objects' (p. 335). Marketers also took absence and presence seriously, practically, and perhaps sceptically. They would ask whether an object is 'a pattern of presences and absences' (Law and Singleton, 2005: 343), wonder why absences and presences matter, and inquire about how to make the object happen. For whom is the object absent or present? How can we identify those artefacts, individuals, audiences who will constitute the absently present object?

10 I am grateful to an anonymous reviewer of Simakova (2010) for suggesting this point.

11 The deadline turned out later to be a preliminary one when readiness for the launch was not achieved.

12 The thrust to demonstrate the scientific background of RFID was also reflected in the way I was introduced to the Expo management in our visits. While inside the company my academic affiliation was rarely mentioned (if not downplayed), in conversations with the Expo managers my role was suddenly articulated as 'a researcher from Oxford', that meant to demonstrate corporate–academic connections.

13 From a conversational analytic point of view, a launch initiates a public conversation by a corporation, and can be treated in terms of *pre-requests*, or 'cautious ways of proceeding' whereby 'you do or do not get sequence with predicted guaranteed results' (Sacks 1992: 691). The example provided is: 'What are those, cigars? – Yeah, you want one? – Sure.' The conversation analyst asserts that 'one thing [a] pre-request regularly elicits is an offer' (Sacks, 1992: 685). I am grateful to Mike Lynch for this observation. Trade shows and tentative launches can indeed be seen as pre-sequences by means of which offers are solicited; however, as the conclusion will further discuss, the tentative or definitive natures of such corporate utterances are differentiated through the performance of the insider/outsider boundary.

14 Although I gained access as a project manager for the demo, this did not involve liaising with other companies to discuss marketing propositions, but rather involved facilitating communication flow between marketing managers and engineers. The boundary between engineering and marketing was defined via assumptions about and distinctions between their constituencies.

15 Shapin (1984: 498) speaks of contesting 'the linguistic signs of competent membership' by Boyle and his opponents who discussed realistic conventions of representations of the pump. Conventions of persuasion ('the modesty of experimental narrative' [p. 494] in Boyle's case) emerged as Boyle struggled to establish his way of talking about the technology. As at the RFID Expo, the politics of representation is about establishing the prevalent conventions of membership talk.

16 Collins (1988) suggests that when approaching scientific demonstrations we need to think in terms of conventions (e.g. demarcating scientific demonstration as a fact-finding activity from stage magic) that both demonstrators and witnesses recognise when participating in the demonstration's performance.

17 This can be usefully compared with the classic picture of the anthropologist 'at work' sitting with a typewriter at a desk surrounded by natives (Woolgar, 1988a: 15). In the photo that I describe, the anthropologist was captured by the natives participating in one of their corporate rituals.

Chapter 8

1 See Cooper and Woolgar (1996) for an examination of tensions associated with ascribing various degrees of importance to researchers' conceptions of the audience.

2 'Awkward student' is Steve Woolgar's phrase (Qualitative Methods course at the Saïd Business School, Oxford, Hilary 2003) echoing Becker's notion of the 'acceptable incompetent'. 'Awkward student' usefully assumes that the ethnographer does not necessarily become accepted, but stresses the continuous 'learning' and awkward attempts to claim membership in a studied tribe. As such, having a novice in the organisation may be perceived as an advantage, enabling a 'fresh look' at things.

3 This way of constructing a boundary between insiders and outsiders recalls Woolgar's (1991a) analysis of the machine case as a boundary between manufactures and users of the machine. Functioning like measures taken to prohibit users from violating the case in attempts to get into the inside of the machine, the Expo website controlled access to the Expo backstage.

4 Snapshots of the website were shown on a couple of conference occasions, where audiences recognised the author as present in the picture. For reasons of anonymity, however, the photos cannot be published.

5 As well as in other settings employing non-disclosure conventions as a feature of organisation of the participants' discourse and relations with an analyst, for example, international relations, policy or weapons control. See Hilgartner (2000) and Rappert (2009) for illuminating examples of experimental writing about such settings.

6 I refer to the special issue of *Organization* on 'Does STS Mean Business? (January 2009) edited by Steve Woolgar, Daniel Neyland and Catelijne Coopmans. The special issue is based on submissions inspired by the series of 'Does STS Mean Business?' workshops that took place in Oxford (2004 and 2005) and at the Academy of Management annual meeting in Philadelphia (2007).

References

Abolafia, Mitchel. 1998. Markets as Cultures: An Ethnographic Approach. In *The Laws of the Markets*, ed. Michel Callon. Oxford: Blackwell, pp. 69–86.

Abrahamson, Eric. 1996. Managerial Fashion. *Academy of Management Review* 21 (1): 254–85.

Agnew, Jean-Christophe. 1986. *Worlds Apart: The Market and the Theater in Anglo-American Thought, 1550–1750*. Cambridge: Cambridge University Press.

Akrich, Madeleine. 1992. The De-Scription of Technical Objects. In *Shaping Technology/Building Society: Studies in Socio-technical Change*, ed. Wiebe Bijker and John Law. Cambridge, MA: MIT Press, pp. 205–24.

Akrich, Madeleine and Bruno Latour. 1992/2000. The Summary of a Convenient Vocabulary for the Semiotics of Human and Nonhuman Assemblies. In *Shaping Technology/Building Society: Studies in Socio-technical Change*, ed. Wiebe Bijker and John Law. Cambridge, Mass.: MIT Press.

Akrich, Madeleine, Michel Callon and Bruno Latour. 2002a. The Key to Success in Innovation Part I: The Art of Intéressement. *International Journal of Innovation Management* 6 (2) (June): 187–206.

Akrich, Madeleine, Michel Callon and Bruno Latour. 2002b. The Key to Success in Innovation Part II: The Art of Choosing Good Spokespersons. *International Journal of Innovation Management* 6 (2) (June): 207–25.

Araujo, Luis. 1999. Exchange, Institutions and Time. In *Rethinking Marketing: Towards Critical Marketing Accountings,* eds Douglas Brownlie, Mike Saren, Robin Wensley and Richard Whittington. London: Sage Publications, pp. 84–106.

Araujo, Luis. 2007. Markets, Market Making and Marketing. *Marketing Theory* 7 (3): 211–26.

Araujo, Luis, John Finch and Hans Kjellberg, eds. 2010. *Reconnecting Marketing to Markets: Practice-Based Approaches*. Oxford: Oxford University Press.

Arnould, Eric and Melanie Wallendorf. 1994. Market-Oriented Ethnography: Interpretation Building and Marketing Strategy Formulation. *Journal of Marketing Research* (JMR) 94 (31/4): 484–504.

Ashmore, Malcolm. 1989. *The Reflexive Thesis. Wrighting Sociology of Scientific Knowledge*. Chicago and London: The University of Chicago Press.

Ashmore, Malcolm. 1993. Behaviour Modification of a Catflap: A Contribution to the Sociology of Things. *Kennis en Methode* 17: 214–29.

Ashmore, Malcolm and Olga Restrepo. 2004. The Authentication Trail: A True Tale, Comical, Tragical and Ironical. Paper presented at the *4S/EASST conference*, Paris (26–28 August).

Ashmore, Malcolm, Greg Myers and Jonathan Potter. 1995. Discourse, Rhetoric, Reflexivity: Seven Days in the Library. In *Handbook of Science and Technology Studies*, eds Sheila Jasanoff, Gerald E. Markle, James C. Petersen, Trevor J. Pinch. London/ Newbury Park, CA/New Delhi: Sage Publications, pp. 321–42.

Barrey, Sophie, Franck Cochoy and Sophie Dubuisson-Quellier. 2000. Designer, Packager and Merchandiser: Trois Professionnels Pour Une Même Scène Marchande. *Sociologie du travail* 42: 457–82.

Barry, Andrew. 2001. *Political Machines: Governing a Technological Society*. London: The Athlone Press.

Barry, Andrew and Don Slater. 2002. Technology, Politics and the Market: An Interview with Michel Callon. *Economy and Society* 31 (2) (May): 285–306.

Beaulieu, Anne. 2004. Mediating Ethnography: Objectivity and the Making of Ethnographies of the Internet. *Social Epistemology* 18 (2–3) (April–September): 139–63.

Beaulieu, Anne. 2010. Research Note: From Co-location to Co-presence: Shifts in the Use of Ethnography for the Study of Knowledge. *Social Studies of Science* 40 (June 2010): 453–70.

Beunza, Daniel, Donald MacKenzie and Iain Hardie. 2006. A Price is a Social Thing: Towards a Material Sociology of Arbitrage. *Organization Studies* 27 (5): 721–45.

Bijker, Wiebe, Thomas P. Hughes and Trevor Pinch. eds. 1987. *The Social Construction of Technological Systems. New Directions in the Sociology and History of Technology*. Cambridge, Mass.: MIT Press.

Bijker, Wiebe and John Law. eds.1992/2000. *Shaping Technology/Building Society: Studies in Socio-technical Change*. Cambridge, Mass.: MIT Press.

Bittner, Egon. 1965. The Concept of Organization. In *People and Organizations*, ed. Graeme Salaman and Kenneth Thompson. Milton Keynes: Open University Press, pp. 264–80.

Bloor, David. 1976. Knowledge and Social Imagery. London: Routledge.

Bloomfield, Brian and Theo Vurdubakis. 2002. The Vision Thing: Constructing Technology and the Future in Management Advice. In *Critical Consulting: New Perspectives on the Management Advice Industry*, ed. Timothy Clark and Robin Fincham. Oxford: Blackwell, pp. 115–29.

Bocock, Robert. 1993. *Consumption*. London: Routledge.

Bowker, Geoffrey C. and Susan Leigh Star. 2000. *Sorting Things Out: Classification and its Consequences*. Cambridge, Mass.: MIT Press.

Brown, Nick, Andrew Webster and Brian Rappert, eds. 2000. *Contested Futures. A Sociology of Prospective Techno-Science*. Aldershot, England: Ashgate Publishing.

Brown, Stephen. 1999. Postmodernism: The End of Marketing? In *Rethinking Marketing: Towards Critical Marketing Accountings*, eds Douglas Brownlie, Mike Saren, Robin Wensley and Richard Whittington. London: Sage Publications, pp. 27–58.

Brownlie, Douglas. 1997. Beyond Ethnography: Towards Writerly Accounts of Organizing in Marketing. *European Journal of Marketing* 31 (3/4): 264–84.

Brownlie, Douglas and Michael M. Saren. 1991. The Four Ps of the Marketing Concept: Prescriptive, Polemical, Permanent and Problematical. *European Journal of Marketing* 26 (4): 34–47.

Brownlie, Douglas, Mike Saren, Robin Wensley and Richard Whittington. 1999a. Marketing Disequilibrium: On Redress and Restoration. In *Rethinking Marketing: Towards Critical Marketing Accountings*, eds Douglas Brownlie, Mike Saren, Robin Wensley and Richard Whittington. London: Sage Publications, pp. 1–23.

Brownlie, Douglas, Mike Saren, Robin Wensley and Richard Whittington. eds. 1999b. *Rethinking Marketing: Towards Critical Marketing Accountings*. London: Sage Publications.

Bucklin, Louis P. ed, 1970. *Vertical Marketing Systems*. Glenview, Ill.: Scott, Foreman.

Burrell, Gibson and Gareth Morgan. 1979. *Sociological Paradigms and Organizational Analysis: Elements of the Sociology of Corporate Life*. London: Ashgate Publishing.

Callon, Michel. 1986. Some Elements of a Sociology of Translation: Domestication of the Scallops and the Fishermen of St Brieuc Bay. In *Power, Action and Belief: A New Sociology of Knowledge?*, ed. John Law. London: Routledge and Kegan Paul, pp. 196–233.

Callon, Michel. 1998a. The Embeddedness of the Economic Markets in Economics. In *The Laws of the Markets*, ed. Michel Callon. Oxford: Blackwell, pp. 1–58.

Callon, Michel. ed, 1998b. *The Laws of the Markets*. Oxford: Blackwell.

Callon, Michel. 1999. Actor-network theory – the market test. In *Actor Network Theory and After*, eds John Hassard and John Law. Oxford: Blackwell Publishers/*The Sociological Review*, pp. 181–95.

Callon, Michel. 2005. 'Why Virtualism Paves the Way to Political Impotence: A Reply to Daniel Miller's Critique of "The Laws of the Markets", *Economic Sociology: European Electronic Newsletter* 6 (2) (February): 3–20. Available online at http://econsoc.mpifg.de/archive/esfeb05.pdf (last accessed 11 April 2012).

Callon, Michel and John Law. 1989. On the Construction of Socio-technical Networks: Content and Context Revisited. *Knowledge and Society* (9): 57–83.

Callon, Michel and Fabian Muniesa. 2005. Economic Markets as Calculative Collective Devices. *Organizational Studies* 26 (8): 1229–50.

Callon, Michel, Cécile Méadel and Vololona Rabeharisoa. 2002. The Economy of Qualities. *Economy and Society* 3 (1/2): 194–217.

Callon, Michel, Yuval Millo and Fabian Muniesa. eds. 2007. *Market Devices*. Oxford: Blackwell.

Carpenter, Philip. 1995. The Rise of the Vertical Market Manager. *MC: Marketing Computers* 15 (10) (November): 28.

Carrier, James. 1997. Introduction. In *Meanings of the Market: The Free Market in Western Culture*, ed. James Carrier. Oxford: Berg, pp. 1–68.

Carrier, James and Daniel Miller. eds. 1998. *Virtualism: A New Political Economy*. Oxford, New York: Berg.

Chapman, Malcolm. 2001. Social Anthropology and Business Studies: Some Considerations of Method. In *Inside Organisations: Anthropologists at Work*, eds David Gellner and Eric Hirsch. Oxford: Berg.

Clark, Timothy and Robin Fincham. eds. 2002. *Critical Consulting*. Oxford: Blackwell.

Cochoy, Franck. 2005. A Short History of 'Customers', or the Gradual Standardization of Markets and Organizations. *Sociologie du Travail* 47 (1) (December): e36–e56.

Cochoy, Franck. 2009. Driving a Shopping Cart from STS to Business, and the Other Way Round: On the Introduction of Shopping Carts in American Grocery Stores (1936–1959). *Organization* 16 (1): 31–55.

Collins, Harry. 1988. Public Experiments and Displays of Virtuosity: The Core-Set Revisited. *Social Studies of Science* 18 (4): 725–48.

Collins, Harry. 1998. The Meaning of Data: Open and Closed Evidential Cultures in the Search for Gravitational Waves. *American Journal of Sociology* 104 (2): 293–338.

Collins, Harry and Steven Yearley. 1992. Epistemological Chicken. In *Science as Practice and Culture*, ed. Andrew Pickering. Chicago: The University of Chicago Press, pp. 301–26.

Cooper, Geoff and Steve Woolgar. 1994. Software Quality as Community Performance. In *The Management of Information and Communication Technologies: Emerging Patterns of Control*, ed. Robin Mansell. London: Aslib, pp. 54–68.

Cooper, Geoff and Steve Woolgar. 1996. The Research Process: Context, Autonomy and Audience. In *Methodological Imaginations*, ed. E. Stina Lyon and Joan Busfield. London: Macmillan, pp. 147–63.

Coopmans, Catelijne. 2006. Making Mammograms Mobile: Suggestions for a Sociology of Data Mobility. *Information, Communication and Society*, 9 (1): 1–19.

Cova, Bernard. 1999. From Marketing to Societing. In *Rethinking Marketing: Towards Critical Marketing Accountings*, eds Douglas Brownlie, Mike Saren, Robin Wensley and Richard Whittington . London/Thousand Oaks/New Delhi: Sage Publications, pp. 64–84.

Czarniawska, Barbara. 1997. *Narrating the Organisation: Dramas of Institutional Identity*. Chicago: Chicago University Press.

Daryl Slack, Jennifer. 1996. The theory and method of articulation in cultural studies. In *Stuart Hall: Critical Dialogues in Cultural Studies*, eds David Morley and Kuan-Hsing Chen. London: Routledge, pp. 112–31.

Dawson, John A. and Susan A. Shaw. 1989. The Move to Administered Vertical Marketing Systems by British Retailers. *European Journal of Marketing* 23 (7): 42–52.

De Laet, Marianne and Annemarie Mol. 2000. The Zimbabwe Bush Pump: Mechanics of a Fluid Technology. *Social Studies of Science* (30) 2 (April 2000): 225–63.

Deutsche Welle Online. 2003. High-Tech Supermarket Offers Looks Into the Future (5 May), available at http://www.dw-world.de/dw/article/0,1432,855158,00.html (accessed 27 January 2009).

Dibb, Sally and Peter Stern. 1999. Research, Rhetoric and Reality: Marketing's Trifid. In *Rethinking Marketing: Towards Critical Marketing Accountings,* eds Douglas Brownlie, Mike Saren, Robin Wensley and Richard Whittington. London: Sage Publications, pp. 230–44.

Dilley, Roy. 1992a. Contesting Markets: A General Introduction to Market Ideology, Imagery and Discourse. In *Contesting Markets: Analyses of Ideology, Discourse and Practice*, ed. Roy Dilley. Edinburgh: Edinburgh University Press, pp. 1–37.

Dilley, Roy. ed. 1992b. *Contesting Markets: Analyses of Ideology, Discourse and Practice*. Edinburgh: Edinburgh University Press.

Dilley, Roy. 1999a. Introduction: The Problem of Context. In *The Problem of Context,* ed. Roy Dilley. New York, Oxford: Berghahn Books, pp. 1–47.

Dilley, Roy, ed. 1999b. *The Problem of Context*. New York and Oxford: Berghahn Books.

Douglas, Mary. 1982. *In the Active Voice, Essays*. London/Boston: Routledge Kegan and Paul.

Doyle, Peter. 2003. Managing the Marketing Mix. Chapter 11 in *The Marketing Book*, 4th edition, ed. Michael Baker. Oxford: Butterworth Heinemann.

Dubuisson-Quellier, Sophie and Claire Lamine. 2008. Consumer Involvement in Fair Trade and Local Food Systems: Delegation and Empowerement Regimes. *GeoJournal* 73: 55–65.

Elliott, Richard. 1999. Symbolic Meaning and Postmodern Consumer Culture. In *Rethinking Marketing: Towards Critical Marketing Accountings*, eds Douglas Brownlie, Mike Saren, Robin Wensley and Richard Whittington. London: Sage Publications, pp. 112–26.

Elliott, Richard and Nick Jankel-Elliott. 2003. Using Ethnography in Strategic Consumer Research. *Qualitative Market Research* 6 (4): 215–23.

Elzinga, Aant. 2004. Metaphors, Models and Reification in Science and Technology Policy Discourse. *Science as Culture* 13 (1): 105–22.

Eriksson, Päivi. 1999. The Process of Interprofessional Competition: A Case of Expertise and Politics. In *Rethinking Marketing: Towards Critical Marketing Accountings*, eds Douglas Brownlie, Mike Saren, Robin Wensley and Richard Whittington. London: Sage Publications, pp. 188–205.

Etgar, Michael. 1976. Effects of Administrative Control on Efficiency of Vertical Marketing Systems. *Journal of Marketing Research* (JMR) 13 (1) (February): 12–24.

Fine, Ben. 2003. Callonistics: A Disentanglement. *Economy and Society* 32 (3) (August): 478–84.

Fish, Stanley. 1980. *Is There a Text in This Class? An Authority of Interpretive Community.* Cambridge, Mass.: Harvard University Press.

Foucault, Michel. 1991. *Discipline and Punish: The Birth of the Prison.* Translated from the French by Alan Sheridan. Harmondsworth: Penguin Books.

Fujimura, Joan. 1992. Standardized Packages, Boundary Objects, and 'Translation'. In *Science as Practice and Culture*, ed. Andrew Pickering. Chicago: Chicago University Press, pp. 168–211.

Garfinkel, Harold. 1967. *Studies in Ethnomethodology.* Malden, MA: Polity Press.

Garfinkel, Harold. 2002. *Ethnomethodology's Programme: Working Out Durkheim's Aphorism.* Lanham, MD: Rowman & Littlefield Publishers.

Geertz, Richard. 1973/2000. *Interpretation of Cultures.* New York: Basic Books.

Gieryn, Thomas. 1999. John Tyndall's Double Boundary-work: Science, Religion and Mechanics in Victorian England. Chapter 1 in *Cultural Boundaries of Science: Credibility on the Line*, Thomas Gieryn. Chicago: University of Chicago, pp. 37–65.

Gilbert, Nigel and Michael Mulkay. 1984. *Opening Pandora's Box: A Sociological Analysis of Scientists' Discourse.* Cambridge: Cambridge University Press.

Goffman, Ervin. 1959. *The Presentation of Self in Everyday Life.* London: Penguin.

Goodwin, Andrew and Janet Wolff. 1997. Conserving Cultural Studies. In *From Sociology to Cultural Studies: New Perspectives*, ed. Elizabeth Long. Oxford: Blackwell Publishers, pp. 123–55.

Grafton Small, Robert. 1999. Morality and Marketplace: An Everyday Story of Consumer Ethics. In *Rethinking Marketing: Towards Critical Marketing Accountings*, eds Douglas Brownlie, Mike Saren, Robin Wensley and Richard Whittington. London/Thousand Oaks/New Dehli: Sage Publications, pp. 154–62.

Grandclément-Chaffy, Catherine. 2008. *Vendre Sans Vendeurs: Sociologie des Dispositifs d'Achalandage en Supermarché.* PhD thesis (École des Mines de Paris).

Greimas, Algirdas Julien and Joseph Courtes. 1979. *Sémiotique: Dictionnaire Raisonné de la Théorie du Langage.* Paris: Hachette.

Grint, Keith and Steve Woolgar. 1992. Computers, Guns and Roses: What's Social About Being Shot? *Science, Technology and Human Values* 17 (3): 366–80.

Grint, Keith and Steve Woolgar. 1997. *The Machine and Work.* Cambridge: Polity Press.

Hammersley, Martyn and Paul Atkinson. 1983/2002. *Ethnography: Principles in Practice.* London/New York: Routledge.

Haraway, Donna. 1988. Situated Knowledges: The Science Question in Feminism and the Privilege of the Partial Perspective. In *Feminist Studies* 14 (3) (Autumn): 575–99.

Hennion, Antoine, Cécile Méadel and Geoff Bowker. 1989. The Artisans of Desire: The Mediation of Advertising between Product and Consumer. *Sociological Theory* 7 (2): 191–209.

Herrnstein Smith, Barbara. 1997. *Belief and Resistance: Dynamics of Contemporary IntellectualCcontroversy.* Cambridge, Mass.: Harvard University Press.

Hilgartner, Stephen. 2000. *Science on Stage: Expert Advice as Public Drama*. Stanford, CA: Stanford University Press.

Hine, Christine. 2000. *Virtual Ethnography*. Thousand Oaks, CA: Sage Publications.

Hine, Christine. 2005. Multi-sited Ethnography as a Middle Range Methodology for Contemporary STS. *Science, Technology and Human Values* 32 (6): 652–71.

Hunt, Shelby. 1990. Truth in Marketing Theory and Research. *Journal of Marketing* 54 (3): 1–15.

Hutchby, Ian. 2001. Technologies, Texts and Affordances. *Sociology* 35 (2): 441–56.

Hutchby, Ian. 2003. Affordances and the Analysis of Technologically Mediated Interaction: A Response to Brian Rappert. *Sociology* 37 (3): 581–90.

Ingold, Tim. 2002. Introduction to Culture. In *Companion Encyclopedia of Anthropology*, ed. Tim Ingold. London and New York: Routledge, pp. 329–49.

Jordan, Kathleen and Michael Lynch. 1998. The Dissemination, Standardization and Routinization of a Molecular Biological Technique. *Social Studies of Science* (28) 5/6 (Special Issue on Contested Identities: Science, Law and Forensic Practice): 773–800.

Kapferer, Jean-Noël. 1997. *Strategic Brand Management: Creating and Sustaining Brand Equity Long Term*, 2nd edition. London: Kogan Page.

Kjellberg, Hans. 2001. *Organising Distribution. Hakonbolaget and the Efforts to Rationalize Food Distribution, 1940–1960*. Stockholm: EFI (PhD thesis).

Klein, Naomi. 2000. *No Logo: Taking Aim at the Brand Bullies*. New York, NY: Picador.

Knorr Cetina, Karin. 1981. *The Manufacture of Knowledge: An Essay on the Constructivist and Contextual Nature of Science*. Oxford and New York: Pergamon.

Kosnik, Thomas J. 1990. Perennial Renaissance: The Marketing Challenge in Hi-Tech Settings. In *Managing Complexity in Hi-Tech Organisations*, eds Mary Ann Von Glinow and Susan Mohrman. Oxford: Oxford University Press, pp. 119–46.

Kotler, Philip. 1972. A Generic Concept of Marketing. *Journal of Marketing* 36 (2): 46–54.

Lampel, Joseph. 2001. Show-and-Tell: Product Demonstrations and Path Creation of Technological Change. In *Path Dependence and Creation*, eds Raghu Garud and Peter Karnoe. Mahwah, NJ: Lawrence Earlbaum, pp. 303–28.

Latour, Bruno. 1987. *Science In Action*. Milton Keynes: Open University Press.

Latour, Bruno. 1988. *The Pasteurization of France*. Translated by Alan Sheridan and John Law. Cambridge, MA: Harvard University Press.

Latour, Bruno. 1990. Drawing Things Together. In *Representation in Scientific Practice*, eds Michael Lynch and Stephen Woolgar. Cambridge, Mass.: MIT Press, pp. 19–69.

Latour, Bruno. 1991. Technology is Society Made Durable. In *A Sociology of Monsters: Essays on Power, Technology and Domination*, ed. John Law. London: Routledge, pp. 103–32.

Latour, Bruno. 1992/2000. Where Are the Missing Masses? The Sociology of a Few Mundane Artifacts. In *Shaping Technology/Building Society: Studies in Socio-technical Change*, eds Wiebe Bijker and John Law. Cambridge, Mass.: MIT Press, pp. 225–59.

Latour, Bruno. 1994. Foreword. In *Accounting and Science: Natural Inquiry and Commercial Reason,* ed. Michael Power: Cambridge: Cambridge University Press, pp. xi–xvii.

Latour, Bruno. 1996. *Aramis or the Love of Technology*. Cambridge, MA: Harvard University Press.

Latour, Bruno. 1999a. Give Me a Laboratory and I Will Raise the World. In *The Science Studies Reader*, ed. Mario Bagioli. New York: Routledge.

Latour, Bruno. 1999b. One More Turn After the Social Turn. In *The Science Studies Reader*, ed. Mario Bagioli. New York: Routledge, pp. 276–90.

Latour, Bruno and Steve Woolgar. 1979/1986. *Laboratory Life: The Construction of Scientific Facts*, 2nd edition. Princeton: Princeton University Press.

Laurent, Gilles and Bernard Pras. 1999. Research in Marketing: Some Trends, Some Recommendations, in *Rethinking Marketing: Towards Critical Marketing Accountings*, eds Douglas Brownlie, Mike Saren, Robin Wensley and Richard Whittington. London: Sage Publications, pp. 245–62.

Law, John. 1987. Technology and Heterogeneous Engineering: The Case of Portuguese Expansion. In *The Social Construction of Technological Systems: New Directions in the Sociology and History of Technology*, eds Wiebe Bijker, Thomas Hughes and Trevor Pinch. Cambridge, MA: MIT Press, pp. 111–34.

Law, John. ed. 1991. *A Sociology of Monsters: Essays on Power, Technology and Domination*. New York: Routledge.

Law, John. 2002a. *Aircraft Stories: Decentering the Object in Technoscience*. Durham, NC and London: Duke University Press.

Law, John. 2002b. Objects and Spaces. *Theory, Culture and Society*, 19: 91–105.

Law, John. 2004. *After Method: Mess in Social Science Research*. London: Routledge.

Law, John and Michel Callon. 1989. On the Construction of Sociotechnical Networks: Content and Context Revisited. *Knowledge and Society* 9: 57–83.

Law, John and John Hassard. 1999. *Actor Network Theory and After*. Oxford: Blackwell and *The Sociological Review*.

Law, John and Annemarie Mol. 2001. Situating Technoscience: An Inquiry into Spatialities. *Environment and planning D: Society and Space* 19: 609–21.

Law, John and Vicky Singleton. 2005. Object Lessons. *Organisation* 12 (3): 331–55.

Lee, Nick and Steve Brown. 1994. Otherness and the Actor Network: The Undiscovered Continent. *American Behavioral Scientist* 37 (6): 772–90.

Lenoir, Timothy. 1999. Was the Last Turn the Right Turn? The Semiotic Turn and A.J. Greimas. In *The Science Studies Reader*, ed. Mario Bagioli. New York: Routledge, pp. 290–301.

Levitt, Theodore. 1975. Marketing Myopia and a Retrospective Commentary. *Harvard Business Review*, 53 (5) (Sept/Oct): 26–44 and 173–81.

Licoppe, Christian. 2004. 'Connected' Presence: the Emergence of a New Repertoire for Managing Social Relationships in a Changing Communication Technoscape. *Environment and Planning D: Society and Space* 22 (1): 135–56.

Licoppe, Christian and Elena Simakova. 2007. Innovation as Encountering: Interrogating Product Launch in Telecom Industries. Unpublished discussion paper for CSI Colloquium 'Expérimenter, éprouver, assembler', Paris (27 and 28 September).

Lien, Marianne E. 1997. *Marketing and Modernity*. Oxford: Berg.

Lien, Marianne E. 2003. Fame and the Ordinary: 'Authentic' Constructions of Convenience Foods. In *Advertising Cultures*, eds Brian Moeran and Timothy Malefyt. Oxford: Berg, pp. 165–87.

Linstead, Stephen. 1999. An Introduction to the Textuality of Organisations. In *Studies of Cultures, Organisations and Societies* 5: 1–10.

Little, Robert W. 1970. The Marketing Channel: Who Should Lead This Extra-corporate Organisation? *Journal of Marketing*, 34 (January): 31–8.

Livingston, Eric. 1999. Cultures of Proving. *Social Studies of Science* 29 (6): 867–88.

Lucas, A. and G. Conlon. 1996. One to a Customer. *Sales & Marketing Management* 148 (1): 91.

Lury, Celia. 1996. *Consumer Culture*. Cambridge: Polity Press and New Brunswick: Rutgers Press.

Lynch, Michael. 1985. *Art and Artefact in Laboratory Science: A Study of Shop Work and Shop Talk in a Research Laboratory*. London: Routledge.

Lynch, Michael and Steve Woolgar. eds. 1990. *Representation in Scientific Practice*. Cambridge, Mass.: MIT Press.

McFall, Liz. 2004. *Advertising: A Cultural Economy*. London: Sage Publications.

McGrath, Mary Ann. 1989. An Ethnography of a Gift Store: Wrappings, Trappings and Rapture. *Journal of Retailing*, 65 (4): 421–4.

MacKenzie, Donald. 1990. *Inventing Accuracy: A Historical Sociology of Nuclear Missile Guidance*. Cambridge, Mass.: MIT Press.

MacKenzie, Donald and Judy Wajcman. eds. 1985. *The Social Shaping of Technology*. Milton Keynes: Open University Press.

MacKenzie, Donald, Fabian Muniesa and Lucia Siu. eds. 2007. *Do Economists Make Markets? On the Performativity of Economics*. Princeton, NJ: Princeton University Press.

Malefyt, Timothy. 2003. Models, Metaphors and Client Relations: The Negotiated Meanings of Advertising. In *Advertising Cultures*, eds Brian Moeran and Timothy Malefyt. Oxford: Berg.

Marcus, George. 1995. Ethnography In/Of the World System: The Emergence of Multi-Sited Ethnography. *Annual Review of Anthropology* (24): 95–117.

Michael, Mike. 1998. Between Citizen and Consumer: Multiplying the Meanings of the 'Public Understanding of Science'. *Public Understanding of Science* 7: 313–27.

Michael, Mike and Nick Brown. 2004. The Meat of the Matter: Grasping and Judging Xenotransplantation. *Public Understanding of Science* 13: 379–97.

Middleton, David and Steven Brown. 2002. The Baby as a Virtual Object: Agency and Stability in a Neonatal Care Unit. Athenea Digital 1. Available at http://antalya.uab.es/athenea/num1/mmiddleton.pdf (last accessed 2 July 2010).

Miller, Daniel. 1987. *Material Culture and Mass Consumption*. Oxford: Basil Blackwell.

Miller, Daniel. 2002a. Turning Callon the Right Way Up. *Economy and Society* 31 (2): 218–33.

Miller, Peter and Nikolas Rose. 1996. Mobilising the Consumer: Assembling the Subject of Consumption. *Theory, Culture and Society* 14 (1): 1–36.

Mirowski, Philip and Nik-Khah, Edward. 2007. Markets Made Flesh: Callon, Performativity and a Problem in Science Studies, Augmented with Consideration of the FCC Auctions. In *Do Economists Make Markets? On the Performativity of Economics*, eds Fabian Muniesa, Donald MacKenzie and Lucia Siu. Princeton, NJ: Princeton University Press, pp. 190–225.

Moeran, Brian. 1996. *A Japanese Advertising Agency*. London: Curzon.

Moeran, Brian. ed. 2001. *Asian Media Productions*. ConsumAsiaN Series. London: Curzon.

Moeran, Brian. 2005. Tricks of the Trade: The Performance and Interpretation of Authenticity. *Journal of Management Studies* 42 (5) (July): 901–22.

Moeran, Brian and Timothy Malefyt. 2003a. Introduction: Advertising Cultures – Advertising, Ethnography and Anthropology. In *Advertising Cultures*, eds Brian Moeran and Timothy Malefyt. Oxford: Berg, pp. 1–35.

Moeran, Brian and Timothy Malefyt. eds. 2003b. *Advertising Cultures*. Oxford: Berg.

Moerman, Michael. 1965. Ethnic Identification in a Complex Civilization: Who are the Lue? *American Anthropologist* 67: 1215–30.

Mol, Annemarie. 2002. *The Body Multiple: Ontology In Medical Practice*. Durham, NC: Duke University Press.

Mol, Annemarie and John Law. 2005. Guest Editorial: Special Issue on Boundaries. In *Environment and Planning D: Society and Space* 23: 637–42.

Moore, Geoffrey. 1999. *Crossing the Chasm: Marketing and Selling Technology Products to Mainstream Customers*, 2nd edition. Oxford: Capstone.

Moyer, Mel S. 1975. Toward More Responsive Marketing Channels. *Journal of Retailing*, 75 (51/1) (Spring): 7–12.

Muniesa, Fabian and Callon, Michel. 2004. The Validity of Economic Experiments. Presented at the session On Social and Consumer Sciences Shaping Market(-ing) Practices, 4S/EASST conference, August 2004.

Munro, Rolland and Jan Mouritsen. eds. 1996. *Accountability: Power, Ethos and the Technologies of Management*. London: International Thomson Business Press.

Myers, Greg. 1991. Conflicting Perceptions of Plans For An Academic Research Centre. *Research Policy* 20: 217–35.

Myers, Greg. 1993. The Rhetoric of Disciplines in Proposals For An Interdisciplinary Research Centre. *Science, Technology and Human Values* 18: 433–59.

Neyland, Daniel. 2005. *Privacy, Surveillance and Public Trust: Closed-Circuits of Interaction CCTV Systems*. London: Palgrave/Macmillan.

Neyland, Daniel. 2008. *Organizational Ethnography*. Los Angeles: Sage Publications.

Neyland, Daniel and Elena Simakova. 2009. How Far Can We Push Sceptical Reflexivity? An Analysis of Marketing Ethics and the Certification of Poverty. *Journal of Marketing Management* Special Issue on Expanding the Disciplinary Space: On the Potential of Critical Marketing 25 (7–8): 777–94.

Neyland, Daniel and Elena Simakova. 2010. Trading Bads and Goods: Market Practices. In *Reconnecting Marketing to Markets: Practice-Based Approaches*, eds Luis Araujo, John Finch and Hans Kjellberg. Oxford: Oxford University Press.

Neyland, Daniel and Steve Woolgar. 2002. Accountability in Action? The Case of a Database Purchasing Decision. *British Journal of Sociology* 53 (2): 259–74.

Nowotny, Helga, Peter Scott and Michael Gibbons. 2001. *Re-Thinking Science: Knowledge and the Public in the Age of Uncertainty*. London: Polity Press.

Olsen, Bjørnar. 1990. Roland Barthes: From Sign to Text. In *Reading Material Culture: Structuralism, Hermeneutics and Post-Structuralism*, ed. Christopher Tilley. Oxford: Basil Blackwell, pp. 163–205.

Ong, Aihwa and Stephen Collier. eds. 2005. *Global Assemblages: Technology, Politics, and Ethics as Anthropological Problems*. Malden, MA: Blackwell Publishing.

Ong, Walter. 1982/2002. *Orality and Literacy*. New York, NY: Routledge.

Oudshoorn, Nelly and Trevor Pinch. eds. 2003. *How Users Matter: The Co-construction of Users and Technology*. Cambridge, Mass.: MIT Press.

Pearson, M. 1998. The Vertical Mambo. *Computer Dealer News* 14 (21) (6 January): 36.

Pels, Dick, Kevin Hetherington and Frédéric Vandenberghe. eds. 2002. Special Issue, Materiality/Sociality of *Theory, Culture & Society* 19 (5–6) (December).

Peter, J. Paul and Jerry C. Olson. 1983. Is Science Marketing? *Journal of Marketing* 47: 111–25.

Pfaffenberger, Bryan. 1992. Technological Dramas. *Science, Technology and Human Values* 17: 282–312.

Pickering, Andrew. ed. 1992. *Science as Practice and Culture*. Chicago: The University of Chicago Press.

Pickering, Andrew. 1993. The Mangle of Practice: Agency and Emergence in the Sociology of Science. *The American Journal of Sociology* 99 (33): 559–89.

Pinch, Trevor. 1993. Turn, Turn, and Turn Again: The Woolgar Formula. *Science, Technology and Human Values* 18 (4): 511–22.

Pinch, Trevor and Wiebe Bijker. 1984. The Social Construction of Facts and Artefacts: Or How the Sociology of Science and Sociology of Technology Might Benefit Each Other. *Social Studies of Science* 14 (3): 399–441.

Pinch, Trevor and Richard Swedberg. eds. 2008. *Living in a Material World. Economic Sociology Meets Science and Technology Studies.* Cambridge, Mass.: MIT Press.

Pinch, Trevor, Malcolm Ashmore and Michael Mulkay (1992/2000) Technology, Testing, Text: Clinical Budgeting in the UK National Health Service. In *Shaping Technology/ Building Society: Studies in Socio-technical Change*, eds Wiebe Bijker and John Law. Cambridge, Mass.: MIT Press, pp. 265–90.

Pollner, Melvin. 1987. Mundane Reason: Reality in Everyday and Sociological Discourse. Cambridge: Cambridge University Press.

Pollner, Melvin. 2002. Inside the Bubble: Communion, Cognition, and Deep Play at the Intersection of Wall Street and Cyberspace. Chapter 13 in *Virtual Society? Technology, Hyperbole, Reality*, ed. Steve Woolgar. Oxford: Oxford University Press, pp. 231–46.

Potter, J. and Wetherell, M. 1987. *Discourse and Social Psychology: Beyond Attitudes and Behaviour.* London: Sage Publications.

Power, Michael. 1999. *The Audit Society: Rituals of Verification.* Oxford: Oxford University Press.

Power, Michael. 2003. Evaluating the Audit Explosion. *Law and Policy* 25 (3) (July): 185–202.

Pratt, Mary Louise. 1987. Fieldwork in common places. In *Writing Culture: The Poetics and Politics of Ethnography*, eds James Clifford and George Marcus. Berkeley, CA: University of California Press, pp. 27–50.

Prus, Robert. 1989. Pursuing Customers: An Ethnography of Marketing Activities. *Sage Library of Social Research* 171. London: Sage Publications.

Quattrone, Paolo and Trevor Hopper. 2006. What is IT? SAP, Accounting, and Visibility in a Multinational Organisation. *Information and Organisation* 16: 212–50.

Rabinow, Paul. 2005. Midst Anthropology's Problems. In *Global Assemblages: Technology, Politics, and Ethics as Anthropological Problems*, ed. Aihwa Ong and Stephen J. Collier. Malden, MA: Blackwell Publishing, pp. 40–55.

Randles, Sally and Alan Warde. 2003. Ethics, Transformation and Market Research, The Organisation of Exchange, Market Regulation and Interdependencies of Markets. Paper presented at *Joint Workshop, CRIC-CEPN*, Manchester, 5–6 June.

Rappert, Brian. 1999. The Uses of Relevance: Thoughts on a Reflexive Sociology. *Sociology* 33 (4): 705–23.

Rappert, Brian. 2001. The Distribution and Resolution of the Ambiguities of Technology, or Why Bobby Can't Spray. *Social Studies of Science* 31 (4) (August): 557–91.

Rappert, Brian. 2003. Technologies, Texts, and Possibilities. *Sociology* 37 (3): 565–80.

Rappert, Brian. 2005. Prohibitions, Weapons and Controversy: Managing the Problems of Ordering. *Social Studies of Science* 35 (2): 211–40.

Rappert, Brian. 2009. *Experimental Secrets: International Security, Codes, and the Future of Research.* New York: University Press of America.

Rappoport, Amos. 2002. Spatial Organisation and the Built Environment. In *Companion Encyclopedia of Anthropology*, ed. Tim Ingold. London and New York: Routledge, pp. 460–502.

Riles, Annelise. 2000. *The Network Inside Out.* Ann Arbor: University of Michigan Press.

Riles, Annelise. ed. 2006. *Documents: Artifacts of Human Knowledge*. Ann Arbor: University of Michigan Press.

Robbins, John, Thomas Speh and Morris Mayer. 1982. Retailers' Perceptions of Channel Conflict Issues. *Journal of Retailing* 58 (4) (Winter): 46–67.

Rosental, Claude. 2002. De la démo-cratie en Amérique. Formes actuelles de la démonstration en intelligence artificielle. *Actes de la Recherche en Sciences Sociales* 141–2 (mars): 110–20.

Rossiter, John. 2002. The Five Forms of Transmittable, Usable Marketing Knowledge. *Marketing Theory*, Special Issue on Marketing Knowledge, 2 (4): 369–80.

Rust, Roland T., Tim Ambler, Gregory S. Carpenter, V Kumar and Rajendra K. Srivastava. 2004. Measuring Marketing Productivity: Current Knowledge and Future Directions. *Journal of Marketing* (October): 76–89.

Ryder, Ian. 2004. Anthropology and the Brand. *Journal of Brand Management* 11 (5): 346–56.

Sacks, Harvey. 1992. Lectures on Conversation, Volume 1, ed. Gail Gefferson. Oxford: Blackwell.

Shackley, Simon and Brian Wynne. 1996. Representing Uncertainty in Global Climate Change Science and Policy: Boundary-Ordering Devices and Authority. *Science, Technology and Human Values* 21 (3) (Summer): 275–302.

Shapin, Stephen. 1984. Pump and Circumstance: Robert Boyle's Literary Technology. *Social Studies of Science* 14 (4): 481–520.

Shapin, Stephen and Simon Schaffer. 1985. *Leviathan and the Air-Pump: Hobbes, Boyle, and the Experimental Life*. Princeton: Princeton University Press.

Sherry, John F. Jr. 1989. Postmodern Alternatives: The Interpretive Turn in Consumer Research. In *Handbook of Consumer Theory and Research*, eds Harold Kassarjian and Thomas Robertson. Englewood Cliffs, NJ: Prentice Hall, Inc., pp. 548–91.

Sherry, John F. Jr. 1995. *Contemporary Marketing and Consumer Behavior: An Anthropological Sourcebook*. Thousand Oaks, CA: Sage Publications.

Shimp, Terence A. 2003. *Advertising, Promotion and Supplemental Aspects of Integrated Marketing Communication*. Mason, Ohio: Thomson, South-Western.

Schudson, Michael. 1984. *Advertising, The Uneasy Persuasion*. London: Routledge.

Shove, Elisabeth and Arie Rip. 2000. Users and Unicorns: A Discussion of Mythical Beasts in Interactive Science. *Science and Public Policy* 27 (3): 175–82.

Siegel, Harvey. 1988. Relativism for Consumer Research? (Comments on Anderson). *Journal of Consumer Research* 15(1) (June): 129–32.

Simakova, Elena. 2007. *Marketing Technologies: An Ethnographic Study of the Performative Properties of Narratives, and of Accountability Relations, in Hi-Tech Marketing*, unpublished DPhil thesis, Saïd Business School/St Cross College. University of Oxford.

Simakova, Elena. 2010. RFID 'Theatre of the Proof': Product Launch and Technology Demonstration as Corporate Practices. *Social Studies of Science* 40 (4) (August): 549–76.

Simakova, Elena. 2012. Making Nano Matter: An Inquiry into the Discourses of Governable Science, in *Science, Technology and Human Values* First published 16 April 2012 as doi: 10.1177/0162243911429334.

Simakova, Elena and Daniel Neyland. 2008. Marketing Mobile Futures: Assembling Constituencies and Creating Compelling Stories for an Emerging Technology. *Marketing Theory* (8): 91–116.

Slater, Don. 1997. *Consumer Culture and Modernity*. Cambridge: Polity Press.

Slater, Don. 2002. From Calculation to Alienation: Disentangling Economic Abstractions. *Economy and Society* 31 (2) (May): 234–49.

Slater, Don. 2003. Introduction: Innovating Markets. Paper presented at the *Innovating Markets Workshop* (London School of Economics, London, UK, 28 March).

Smith, Dorothy E. 1978. K is Mentally Ill: The Anatomy of a Factual Account. *Sociology* 12 (1): 23–53.

Smith, Dorothy E. 2001. Texts and the Ontology of Organisations and Institutions. *Studies in Cultures, Organizations and Societies* 7 (2): 159–98.

Smith, Wally. 2009. Theatre of Use: A Frame Analysis of IT Demonstrations. *Social Studies of Science* 39: 449–80.

Strathern, Marilyn. 1996. Cutting the Network. *Journal of the Royal Anthropological Institute* 2: 517–35.

Strathern, Marilyn. 2005. Robust Knowledge and Fragile Futures. In *Global Assemblages: Technology, Politics, and Ethics as Anthropological Problems,* eds Aihwa Ong and Stephen Collier. Malden, MA: Blackwell Publishing, pp. 464–82.

Suchman, Lucy. 1993. Technologies of Accountability: Of Lizards and Airplanes. In *Technology in working order: studies of work, interaction and technology,* ed. Graham Button. London: Routledge, pp. 113–26.

Suchman, Lucy. 2005. Affiliative Objects. *Organization* 12 (3): 379–99.

Suchman, Lucy, Randall Trigg and Jeanette Blomberg. 2002. Working Artefacts: Ethno-methods of the Prototype. *British Journal of Sociology* 53 (2): 163–79.

Thrift, Nigel. 1998. Virtual Capitalism: The Globalisation of Reflexive Business Knowledge. In *Virtualism: A New Political Economy,* eds James G. Carrier and Daniel Miller. Oxford: Berg, pp. 161–87.

Tilley, Christopher. 1990a. Michel Foucault: Towards an Archaeology of Archaeology. In *Reading Material Culture: Structuralism, Hermeneutics and Post-Structuralism,* ed. Christopher Tilley. Oxford: Basil Blackwell, pp. 281–347.

Tilley, Christopher. ed. 1990b. Reading Material Culture: Structuralism, Hermeneutics and Post-Structuralism. Oxford: Basil Blackwell.

Tilley, Christopher. 1991. *Material Culture and Text: The Art of Ambiguity.* London: Routledge.

Tsoukas, Haridimos and Mary Jo Hatch. 2001. Complex Thinking, Complex Practice: The Case for a Narrative Approach to Organizational Complexity. In *Human Relations* 54 (8): 979–1013.

Van Waterschoot, W. (2000). The Marketing Mix as a Creator of Differentiation. In *The Oxford Textbook of Marketing,* ed. K. Blois. Oxford: Oxford University Press, pp. 183–211.

Webster, Frederick. E. Jr. 1992. The Changing Role of Marketing in the Corporation. *Journal of Marketing* 56 (October): 1–17.

Wensley, Robin. 1990. The Voice of the Consumer? Speculations on the Limits to Marketing Analogy. *European Journal of Marketing* 24 (7): 49–60.

Wensley, Robin. 1999. Falling in Love with a Marketing Myth: The Story of Segmentation and the Issue of Relevance. In *Romancing the Market,* eds Stephen Brown, Bill Clarke and Anne Marie Doherty. London: Routledge, pp. 74–86.

Willmott, Hugh. 1999. On the Idolisation of Markets and the Denigration of Marketers: Some Critical Reflections on a Professional Paradox. In *Rethinking Marketing: Towards Critical Marketing Accountings,* eds Douglas Brownlie, Mike Saren, Robin Wensley and Richard Whittington. London: Sage Publications, pp. 205–23.

Winick, Charles. 1961. Anthropology's Contributions to Marketing. *Journal of Marketing*, 61 (25/5) (July): 53–60.

Winner, Langdon. 1993. Upon Opening the Black Box and Finding It Empty: Social Constructivism and the Philosophy of Technology. *Science, Technology and Human Values* 18 (3): 362–78.

Woolgar, Steve. 1981. Discovery: Logic and Sequence in a Scientific Text. In *The Social Process of Scientific Investigation*, eds Karin D. Knorr, Roger Krohn and Richard Whitley. Dordrecht: Reidel, pp. 239–68.

Woolgar, Steve. 1988a. Reflexivity is the Ethnographer of the Text. In *Knowledge and Reflexivity. New frontiers in the Sociology of Knowledge*, ed. Steve Woolgar. London: Sage Publications, pp. 14–35.

Woolgar, Steve. ed. 1988b. *Knowledge and Reflexivity*. New frontiers in the Sociology of Knowledge. London: Sage Publications.

Woolgar, Steve. 1988c. *Science: The Very Idea*. London: Routledge.

Woolgar, Steve. 1989. "Stabilization Rituals: Steps in the Socialisation of a New Machine." Paper presented at the *PICT conference*, Brunel University, May.

Woolgar, Steve. 1991a. Configuring the User. The Case of Usability Trials. In *A Sociology of Monsters? Essays on Power, Technology and Domination*, ed. John Law. London: Routledge, pp. 57–102.

Woolgar, Steve. 1991b. The Turn to Technology in Social Studies of Science. *Science, Technology and Human Values* 16 (1): 20–50.

Woolgar, Steve. 1993a. The User Talks Back. *CRICT Discussion Paper No. 40*. Brunel University (September).

Woolgar, Steve. 1993b. What's at Stake in the Sociology of Technology? A Reply to Pinch and to Winner. *Science, Technology and Human Values* 18 (4): 523–9.

Woolgar, Steve. 1996. Technologies as Cultural Artefacts. In *Information and Communication Technologies – Visions and Realities*, ed. W. Dutton. Oxford: Oxford University Press.

Woolgar, Steve. 1997. Accountability and Identity in the Age of UABs. *CRICT Discussion Paper* 60, February, Brunel University.

Woolgar, Steve. 1998. A New Theory of Innovation? *Prometheus* 16 (4): 441–53.

Woolgar, Steve. 2000a. Virtual Technologies and Social Theory – A Technographic Approach. In *Preferred Placement: Knowledge Politics on the Web*, ed. Richard Rogers. Maastricht: Jan van Eyck Akademie Editions.

Woolgar, Steve. 2000b. Social Basis of Interactive Social Science. *Science and Public Policy* 27 (3): 165–73.

Woolgar, Steve. 2002a. After Word? – On Some Dynamics of Duality Interrogation. Or: Why Bonfires Are Not Enough. *Theory, Culture and Society* 19 (5/6): 261–70.

Woolgar, Steve. 2002b. Five Rules of Virtuality. In *Virtual Society? Technology, Cyberbole, Reality*, ed. Steve Woolgar. Oxford: Oxford University Press, pp. 1–23.

Woolgar, Steve. 2004. Marketing Ideas. *Economy and Society*, 33 (4) (November): 448–62.

Woolgar, Steve and Geoff Cooper. 1999. Do Artefacts Have Ambivalence? *Social Studies of Science* 29 (3): 433–49.

Woolgar, Steve and Catelijne Coopmans. 2006. Virtual Witnessing in a Virtual Age: A Prospectus for Social Studies of E-Science. Chapter 1 in *New Infrastructures for Knowledge Production: Understanding E-Science*, ed. Christine Hine. Hershey: Idea Group Inc., pp. 1–26.

Woolgar, Steve and Keith Grint. 1991. Computers and the Transformation of Social Analysis. *Science, Technology and Human Values* (16) 3 (Summer): 368–78.

Woolgar, Steve and Elena Simakova. 2003. Marketing Marketing: An Exploratory Paper. Paper presented at the Workshop on Market(-ing) Practices in Shaping Markets. Stockholm: Stockholm School of Economics (June 2003).

Woolgar, Steve, Catelijne Coopmans and Daniel Neyland. 2009a. Does STS Mean Business? In Special Issue 'Does STS Mean Business?', eds Steve Woolgar, Catelijne Coopmans and Daniel Neyland. *Organization* 16 (5): 5–30.

Woolgar, S., Coopmans, C., Neyland, D. And Mouritsen, J. eds. 2009b. Special Issue 'Does STS Mean Business?'. *Organization* 16 (5): 5–30.

Workman, John P. Jr. 1993. Marketing's Limited Role in New Product Development in One Computer Systems Firm. *Journal of Marketing Research* 30 (4) (November): 405–21.

Yates, Timothy. 1990. Jacques Derrida: 'There is nothing outside of the text.' In *Reading Material Culture: Structuralism, Hermeneutics and Post-Structuralism*, ed. Christopher Tilley. Oxford: Basil Blackwell, pp. 206–80.

Zwick, Detlev and Julien Cayla. eds. 2011. *Inside Marketing: Practices, Ideologies, Devices*. Oxford: Oxford University Press.

Index

Printed in the USA/Agawam, MA
October 18, 2013

581095.060

DATE DUE